Pilot Training Manual for the Mitchell Bomber

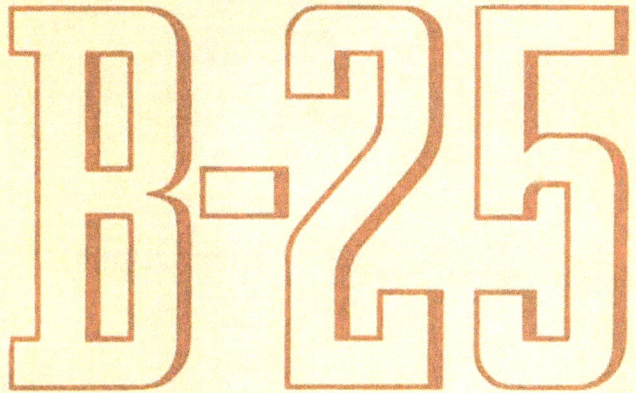

PUBLISHED FOR HEADQUARTERS, AAF

OFFICE OF ASSISTANT CHIEF OF AIR STAFF, TRAINING

BY HEADQUARTERS, AAF, OFFICE OF FLYING SAFETY

THE OTTERBEIN PRESS, DAYTON, OHIO
NOVEMBER, 1944—10,000

Foreword

This manual is the text for your training as a B-25 pilot and airplane commander.

The Air Forces' most experienced training and supervisory personnel have collaborated to make it a complete exposition of what your pilot duties are, how each will be performed, and why it must be performed in the manner prescribed.

The techniques and procedures described in this book are standard and mandatory. In this respect the manual serves the dual purpose of a training checklist and working handbook. Use it to make sure that you learn everything described herein. Use it to study and review the essential facts concerning everything taught. Such additional self-study and review will not only advance your training, but will alleviate the burden of your already overburdened instructors.

This training manual does not replace the Technical Orders for the airplane, which will always be your primary source of information concerning the B-25 so long as you fly it. This is essentially the textbook of the B-25. Used properly, it will enable you to utilize the pertinent Technical Orders to even greater advantage.

H. H. Arnold

GENERAL, U.S. ARMY,
COMMANDING GENERAL,
ARMY AIR FORCES

HISTORY OF THE MITCHELL BOMBER

Welcome to the Mitchell bomber!

You are going to fly a champ with a long line of firsts to her credit!

First to see action on every fighting front.

First Army airplane to sink an enemy sub.

First medium bomber to fly from a carrier deck.

First warplane to pack a 75-mm. cannon.

It all started when the Army asked for designs of a medium bomber to be submitted. That was on 25 January, 1939. Forty days later the B-25 was born!

Daughter of a slide rule, with neither wind-tunnel tests nor prototypes to study, the performance of the B-25 was a series of figures on an engineer's drawing board.

Yet, 19 days after Hitler marched into Poland, in September, 1939, the Army awarded the North American Aviation Company a contract for 148 Mitchell bombers, one of the largest orders written up to that time.

In less than 2 months, following a number of modifications, the mock-up was approved. Exhaustive tests by Army engineers followed, and in August, 1940, the first B-25 was test-flown and its performance found to be better than the claims its designers had made for it.

Since that time, hundreds of changes in design have been made, but the general appearance of all models of the B-25 has not changed.

Designed to carry a bomb load of 3500 lb. and a crew of 5, it has operated efficiently with heavier bomb loads and a crew of 6. Early in the war, when it was engaged in emergency evacuation work, the B-25 carried 26 men and their baggage a distance of 700 miles. On one occasion it carried 32 men and their baggage with auxiliary and main fuel cells full.

Red-lined at 340 mph, cruising easily at 200 mph, the Mitchell, when emergencies have arisen, has exceeded 340 mph, with no disastrous effects.

Its low landing speed has been a boon to flyers who have had to operate from jungle strips and airfields blasted from mountain sides.

Combat experience led to changes in design and armament—more firepower, spare fuel tanks, power-driven turrets, and larger escape hatches, which were added to meet the need for quick exit from a damaged plane.

In April, 1942, the Mitchell made history. Under the leadership of Brigadier General Ralph Royce and Colonel John Davies, 13 B-25's set out from an unidentified base for the island of Mindanao, 2000 miles away. On this, the longest bombing expedition in the history of aerial warfare, the planes flew 2000 miles to a secret base where a store of gasoline was hidden. For 2 days they hit the Japs who were advancing on Bataan, then headed for home without loss.

Less than a week later came the Doolittle raid on Tokyo, with 16 B-25's taking off from the deck of the aircraft carrier Hornet. It can now be told that the tail guns in the B-25's on that raid were painted broomsticks which Major General Doolittle ordered installed after learning that Jap pilots had been ordered to stay out of range of the American tail-stingers.

During the early days of the submarine menace, B-25's were equipped with special wing bomb racks, operating successfully in the submarine hunt and again proving their versatility and capacity for modification.

Arctic operation meant new problems in heating and defrosting for the B-25. They were overcome. Long over-water hops, with hours of precision instrument flying, brought the installation of the automatic pilot, taking the strain off our flyers. For action against the Jap navy, torpedo racks were installed. A multitude of combat problems found the B-25 ready for adaptation to meet them, its most recent and spectacular adaptation being the installation of the 75-mm. cannon in the B-25 G and B-25 H.

The use of the B-25 as a low-altitude attack plane led to the removal of the lower turret. It was replaced by .50-cal. waist guns and a power-operated tail turret. For more effective defense, the upper turret was moved forward.

Package guns—two .50-cal. mounted on each side of the fuselage and firing forward—plus four .50-cal. installed in the nose above the cannon, have transformed the B-25 into a flying machine-gun company, superbly effective for strafing.

The evolution of the Mitchell bomber does not end here. Every day, as experience mounts and new tactics develop, the B-25 proves its versatility, ready to run with the hare or hunt with the hounds—an airplane of which its pilots may well say: It does the job!

DUTIES AND RESPONSIBILITIES OF THE
Airplane Commander

The commander of the B-25 must be more than a pilot. As his title implies, he must be a leader of men—a leader in a special sense. He must not train his crew as automatons, but as a team which will use initiative and perform its tasks to one end only . . . the success of the mission.

You are the leader. The successful coordination of the work involved in getting your plane to its objective and back to its base depends a great deal on the way in which you lead.

When you are thoroughly familiar with the jobs the members of your crew are doing, you've won half the battle of being the commander of your airplane.

The second half of the battle consists in knowing your men as individuals as well as members of the crew. Do you know where your tail gunner was born? Is your crew chief married? What work was your navigator doing before he got in the Army? How does your bombardier like his job on the B-25?

Naturally, you don't ask these questions of your crew as if you were a desk sergeant at the night court. If you're going about things the right way, you may never have to ask. Your men will volunteer the information. Men always talk about themselves when they're fairly sure their listener is really interested.

They'll know whether you're interested if you look out for their comfort on flights and between flights. If you're away from base overnight, you may find it necessary to finance one crew member or another. Be sure that every crew member is properly fed, quartered, and clothed. The manner in which you take care of their needs will make or mar your reputation with your crew.

You need a lot of tact in handling these things. Your best rule of thumb for getting to know and take care of your crew should go something like this: "Is my interest in the crew getting the best out of them for the teamwork I need to fly my plane?" But be sure you don't overdo it. Your tail gunner isn't going to be too happy if you tell him that his crap-shooting is blistering his trigger finger. But you're not overdoing it if you pull a plate of gas-forming food out from under his hungry eyes just before a high-altitude mission.

Crew Discipline

Discipline in an air crew means that you are commanding respect and getting your orders obeyed. It also means that a lot of the time you're not finding it necessary to give orders at all. Your crew members are performing their duties without having to be told.

A good way to develop the jitters about your plane and your crew is by keeping them at a distance, talking to them pompously, and by showing favoritism or uncertainty in your decisions.

In a little while you'll find yourself working on one side of a 10-foot wall while your crew works on the other.

On the other hand, you won't get discipline by dropping all distinctions between commander and crew and letting the waist gunner call you Joe.

Somewhere between these two methods there is a happy medium which will insure that any order you give will bring instant obedience and maintain respect and mutual confidence.

You can be friendly without becoming familiar, understanding without becoming a father-confessor, and firm without emulating Simon Legree. Give direct orders only when there is a need for orders. Once you issue an order, **see that it is always obeyed.**

Ready for Action

Are your guns working? The only way you can be sure is to know how competent and reliable your gunners are. It is disastrous to get caught by a swarm of enemy fighters and find that your guns won't function.

What about your navigator? Does he know his job well enough to get you over that pinpoint target a thousand miles from any visible fix?

Is your bombardier sure that his equipment is in perfect condition? Has he remembered to warm up his bombsight to prevent fogging at the critical moment?

You can't know the precise answers to all the questions involved in having your plane ready for action—but you can know most of the important questions. Learn enough about every man's job so that you can ask the right questions, and you'll find that your crew will be there with the right answers at the right time.

PRACTICAL *Questions*

1. Can all members of your crew fly at high altitudes without discomfort or physical handicap?

2. Does any member of your crew get airsick?

3. Can the copilot take over in emergency?

4. Does the radio operator understand D.F. aids?

5. Do the gunners know how to unload and stow their guns?

6. Do the engineer and the copilot (and do you) know how to use the load adjuster and how to load the airplane properly?

7. Do the engineer and copilot (and do you) use the control charts to check your power settings and the efficient performance of your airplane?

8. Does your crew know emergency procedure and signals?

9. Is each member of your crew properly equipped?

10. What can you do to prevent or relieve anoxia, air sickness, and fatigue?

11. Is your crew familiar with first-aid treatment?

12. Can you improve the morale of your crew?

These are some of the practical questions which you as airplane commander must be able to answer.

THE COPILOT

The copilot is the executive officer—your chief assistant, understudy, and strong right arm. He must be familiar enough with every one of your duties—both as pilot and as airplane commander—to take over and act in your place at any time.

He must be able to fly the airplane under all conditions as well as you would fly it yourself.

He must be proficient in engine operation and know instinctively what to do to keep the airplane flying smoothly, even though he is not handling the controls.

He must have a thorough knowledge of cruising control data and know how to apply his knowledge at the proper time.

He is also the engineering officer aboard the airplane, and maintains a complete log of performance data.

He must be able to fly good formation in any assigned position, day or night.

He must be qualified to navigate by day or at night by pilotage, dead reckoning, and by use of radio aids.

He must be proficient in the operation of all radio equipment in the pilot's compartment.

In formation flying, he must be able to make engine adjustments almost automatically.

He must be prepared to assist on instruments when the formation is climbing through an overcast, so you can watch the rest of the formation.

Remember that the more proficient your copilot is **as a pilot,** the better able he is to perform the duties of the vital post he holds as your second in command.

Be sure that he is always allowed to do his share of the flying, in the copilot's seat, on take-offs, landings, and on instruments.

Bear in mind that the pilot in the right-hand seat of your airplane is preparing himself for an airplane commander's post too. Allow him every chance to develop his ability and to profit by your experience.

THE BOMBARDIER-NAVIGATOR

As a navigator it is the bombardier-navigator's job to direct your flight from departure to destination and return. He must know the exact position of the airplane at all times. For you to understand how to get the most reliable service from your navigator, you must know as much about his job as possible.

Navigation is the art of determining geographic positions by means of (a) pilotage, (b) dead reckoning, (c) radio, or (d) celestial navigation, or any combination of these four methods. By any one or combination of methods the navigator determines the position of the airplane in relation to the earth.

Instrument Calibration

Instrument calibration is an important duty of the navigator. All navigation depends directly on the accuracy of his instruments. Correct

calibration requires close cooperation and extremely careful flying by the pilot. Instruments to be calibrated include the altimeter, all compasses, airspeed indicators, alignment of the astrocompass, astrograph, and drift meter, and a check on the navigator's sextant and watch.

Pilot-Navigator Preflight Planning

1. Pilot and navigator must study the flight plan of the route to be flown, and select alternate airfields.
2. Study the weather with the navigator. Know what weather you are likely to encounter. Decide what action is to be taken. Know the weather conditions at the alternate fields.
3. Inform your navigator at what airspeed and altitude you wish to fly so that he can prepare his flight plan.
4. Learn what type of navigation the navigator intends to use: pilotage, dead reckoning, radio, celestial, or a combination of all methods.
5. Determine check points; plan to make radio fixes.
6. Work out an effective communication method with your navigator to be used in flight.
7. Synchronize your watch with your navigator's.

Pilot-Navigator in Flight

1. **Constant course**—For accurate navigation you must fly a constant course. The navigator has to make many computations and entries in his log. Constantly changing course makes his job more difficult. A good navigator should be able to follow the pilot, but he cannot be taking compass readings all the time.
2. **Constant airspeed**—Hold IAS as nearly constant as possible. This is as important to the navigator as is a constant course in determining position.
3. **Precision flying** greatly affects the accuracy of the navigator's instrument readings, particularly celestial readings. A slight error in celestial reading causes considerable error in determining position. You can help the navigator by providing as steady a platform as possible from which to take readings. The navigator should notify you when he intends to take readings so that you can level off and fly as smoothly as possible, preferably by using the automatic pilot. Do not allow your navigator to be disturbed while he is taking celestial readings.
4. **Notify the navigator of any change in flight,** such as change in altitude, course, or airspeed. Before you change your flight plan, consult the navigator. Talk over the proposed change so that he can plan the flight and advise you concerning it.
5. If there is doubt about the position of the airplane, consult your navigator, refer to his flight log, talk the problem over and decide together the best course of action.
6. Check your compasses at intervals with those of the navigator, noting any deviation.
7. Require your navigator to give position reports at intervals.
8. You are ultimately responsible for getting the airplane to its destination. Therefore, it is your duty to know your position at all times.
9. Encourage your navigator to use as many of the methods of navigation as possible for double-checking. In training, give him a chance to practice. Follow his courses even though you know he is wrong. Keep track of the plane's position but allow him to rectify his errors.

Post-flight Critique

After every flight, get together with the navigator and discuss the flight and compare notes.

Go over the navigator's log. If there have been serious navigational errors, discuss them with the navigator and determine their cause. If the navigator is at fault, caution him that it is his job to see that the same mistake does not occur again. If faulty instruments have caused the error, see that they are corrected before attempting another navigation mission. If your flying has contributed to the inaccuracy of the navigation, try to fly a better course the next mission.

Miscellaneous Duties

As a member of the team, the bombardier-navigator must also have a general knowledge of the entire operation of the airplane.

He must be familiar with the oxygen system, know how to operate the turrets, radio equipment, and fuel transfer system.

He must know the location of all fuses and

spare fuses, lights and spare lights, affecting navigation.

He must be familiar with emergency procedures, such as the manual operation of landing gear, bomb bay doors, and flaps, and the proper procedures for crash landings, ditching, bailout, etc.

Bombardment

Accurate and effective bombing is the ultimate purpose of your entire airplane and crew. Every other function is preparatory to hitting and destroying the target.

Successful bombardment is the primary goal of the bombardier-navigator. The success or failure of the mission depends upon what he accomplishes in that short interval of the bombing run.

A great deal depends on the understanding between bombardier-navigator and pilot. You expect your bombardier to know his job. He expects you to understand the problems involved in his job, and to give him full cooperation. Teamwork between pilot and bombardier is essential.

Under any given set of conditions—ground speed, altitude, direction, etc.—there is only one point in space where a bomb may be released from the airplane to hit a predetermined object on the ground.

There are many things with which a bombardier must be thoroughly familiar in order to release his bombs at the right point to hit this predetermined target.

He must understand his bombsight, what it does, and how it does it.

He must understand the operation and upkeep of his bombing instruments and equipment.

He must know that his racks, switches, controls, releases, doors, linkage, etc., are in first-class operating condition.

He must know how to operate all gun positions in the airplane.

He must know how to load and how to clear simple gun stoppages and jams while in flight.

He must be able to load and fuse bombs.

He must understand the destructive power of bombs and know the vulnerable spots on various types of targets.

He must understand the bombing problem, bombing probabilities, bombing errors, etc.

He must be versed in target identification and in aircraft identification.

The bombardier should be familiar with the duties of all members of the crew.

To enable the bombardier to do his job, you must place the airplane in the proper position to arrive at a point from which he can release his bombs to hit the target.

Unless the pilot performs his part of the bombing run correctly, even the best bombardier in the world cannot bomb accurately.

RADIO OPERATOR

There is a lot of radio equipment in today's B-25's. There is one particular man who is supposed to know all there is to know about this equipment. Sometimes he does, but often he doesn't. His deficiencies often do not become apparent until the crew is in the combat zone when it is too late. Too often pilots and crews lose their lives because the radio operator has accepted his responsibility indifferently.

It is impossible to learn radio in a day. It is imperative that you check your radio operator's ability to handle his job before taking him overseas as part of your crew. To do this you may have to check with the various instructors to find out any weakness in the radio operator's training and proficiency and to help overcome such weaknesses.

The radio operator is required to:
1. Render position reports every 30 minutes.
2. Assist the navigator in taking fixes.
3. Keep the liaison and command sets properly tuned and in good operating order.
4. Understand from an operational point of view:
    (a) Instrument Landing
    (b) IFF
    (c) VHF
    and other navigational aids.
5. Maintain a log.

In addition to being radio operator, the radio man is also a gunner. During combat he leaves his watch at the radio and takes up his guns. He often has to learn photography. Some of the best pictures taken in the Southwest Pacific were taken by radio operators.

THE ENGINEER

Size up the man who is to be your engineer. This man should know more about the airplane you are to fly than any other member of the crew. If there are deficiencies in his training you may be able to fill them in.

Think back on your own training. In many courses of instruction, you had a lot of things thrown at you from right and left. You had to concentrate on how to fly; where your equipment was concerned, you learned to rely more and more on the enlisted men, particularly the crew chief and the engineer, for advice.

Pilot and engineer must work closely together to supplement and fill in the blank spaces in each other's education.

To be a qualified combat engineer, a man must know his airplane, his engines, and his armament equipment thoroughly.

He must work closely with the copilot, checking engine operation, fuel consumption, and the operation of all equipment.

He must be able to work with the bombardier, and know how to cock, lock, and load the bomb racks. It is up to you to see that he is familiar with these duties and, if he is hazy concerning them, to have the bombardier give him special help and instruction.

He should have a general knowledge of radio equipment, and be able to assist in tuning transmitters and receivers.

Your engineer should be your chief source of information about the airplane. He should know more about the equipment than any other member of the crew—yourself included.

You, in turn, are his source of information about flying. Bear this in mind in all your discussions with the engineer. The more complete you can make his knowledge of the reasons behind every function of the equipment, the more valuable he will be as a member of the crew. Someday his extra knowledge may save the day in an emergency.

Generally, in emergencies, the engineer is the man to whom you turn first. Build up his pride, his confidence, his knowledge. Know him personally; check on the extent of his knowledge. Make him a man upon whom you can rely.

THE GUNNERS

Your gunners belong to one of two distinct categories: turret gunners and flexible gunners.

The power turret gunners must have good coordination.

While the flexible gunners do not require the same delicate touch as the turret gunner, they must have a fine sense of timing.

All gunners should be familiar with the coverage area of all gun positions, and be prepared to bring the proper gun to bear on the target.

They must be experts in aircraft identification.

They must be thoroughly familiar with the machine guns. They should know how to maintain the guns, how to clear jams and stoppages, and how to harmonize the sights with the guns.

During training flights, the gunners should be in their turrets, tracking with the guns even when actual firing is not practicable. Other aircraft flying in the vicinity offer excellent tracking targets, as do automobiles, houses, and other ground objects during low-altitude flights.

Keep your gunners' interest alive at all times. Any form of competition among the gunners themselves should stimulate their interest.

Finally, each gunner should fire the guns at each station to familiarize himself with the other positions.

Rules to Be Enforced on Every Flight

Smoking

1. No smoking in airplane at an altitude below 1000 feet.
2. No smoking during fuel transfer.
3. Never attempt to throw a lighted cigarette from the airplane. Put it out first.

Parachutes

1. All persons aboard will wear parachute harness at all times from takeoff to landing.
2. Each person aboard will have a parachute on every flight.
3. Carry at least one spare parachute in the plane.

Propellers

1. Always enter and leave the plane to and from the rear.
2. No person will leave the airplane when propellers are turning unless ordered to do so by the airplane commander.

Oxygen Masks

1. Oxygen masks will be carried on all flights where altitude **may** exceed 10,000 feet.
2. Day: All persons will use oxygen starting at 7000 to 10,000 feet on all day flights where altitude at any time may exceed 12,000 feet.
3. Use oxygen for all flights at 8000 ft. or above when the duration of the flight may exceed 4 hours.
4. Night: All persons will use oxygen from the ground up on all flights during which altitude may reach 10,000 feet.

Training

1. Tell your crew the purpose of each mission and what you expect each to accomplish.
2. **Keep the crew busy throughout the flight.** Get position reports from the navigator; send them out through the radio operator. Put the engineer to work on the cruise control and maximum range charts. Require the copilot to keep a record of engine performance. Give them a workout. Encourage them to use their skill. A team is an active outfit. Make the most of every practice mission.
3. **Practice all emergency procedures as often as possible**—bailout, ditching and fire drill.

Inspections

1. Check your airplane with reference to the particular mission you are undertaking. **Check everything.**
2. Check your crew for equipment, preparedness, and understanding of what you expect from them.

Interphone

1. Assure yourself that all members of the crew are standing by their interphones at all times. **Insist on clear, well-controlled voices. Speak slowly and clearly.**
2. Require reports by interphone every 15 minutes from all crew members when on oxygen.

General Description

★ The Mitchell medium bomber is a high-speed, mid-wing land monoplane. Positive dihedral in the inner and negative dihedral in the outer wing panels give the plane a gull-wing appearance, while adding control and maneuverability. ★ A twin tail section with large rudders increases stability and maneuverability and allows a greater concentration of firepower to the rear.

A tricycle landing gear adds to the ease of landing, prevents groundlooping, and provides the pilot with maximum visibility during ground operation. It also permits a wide range of loading to obtain maximum bomb and weight carrying capacity.

Underslung Wright Cyclone engines drive Hamilton hydromatic propellers and deliver 1700 Hp each at full power.

The fuselage is a semi-monocoque, four-longeron, stressed skin structure. The bombardier's, pilot's, and navigator's compartments are located in that order, forward of the bomb bay. The radio operator's, gunner's, and photographer's compartments are located in that order aft of the bomb bay.

Each engine has individual self-sealing fuel and oil systems. Fuel transfer systems allow extra fuel, carried in fuselage tanks, to be transfered to the main system. There is a cross-feed in the fuel system for emergency operations.

Two 24-volt batteries supply electric power for starting and initial operation. Two generators recharge the batteries and supply power when engine speed permits their operation. Each engine has a dual-ignition system.

The B-25 has standard communication and bombardment equipment. Its armament is varied but follows AAF standards. Models of the plane have been converted for varying tactical needs by the addition of .50-cal. machine guns and the 75-mm. cannon.

There are electrically driven power turrets on some models and a hydraulically driven tail turret on others.

The plane has standard lighting, heating and hydraulic systems.

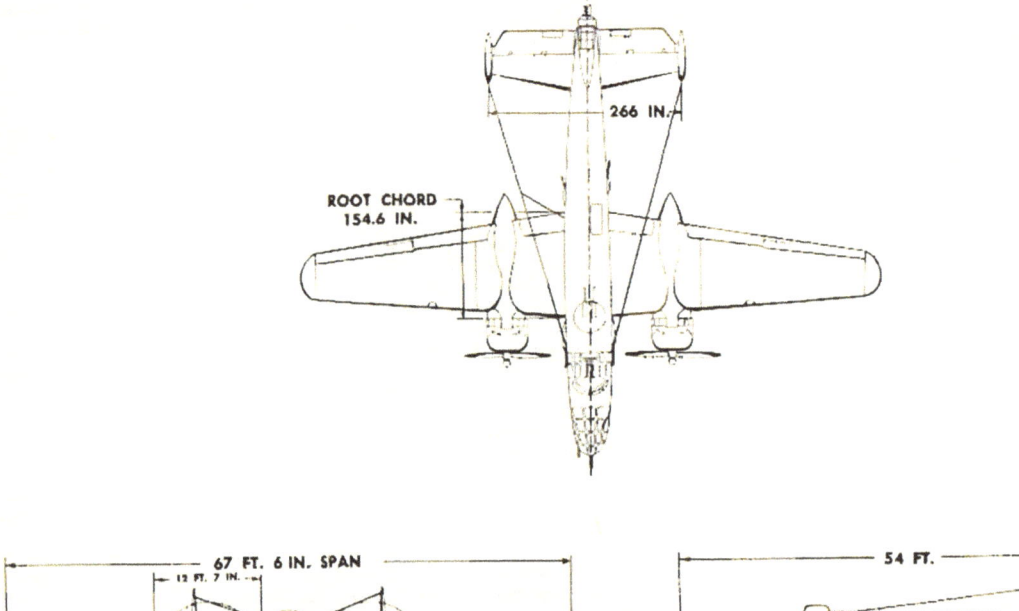

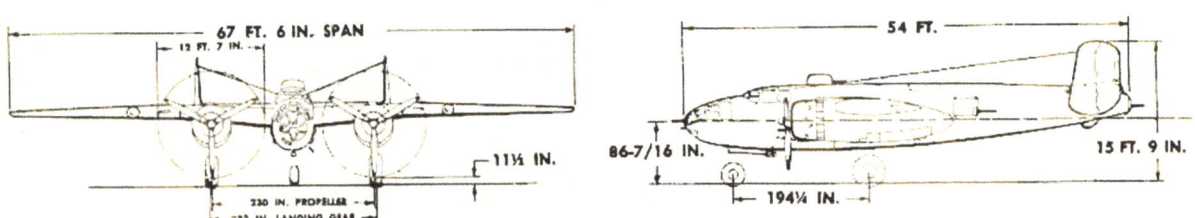

The airplane dimensions are: Span 67 feet 6 inches, length 54 feet, height 15 feet 9 inches. The airplane empty weighs approximately 20,300 lb.; loaded to maximum capacity, 35,500 lb.

Location of Controls
B-25 C and D

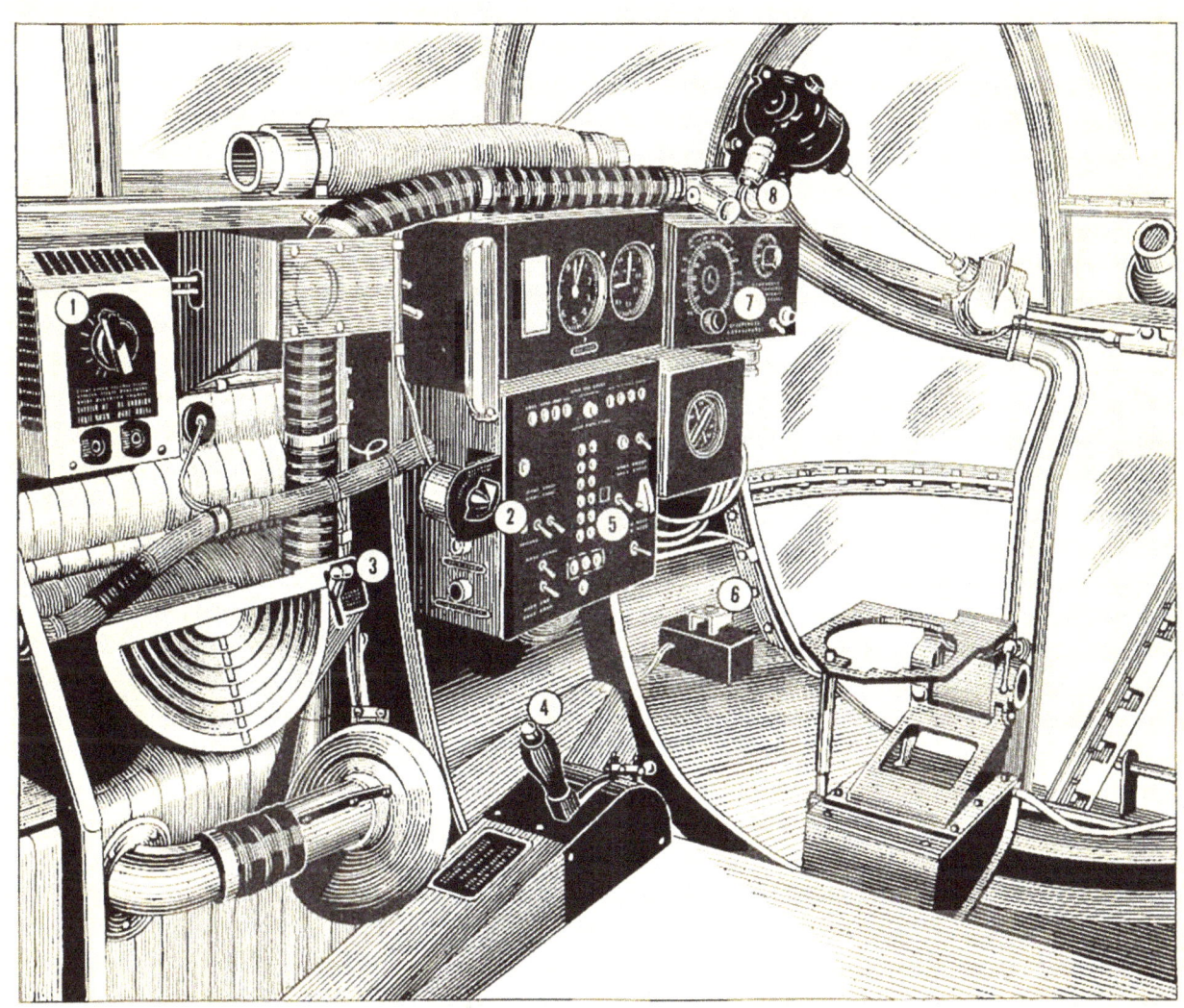

BOMBARDIER'S COMPARTMENT — LEFT SIDE

1. Heated Clothing Electrical Outlet Control
2. Bombsight Window Anti-Icer Rheostat
3. Ventilation Outlet Control
4. Bomb Bay Door and Bomb Control Handle
5. Bomb Control Panel
6. Bomb Release Switch
7. Selective Train Switch Interval Control
8. Bombsight and Windshield Defrosting Unit

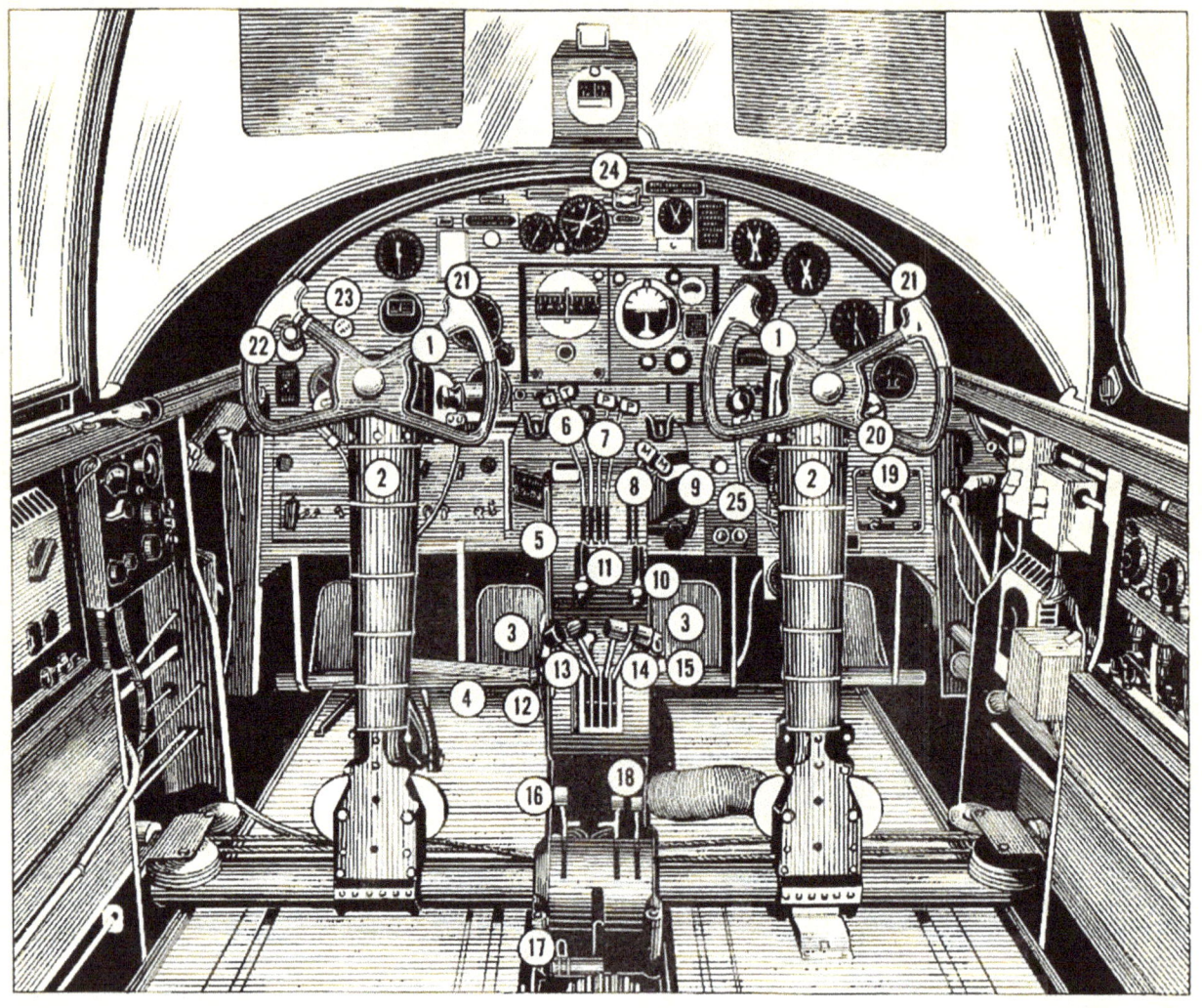

PILOT'S COMPARTMENT—GENERAL FORWARD VIEW

1. Aileron Controls
2. Elevator Controls
3. Rudder Controls
4. Surface Control Lock
5. Elevator Trim
6. Throttles
7. Propeller Controls
8. Mixture Controls
9. Parking Brake Handle
10. Propeller & Mixture Control Lock
11. Throttle Control Lock
12. Auto-Pilot OFF-ON Control
13. Supercharger Controls
14. Oil Cooler Shutters
15. Carburetor Air Heat Controls
16. Wing Flaps
17. Landing Gear
18. Engine Cowl Flaps
19. Engine Fire Extinguisher
20. Instrument Panel Fluorescent Light Switch
21. Throat Microphone Switches
22. Gun Trigger Switch
23. Bomb Release Button
24. Emergency Bomb Release
25. Detonator Switch

PILOT'S INSTRUMENT PANEL

* Provision only.

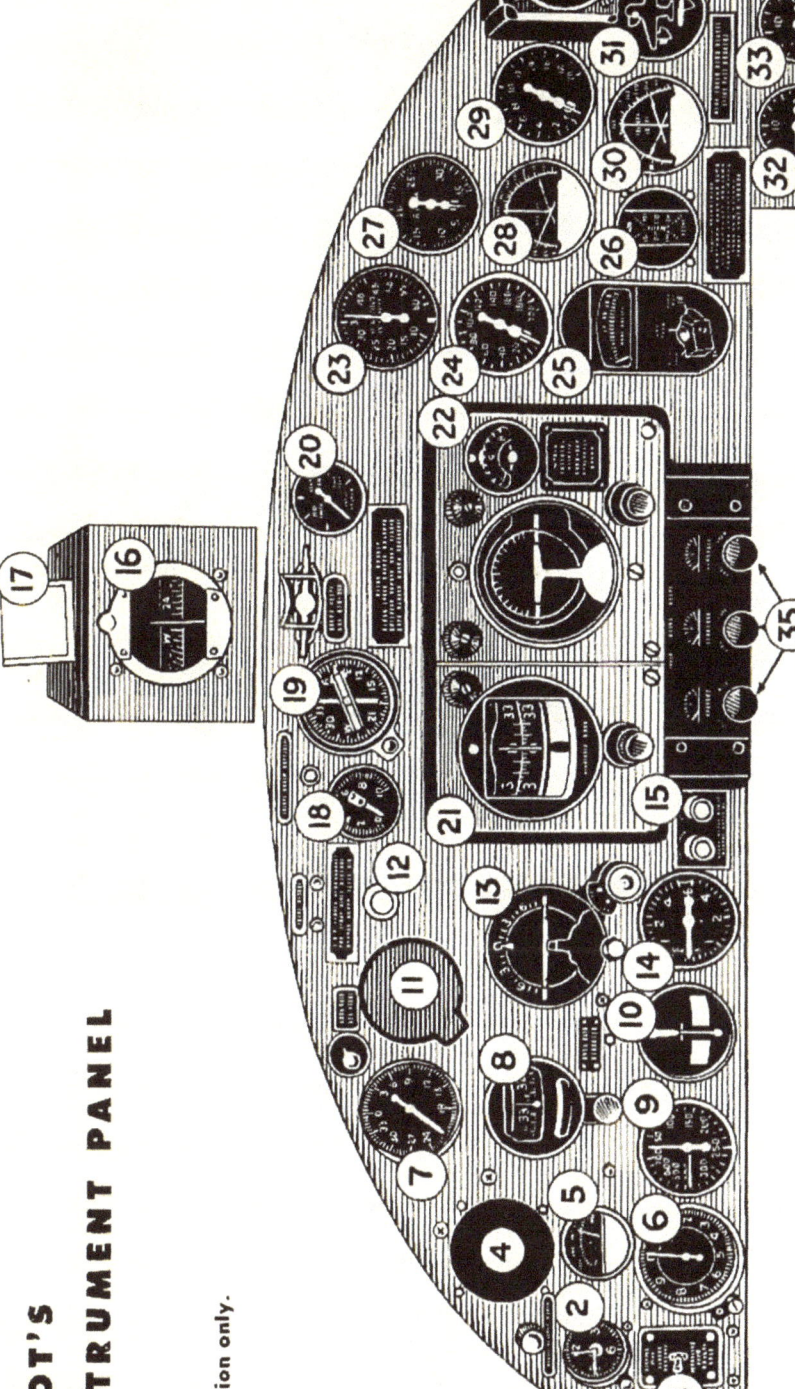

1. Altimeter Correction Card
2. Pilot's Clock
3. Static Pressure Selector Valve
*4. Pilot Director Indicator
5. Free Air Temperature Indicator
6. Altimeter
7. Radio Compass
8. Directional Gyro
9. Airspeed Indicator
10. Bank and Turn Indicator
*11. Accelerometer
12. Bank and Turn Needle Valve
13. Flight Indicator
14. Rate of Climb Indicator
15. Nose Wheel Turn Indicator
16. Magnetic Compass
17. Compass Correction Card
18. Suction (Vacuum) Gage
19. Remote Reading Compass
20. Auto Pilot Oil Pressure Gage
21. Auto Pilot Directional Gyro Unit
22. Auto Pilot Bank and Climb Gyro Unit
23. Manifold Pressure Gage
24. Oil Pressure Gage
25. Main Tanks Fuel Level Indicator
26. Auxiliary Tanks Fuel Level Indicator
27. Tachometer Indicator
28. Oil Temperature Indicator
29. Fuel Pressure Indicator
30. Cylinder Head Temperature Indicator
31. Landing Gear and Flap Position Indicator
32. Hydraulic Pressure Gage
33. Brake Pressure Gage
34. Carburetor Air Temperature Indicator
35. Auto-Pilot Servo Speed Control Knobs

PILOT'S SWITCH PANEL AND CONTROL PEDESTAL PANEL

1. Propeller Anti-Icing Rheostat
2. Compass Light Rheostat
3. Formation Light Rheostat
4. Torpedo Director Light Rheostat
5. Propeller Feathering Buttons
6. Servo Speed Control Knobs
7. Ignition Safety Switch
8. Ignition Switches
9. Recognition Light Keying Switch
10. Landing Light Switches
11. Fuel Booster Pump Switches
12. Engine Primer Switch
13. Starter Switches
14. Auxiliary Wing Tank Transfer Pump Switches
15. Pilot's Auxiliary Bomb Door Control
16. Recognition Light Switches
17. Bombardier's Signal Switch
18. Radio Compartment Heater Control
19. Oil Dilution Switch
20. Position Light Switches
21. Cockpit Lights
22. Dome Light Switch
23. Pitot Heat Switch
24. Battery Disconnect Switches
25. Passing Light Switch
26. Carburetor De-Icer Switch
27. Windshield Defrosting Blower Switch
28. Alarm Bell Switch
29. Gun Safety Switch

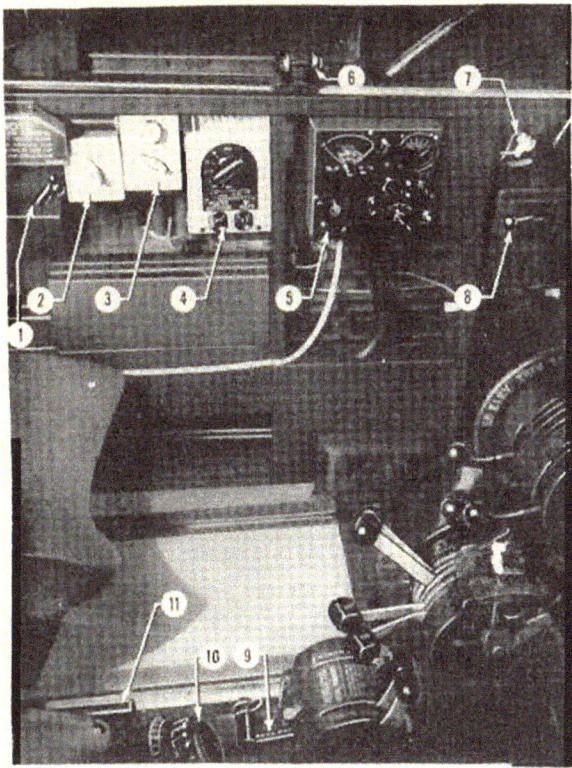

PILOT'S COMPARTMENT— RIGHT SIDE

1. Radio Transmitters
2. Radio Receivers
3. Heated Clothing Electrical Control
4. Filter Switch Box
5. Radio Jack Box
6. Adjustable Spotlight
7. Co-Pilot's Sliding Window Control
8. Ventilation Inlet

PILOT'S COMPARTMENT— LEFT SIDE

1. Pilot's Air Flow Control
2. Filter Switch Box
3. Radio Jack Box
4. Heated Clothing Electrical Control
5. Radio Compass Control Unit
6. Pilot's Sliding Window Control
7. Adjustable Spotlight
8. Ventilation Inlet
9. Landing Gear
10. Aileron Trim
11. Hydraulic Hand Pump

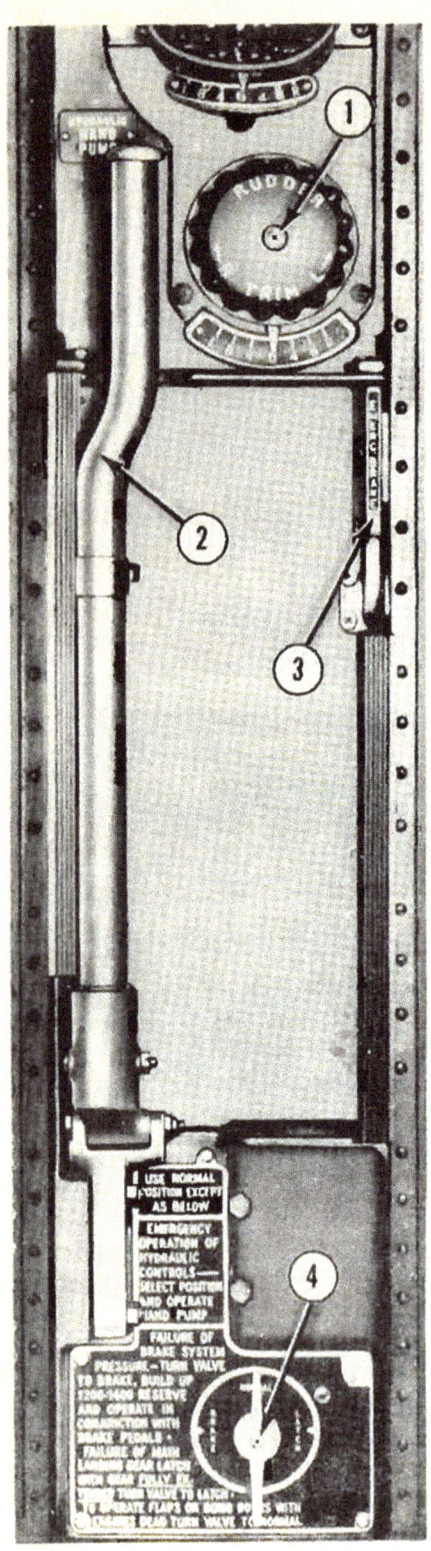

HYDRAULIC HAND PUMP AND EMERGENCY AIR BRAKE CONTROL

Located Rear of Pilot's Pedestal on Floor Between Pilot's and Copilot's Seats.

1. Rudder Trim
2. Hydraulic Hand Pump
3. Emergency Air Brake Handle
4. Emergency Hydraulic Selector

NAVIGATOR'S COMPARTMENT —FORWARD VIEW

1. Radio Compass Control Unit
2. Main Landing Gear and Nose Gear Emergency Hydraulic Lowering Handle
3. Emergency Air Brake Pressure Gage
4. Hand Fire Extinguisher (CO_2)
5. Accumulator Hydraulic Pressure Gages

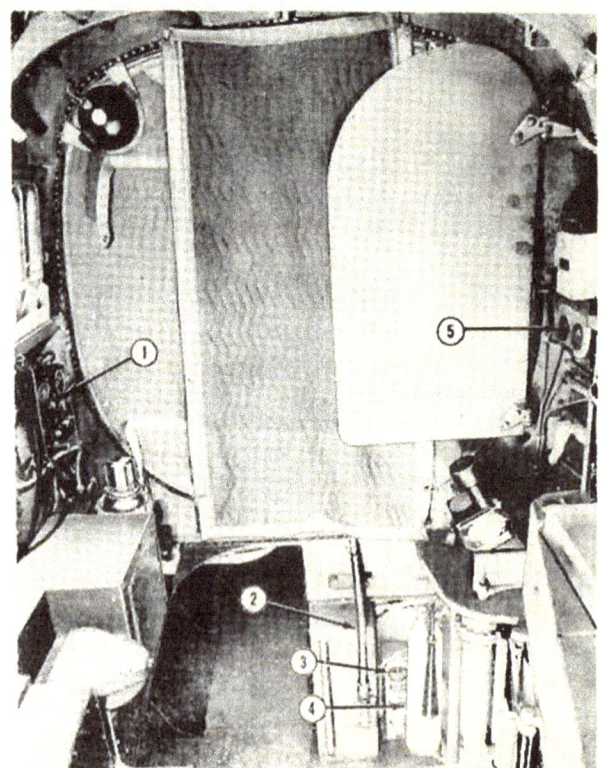

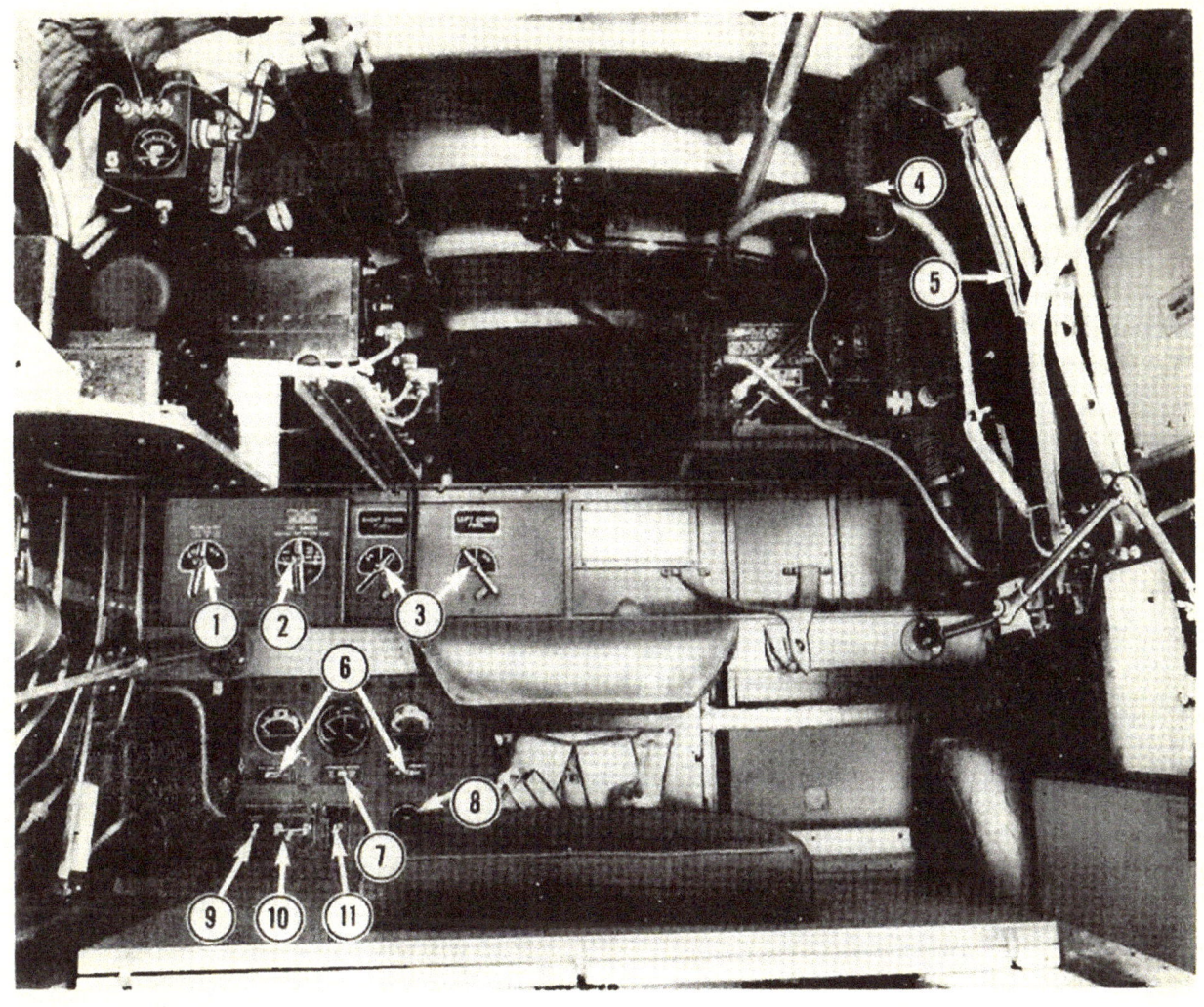

NAVIGATOR'S COMPARTMENT—REAR VIEW

1. Fuel Cross Feed Shut-off Valve
2. Fuselage Tank Transfer Valve
3. Emergency Fuel Shut-off Valves
4. Astro Dome Defrosting Tube
5. Astrograph Mounting Bracket
6. Generator Main Line Switches
7. Generator Voltmeter Switch
8. Chart Table Lamp Rheostat
9. Inverter Cut-off Switch
10. Inverter Active and Spare Change-over Switch
11. Fuselage Tank Transfer Pump Switch

RADIO OPERATOR'S COMPARTMENT—FORWARD VIEW

1. Life Raft Release
2. Radio Transmitting Key
3. Radio Jack Box
4. Emergency Wing Flap Crank
5. Emergency Escape Hatch Release
6. Hand Fire Extinguisher (CO_2)
7. Ventilation Inlet
8. Oxygen Regulator
9. Dome Light Switch

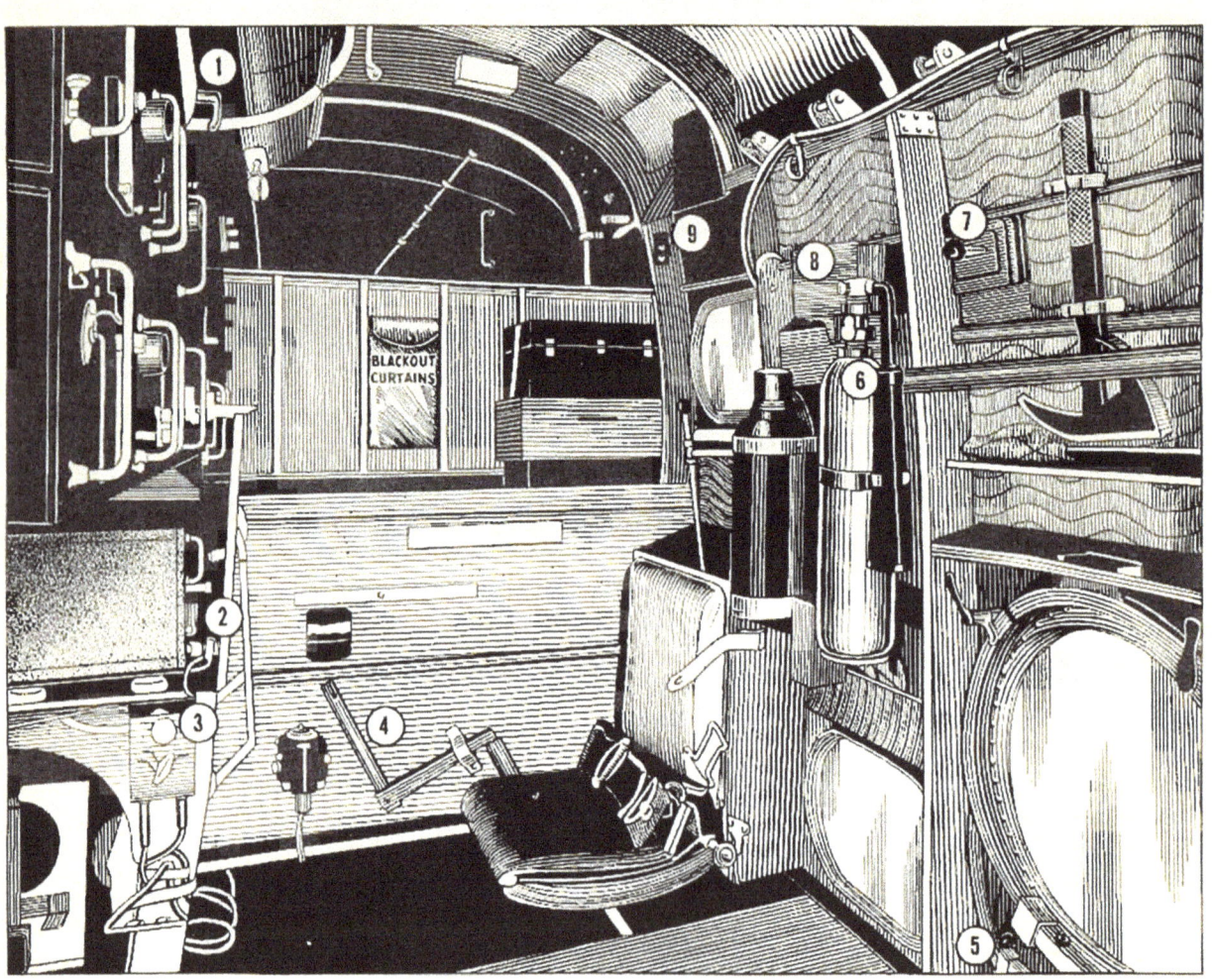

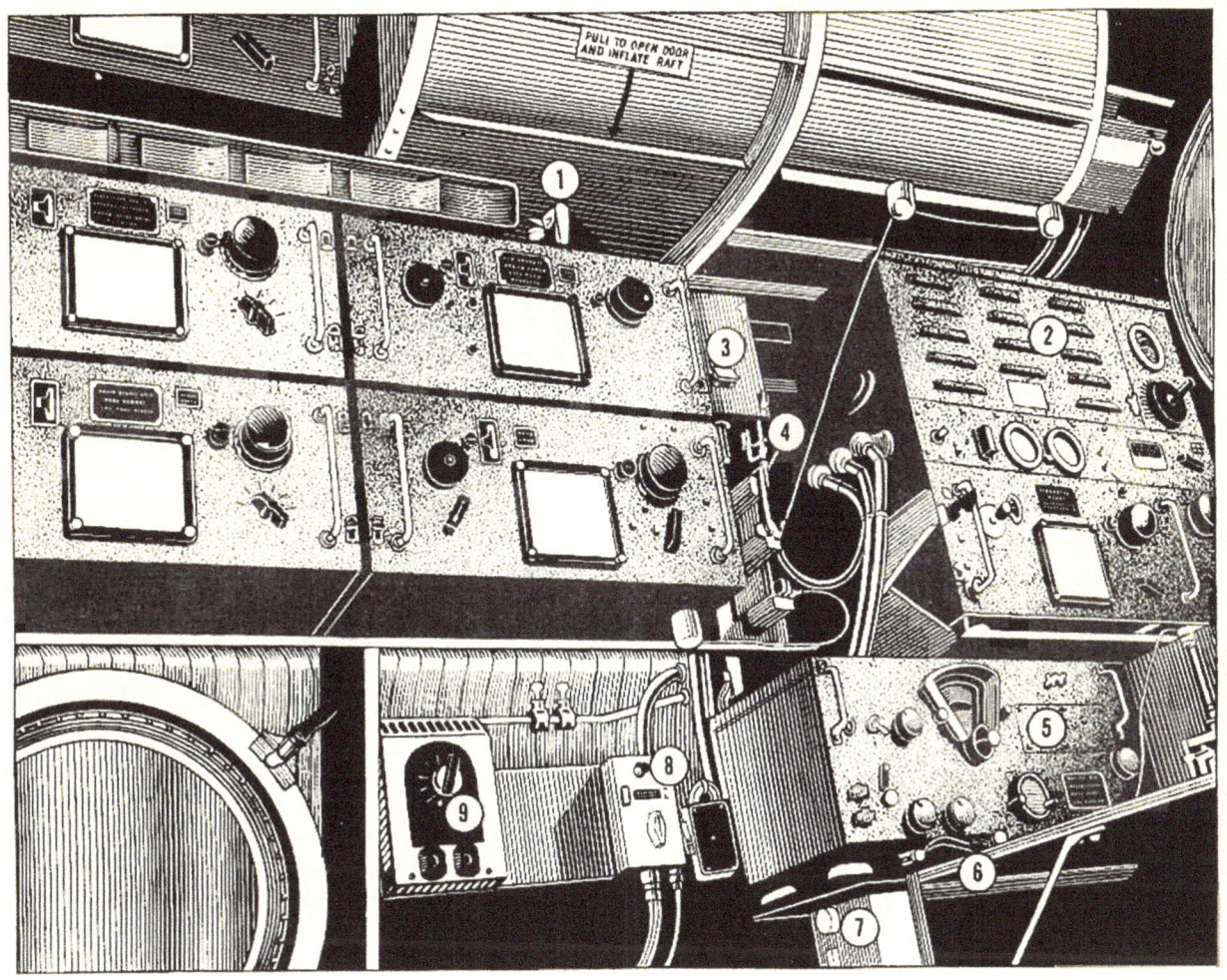

RADIO OPERATOR'S COMPARTMENT — LEFT SIDE

1. Life Raft Release
2. Liaison Transmitter Unit
3. Liaison Monitor Switch
4. Antenna Change-over Switch
5. Liaison Receiver Unit
6. Radio Transmitting Key
7. Radio Jack Box
8. Trailing Antenna Reel Control Box
9. Heated Clothing Electrical Control

FOR CHANGED LOCATION OF CONTROLS IN OTHER MODELS SEE PAGE 58

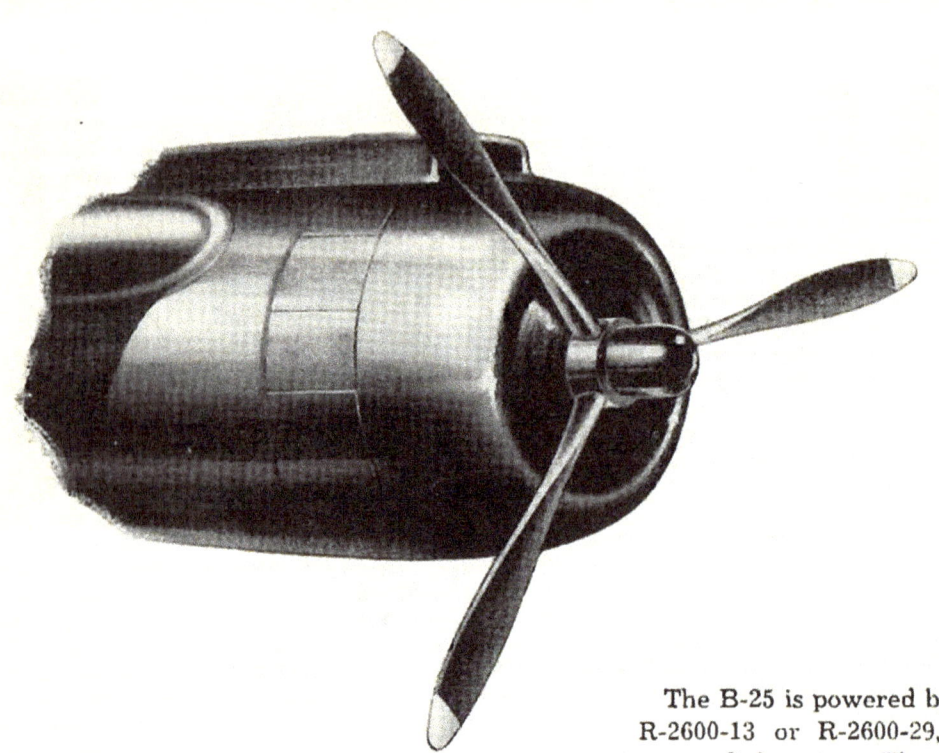

POWER PLANT

The B-25 is powered by two Wright Cyclone R-2600-13 or R-2600-29, 14-cylinder, double-row radial engines. The operation of these two series is similar. Primarily aircooled, these engines have two secondary methods of cooling:

1. Scavenged engine oil is cooled by 2 oil coolers located in the outboard section of each wing before it is returned to the engines.

2. Rich fuel mixtures cool the engines at high power settings.

3. Individual flame-damping exhaust stacks reduce exhaust flame visibility at night.

ENGINE POWER RATINGS

RATINGS	BRAKE HP	RPM	BLOWER
Sea Level	1500	2400	Low
Takeoff	1700	2600	Low
Normal	1500	2400 at 6700 feet	Low
	1350	2400 at 13,000 feet	High
Military	1700	2600 at 5500 feet	Low
	1450	2600 at 13,500 feet	High

Supercharger

A supercharger is to an internal-combustion engine what an oxygen mask and a supply of oxygen is to a pilot.

An integral part of the R-2600 engine is the internal 2-speed, gear-driven supercharger. It supplies the necessary manifold pressures for high-altitude operation.

The impeller, acting as a power fan, is driven at a 7.06:1 ratio in low blower and 10.06:1 in high blower. This passes the fuel-air mixture from the carburetor and adapter at increased pressures to the manifold. The manifold distributes the mixture to the intake ports and the cylinder heads.

Accessory Section

The accessory section, on the rear of the engine, contains various devices for supplying pressures and operational action to the airplane. These are:

Right and left scintilla magnetos
Generator
Inertia starter
Fuel pump
Oil pump
Scavenger pump
Hydraulic pump
Vacuum pump
Cuno automatic filter
Tachometer drive gear

A number of instrument fittings complete this section.

Carburetor

Holley variable-venturi carburetors operating at pressures of 6 to 7 lb. sq. in. supply the engines with fuel.

The carburetors are the pressure-metering type. By operating the throttles, you control the amount of air passing the venturi throats; the air, by its varying pressures, measures the amount of fuel allowed to enter the adapter section and mix with the air. This establishes a predetermined fuel-air ratio.

These carburetors incorporate several devices to increase and decrease the fuel-air ratio in relation to the engine power output.

1. **Compensator System**—A bleed line operated by a spring-loaded check valve and diaphragm. When you use high throttle settings, it allows a richer mixture to reach the cylinders to cool the cylinder heads properly.

2. **Accelerating Pump**—A device to supply an additional charge of fuel when you open throt-

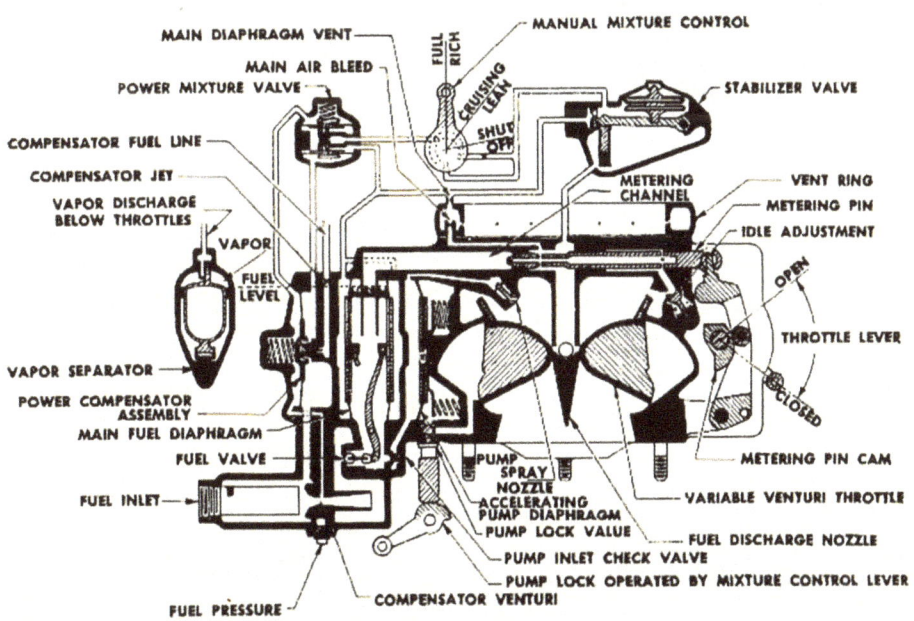

THE HOLLEY CARBURETOR

tles suddenly. It corrects for a time lag in the regular supply. It is diaphragm operated and cuts out when the mixture control is in "IDLE CUT-OFF."

3. **Mixture Control**—Allows you to set the carburetor for cruising lean which improves fuel economy and fuel mixtures under all operating conditions.

4. **Stabilizer Valve**—A slide valve which acts as an automatic mixture control, compensating for changes in temperature and pressure.

5. **Power Mixture Valve**—A diaphragm-operated bypass valve. When you open throttles to high power settings, it cuts the manual mixture control out of the system, and prevents you from taking off with cruising mixtures.

6. **Vapor Separator**—A needle-valve and float device for diverting fuel vapor into the adapter where they mix with the normal mixture and pass to the impeller section.

7. **Primer**—A needle valve in the fuel inlet casting to facilitate starting the engine.

AIR INDUCTION SYSTEM

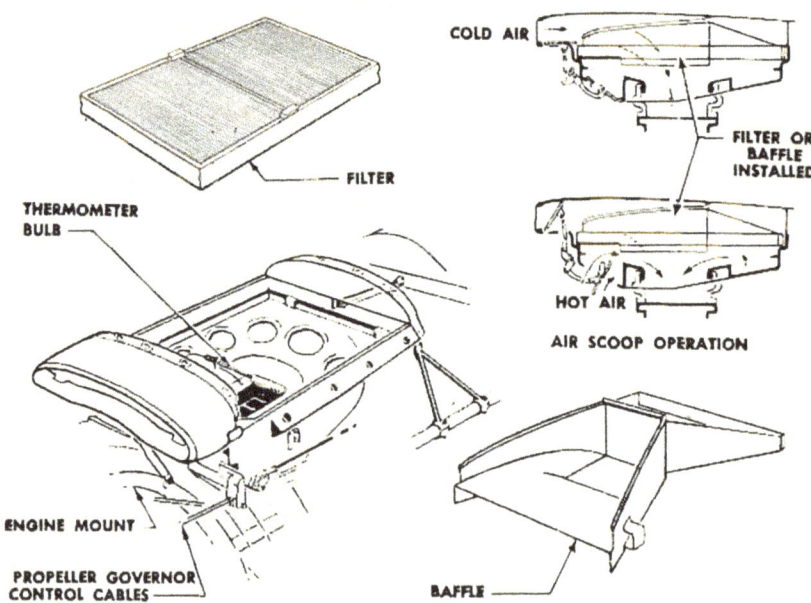

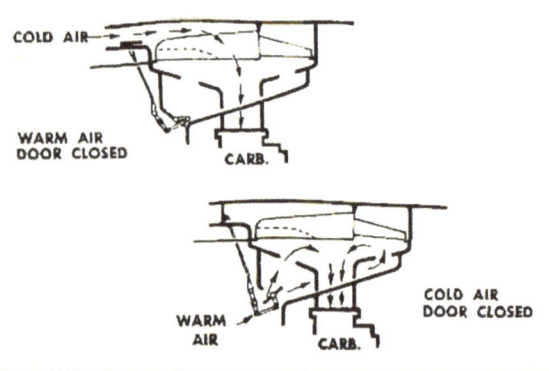

Air enters the induction system through air scoops above the nacelle. The ram action of the air mass supplies the energy to move cold air through the system.

A carburetor heat control provides an alternate source of air, allowing heated air to flow from around the cylinder heads to the system.

Normally there is a baffle in the air-mixing chamber. Air entering horizontally through the cold-air intake is deflected down into the carburetor inlet. Under dusty atmospheric conditions an air filter in the air-mixing chamber replaces the baffle.

FUEL SYSTEM

Each engine has an independent fuel supply, interconnected by fuel transfer and fuel cross-feed systems. The fuel lines and cells are self-sealing.

The main fuel supply is carried in 4 large fuel cells, 2 in each wing center section between the fuselage and the nacelle. The front cell in each wing has a capacity of 184 gallons, the rear cell 151 gallons.

To reduce the fuel system's vulnerability to enemy fire, the engine is supplied only from the main cells. A flutter valve in the adapter between the front and rear cells allows fuel to flow from rear to front but restricts a reverse flow. Thus, if the rear cell is damaged you lose the fuel in the rear cell, but you don't lose the remaining fuel supply in other cells.

An electric fuel booster pump mounted below the adapter serves 3 important functions:

1. Furnishes adequate pressure for engine starting.
2. Provides emergency fuel pressure for operation below 1000 feet.
3. Provides additional fuel pressure above 10,000 feet to prevent vapor lock.

All fuel flow, whether for transfer or normal operation, is from rear to front. The main cells supply fuel to the engines through the adapter and the booster pump. Fuel leaving the booster pump flows to the cut-off valves, thence to the fuel strainers and the fuel pump. The pump boosts pressure to 6-7 lb. sq. in. before the fuel enters the carburetor.

There are three interconnected fuel cells with a common filler cap outboard of the nacelle in each wing. The total capacity of this auxiliary fuel supply in each wing is 152 gallons. Because all 3 cells are filled, measured, and distribute their fuel through common lines, they are considered as a single tank.

This fuel is transferred to the front main tank in each wing by an electric transfer pump, controlled by a switch on the pilot's pedestal.

Additional fuel for long-range and ferry missions may be carried by the installation of a fuselage fuel cell. A 215-gallon self-sealing fuel cell is strapped into the top of the bomb bay and becomes an integral part of the airplane. You can carry only partial bomb loads when this cell is installed.

If no bombs are to be carried, a 335-gallon metal tank may be suspended from the bomb shackles and salvoed in an emergency.

Transfer fuel from the fuselage tanks to the front main cell by an electric centrifuge pump and in emergencies by a double-action hand pump.

Fuel transfer valves for the fuselage tanks are on the forward wall of the bomb bay.

Use the crossfeed system for emergency operation only. By using the crossfeed, you can supply fuel from one or both tanks to one or both engines.

LOCATION OF FUEL CELLS

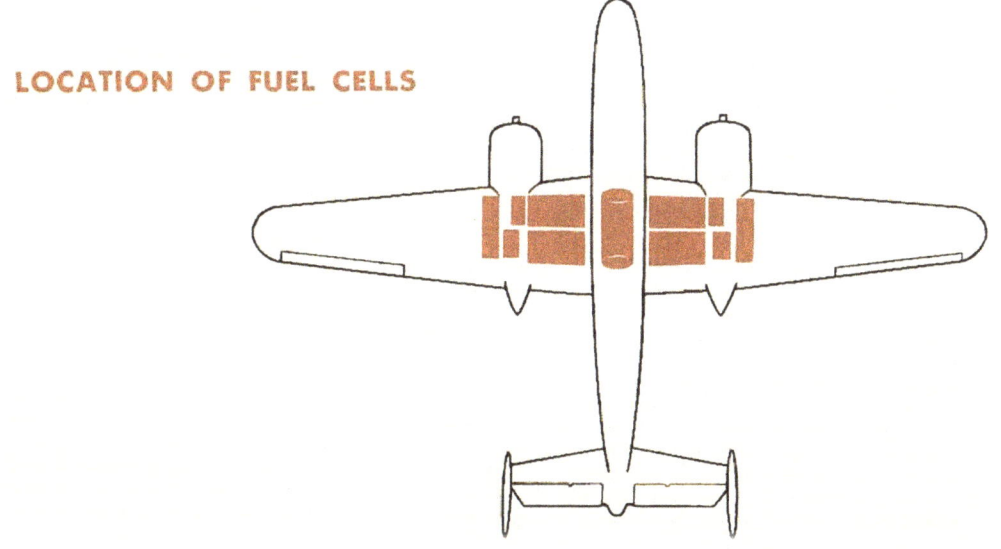

FUEL SYSTEM

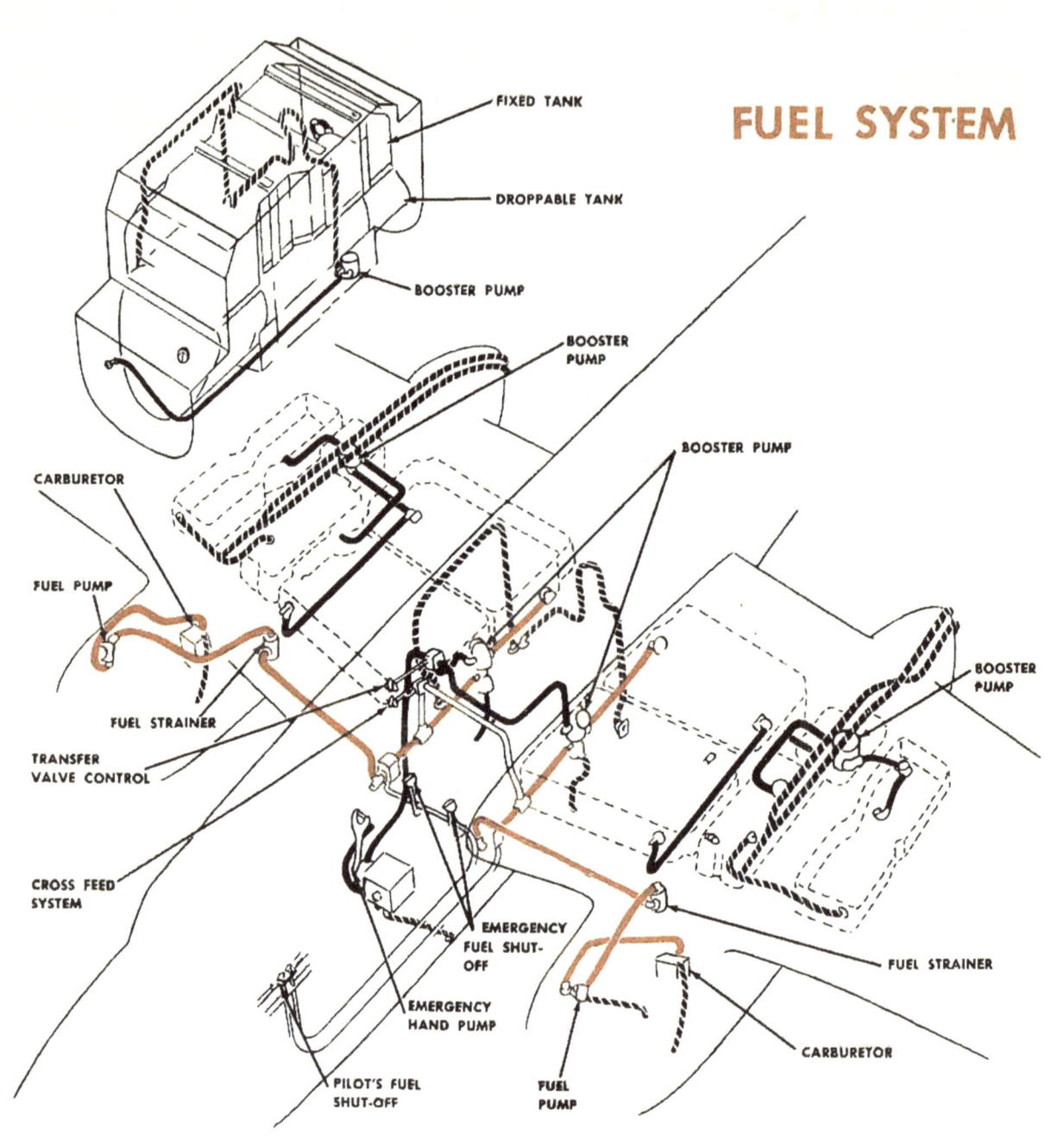

OIL SYSTEM

Each engine has an independent oil supply. The self-sealing oil tank mounted behind the firewall on each nacelle has a capacity of 34 gallons. It contains a hopper tank to accelerate oil warming and facilitate oil dilution. A sump and standpipe in the lower part of the tank insure a supply of 1½ gallons of oil for the propeller feathering system even if the main oil system is dry.

On early models not equipped with self-sealing tanks, the tank is of the same outward size but will hold 37½ gallons of oil.

The Y drain for each oil system is in the lowermost part of the system. This unit contains a bulb which is connected to the oil temperature gage, and also an inlet leading from the oil dilution valve to insure gasoline reaching every part of the oil system.

Check this drain frequently for leaks. A leak will cause the loss of the entire oil supply.

The oil pump is a gear-type, positive displacement pump incorporating 3 pumps in one housing: a pressure pump and 2 return or scavenger pumps—one for the forward and one for the rear sump of the engine.

A spring-loaded valve adjusts the pressure pump, bypassing the oil side to the inlet side. Turning the adjustment clockwise increases the pressure.

The oil pressure system is relieved by a spring-loaded check valve in the line between the oil pump and the oil cuno. It is set to open at a pressure of 90 lb. sq. in. Pressure greater than 90 lb. forces this valve off its seat and allows oil to bypass and return to the main tank. This keeps the pressure constant within a + or —1 lb.

The cuno strainer is made up of many metal discs, with a small metal plate between each pair of discs. It strains out foreign particles. A small flange operated by oil pressure turns the discs, making the cuno self-cleaning.

The cuno incorporates an automatic bypass valve. This valve opens and allows the oil to flow around the strainers if the plates become badly clogged.

The oil temperature regulators are outboard of the engine nacelle in each wing, with 2 regulators connected in parallel for each system.

Each regulator consists of a 10-inch-diameter oil cooler controlled by a thermostatic valve. Each cooler comprises a cooling element, serving as a core, enclosed by a shell and surrounded by a warming jacket. It is similar to the radiator of an automobile.

The oil has 2 paths of flow. One is through the warming jacket past a relief valve and out, thus bypassing the cooling element. The other path is around the warming jacket to the cooling element inlet, through the cooling element and out.

The position of the thermostatic valve determines the path to be used. Regulation of the oil temperature is fully automatic once the valve is calibrated.

Air for cooling enters the leading edge of the wing. The amount of cooling effected is in proportion to the mass of air flowing through the air ducts. On early models the amount of air flow can be manually controlled from the cockpit by direct linkage with the oil cooler shutters. On models H and J, the operation of the oil coolers is automatic.

If the oil temperature rises abnormally, it may be the result of clogged cooling elements. Rectify this condition by closing the oil cooler shutters for a maximum of 2 minutes. This builds up an extremely high oil temperature and cleans the cooling element of sludge or gum. Then resume normal operation. On models H and J, a surge valve allows the oil to bypass the cooling element entirely. The oil pressure gage in older planes is an autosyn-type instrument on one of the engine mounts. In the newer planes it is a pressure transmitter.

The pressure transmitter is described in the section dealing with instruments.

The temperature bulb in the Y drain is connected directly to a bourdon-tube gage on the instrument panel calibrated to read temperature directly.

The drain plug in the front sump of the engine is magnetic, to aid in clearing steel particles from the oil. It is also an aid in indicating internal damage in the engine.

The maximum oil consumption of the engine at cruising throttle setting is 16 quarts per hour; at takeoff throttle setting it is 28.2 quarts per hour.

The airplane should have full oil cells (34 gallons each) for takeoff. However, in an emergency it may be flown with a minimum of 21 gallons in each cell.

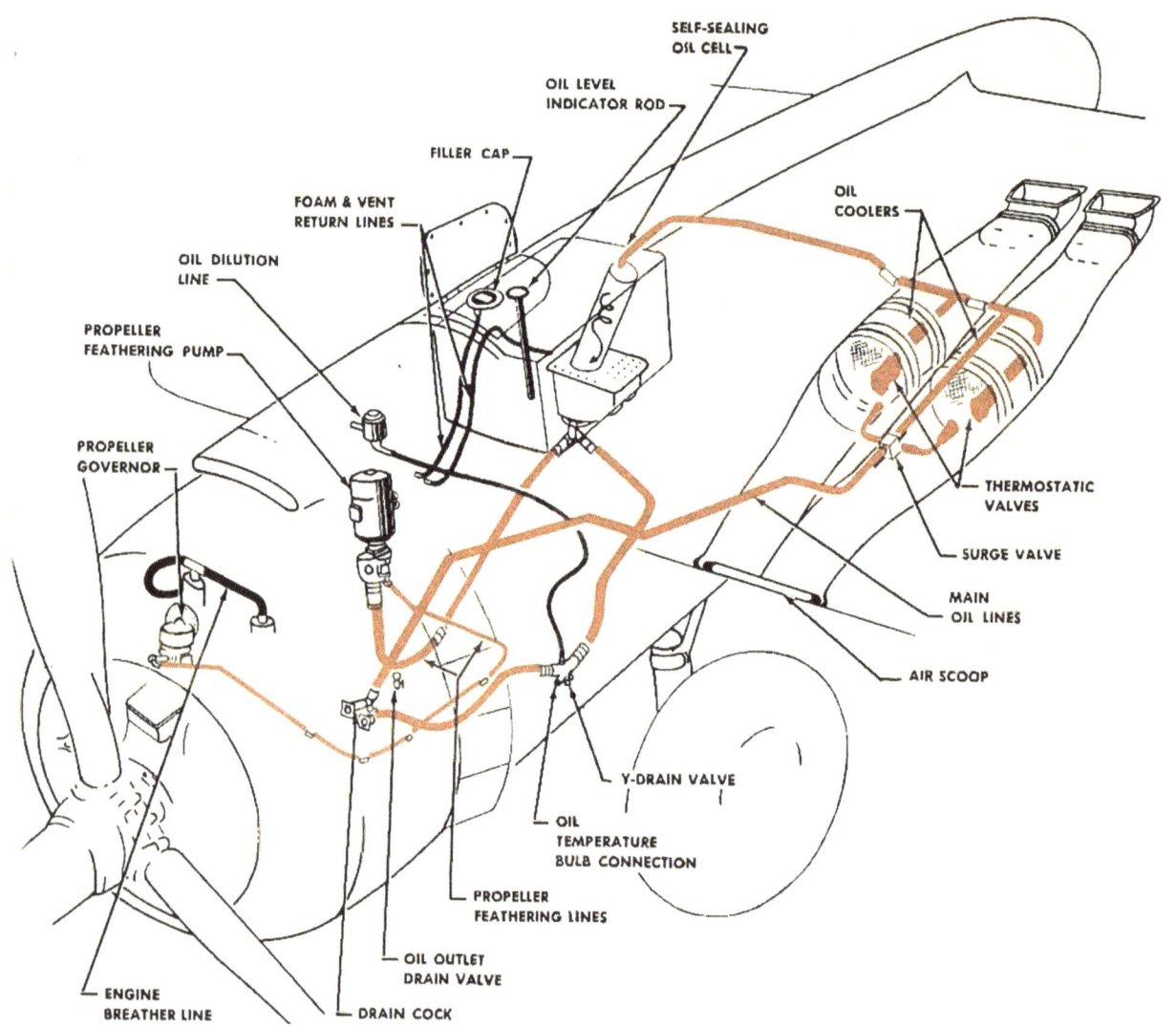

DUAL IGNITION SYSTEM

The ignition system, except for the induction vibrator coil, is independent of all other electrical power sources.

There are 2 magnetos on each engine. The right magneto furnishes spark to the front plugs and the left to the rear plugs in both banks of cylinders.

Dual ignition provides more efficient combustion, decreasing the possibility of detonation. It also acts as a safety factor by providing 2 separate ignition systems on each engine.

Since the magnetos do not furnish sufficient spark until they are turning 75 to 85 rpm, it is necessary to provide starting spark from an induction vibrator coil. It is in the power panel junction box and steps up 24-volt current to 20,000-25,000 volts at a low amperage output. To operate it, engage the starter with the meshing switch. High-voltage spark is sent to the right magneto, firing the front plugs as they are less likely to foul. The induction coil continues to operate until the meshing switch is released.

Caution

Never keep the induction vibrator coil in continuous operation, as tremendous heat is generated, and the coil will burn out.

Necessary lines, fuses, and switches complete the ignition system.

ELECTRICAL SYSTEM

The electrical power which operates and controls the various units of the B-25 is supplied by 2 generators, supplemented by 2 storage batteries connected in parallel.

The batteries, behind the firewall in each nacelle, furnish 24-volt current to the electrical equipment when the generators are not operating.

Battery-disconnect solenoids connect the batteries to the electrical system. (On late series aircraft B-4 relays replace these solenoids.) The solenoids are in the power panel junction box and are controlled by switches on the pilot's switch panel. Both are "ON" for normal operation.

There is an outlet in the right nacelle for the use of external power. (All electrical switches must be "OFF" before applying external power.)

There is a 30-volt, 200-ampere, blast-cooled generator on the accessory section below the starter of each engine. They are geared to the engine drive shafts at a 1.38:1 ratio.

The generators recharge the batteries and furnish all necessary electrical power. The voltage output of the generators is kept at 28 to 28.5 volts by 2 voltage regulators in the navigator's junction box.

Two switches on the navigator's switch panel control the generators.

Reverse-current relays in the power panel

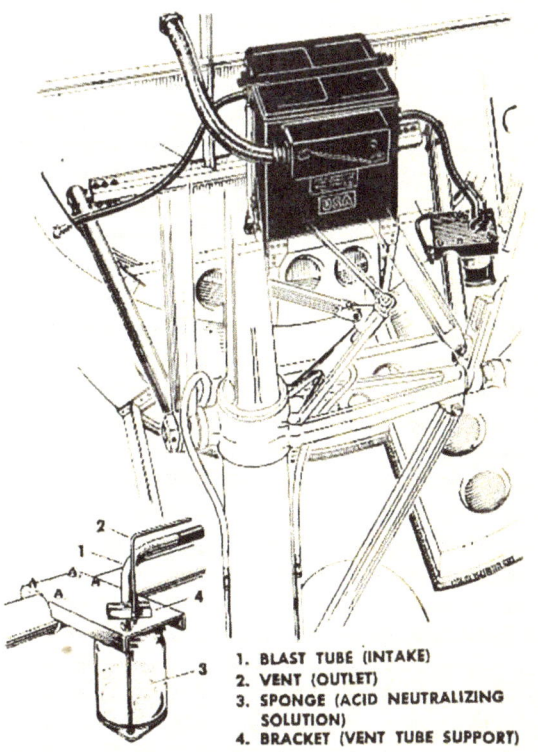

1. BLAST TUBE (INTAKE)
2. VENT (OUTLET)
3. SPONGE (ACID NEUTRALIZING SOLUTION)
4. BRACKET (VENT TUBE SUPPORT)

STORAGE BATTERY

junction box prevent a reverse flow of current, avoiding loss of battery charge when generator output is low.

Instruments for checking generator output are on the navigator's switch panel.

Inverters change direct current to alternating current for certain electrical units. These units are: radio compass, marker beacon, autosyn instruments, remote indicating compass, magnetic compass light, drift meter, bomb indicating lights, A-8 fluorescent lights, and heated clothing.

The inverter is a combination motor-generator. The 24-volt current drives the motor, which in turn drives the generator and produces 26-volt and 110-volt alternating current.

There is a combination inertia and direct-cranking starter on each engine. The motor is a part of the inertia system developing 22,000 rpm. This is reduced to 90 rpm for cranking the engine.

The current to the starter passes through the starter solenoid in the power panel junction box. This solenoid is operated by the energizing switch on the pilot's pedestal. After the inertia is built up, 2 jaws—one on the starter and one on the end of the engine crankshaft—transfer it to the engine. This action is accomplished by the meshing solenoid in the starter operated by the meshing switch on the pilot's pedestal.

These switches, used for both engines, are 3-position, spring-loaded switches.

Various circuits, switches, and fuses complete the system.

On late-model airplanes, circuit breakers replace the fuses in the electric system.

B-25 LIGHTING EQUIPMENT

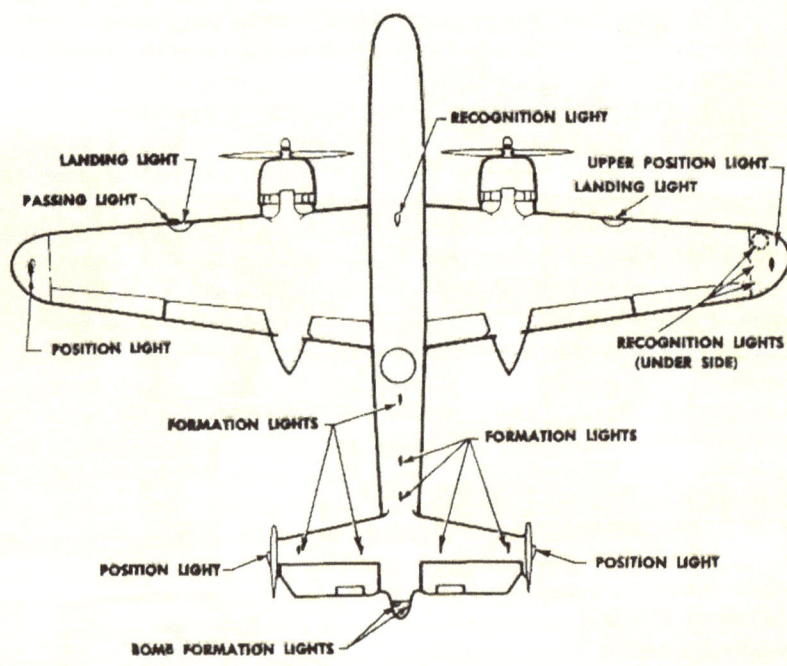

Exterior Lighting

Landing Lights—An 8-inch, sealed-beam landing light is in the leading edge of each outer wing panel and is operated by a switch on the pilot's control pedestal.

Passing Light—Located beside the landing light in the left outboard wing panel, it is controlled by a switch on the pilot's switch panel (not installed on late series B-25).

Position Lights—The position lights consist of a red light on the outer edge of the left wingtip, a green light on the outer edge of the right wingtip, and a white frosted light on the outboard surface of each vertical stabilizer. Two switches on the pilot's switch panel operate these lights. Each switch has an independent "BRIGHT" and "DIM" position for the wing and tail lights, separately controlled.

Formation Lights—The formation lights, colored blue, are mounted on the upper surface of the fuselage and horizontal stabilizer so they will not be visible from the ground. There are 3 lights aft of the upper turret on the center line of the fuselage and 4 lights on the horizontal stabilizer approximately 3 inches forward of the elevators. A rheostat, acting as both switch and intensity adjustment, controls all 7 lights (not installed on late series B-25's).

Recognition Lights—The recognition lights comprise a white lamp on the upper surface of the fuselage above the radio compartment, and red, green and amber lights on the lower surface of the right wingtip. A bank of 4 toggle switches on the left side of the pilot's control pedestal operates the lamps in any desired combination. They can be set to burn continuously or to flash off and on by means of a keying switch on the toggle switch box. **Caution: Do not keep the recognition lights on for more than a few seconds with the airplane on the ground, as serious damage to the lenses will result.**

Interior Lighting

Dome lights are located in the pilot's, bombardier's, navigator's, bomb bay, and radio compartments. The controls for the dome lights are in their respective compartments.

Extension lights are in the pilot's, bombardier's, and navigator's compartments. Switch controls of these lights are on each unit. They can be extended approximately 4 feet.

Instrument Lighting

Fluorescent lamps are in the bombardier's compartment and on the pilot's and copilot's control columns. Intensity of these lights is adjustable by rheostats, adjacent to the lamps.

The pilot's magnetic compass light is in the compass itself; a rheostat on the pilot's switch panel controls it.

All optical gunsight lights are inside the sights. The rheostats which control them are near each unit.

HAMILTON HYDROMATIC PROPELLERS

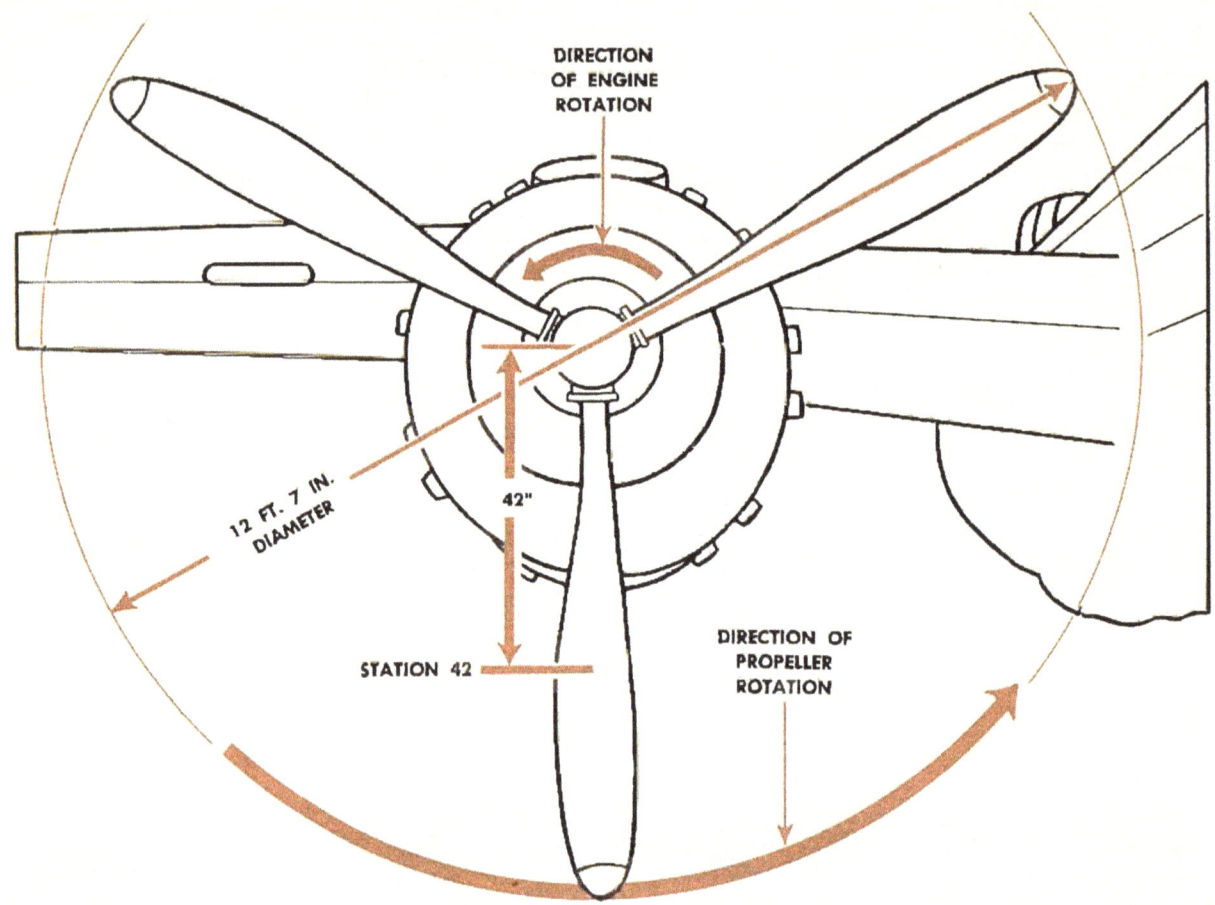

The Hamilton hydromatic propellers of the B-25 are hydraulically operated. Their special features are automatic constant-engine-speed operation and the ability to feather and unfeather quickly in an emergency.

The actuating mechanisms operate in an oil bath, thereby minimizing wear and the chance of mechanical failure.

Constant-engine-speed control is achieved by an engine-driven governor metering oil to and from the actuating dome assembly. Engine oil under 75-90 lb. sq. in. pressure, plus the centrifugal twisting moment of the blade, decreases blade angle. Engine oil at a boosted pressure of 180-200 lb. sq. in. pressure increases blade angle.

Feathering and unfeathering is accomplished by an independent auxiliary oil system controlled from the cockpit.

Principle of Operation

Angular blade movement of the propellers is obtained by converting the straight-line motion of the piston to circular movement by the cams. Oil pressure drives the piston forward or backward.

Constant-speed Control

The propeller governor assembly maintains rpm settings established by the pilot.

The governor consists of 2 flyweights geared to the operation of the crankshaft. These fly-

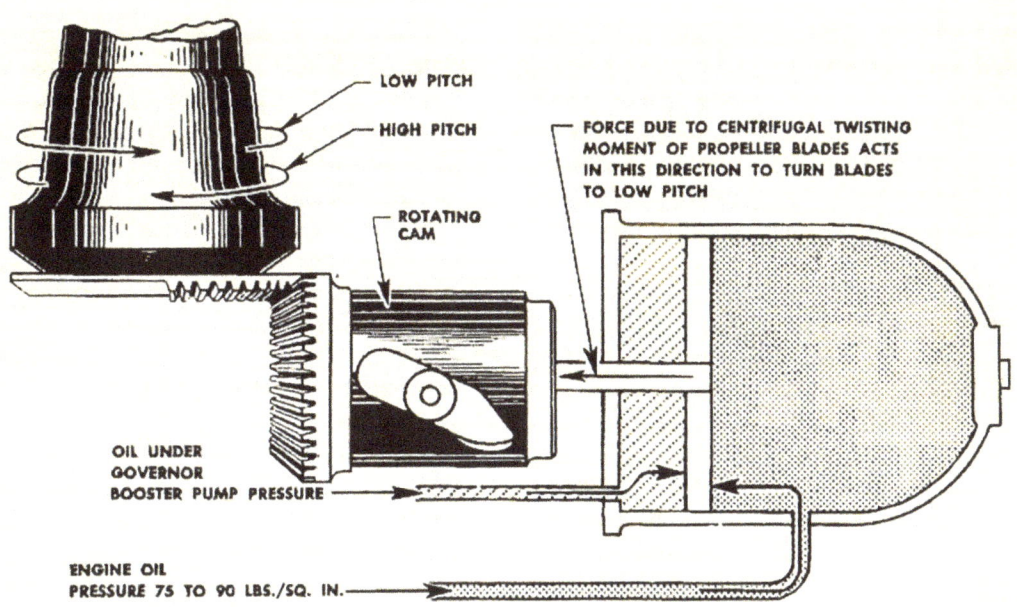

weights adjust the load on the engine by raising or lowering a pilot valve which allows oil under pressure to be metered to the propeller dome, thereby increasing or decreasing the blade angle.

On-speed—An on-speed condition exists when the engine is turning at the selected rpm. The pilot valve has closed the pressure and drain ports in the governor, maintaining the blades at a fixed blade angle.

Overspeed—An overspeed condition indicates that the engine rpm has increased beyond the original setting. To counteract this condition, engine oil flows to the governor. There a booster pump increases pressure of the oil to 180-200 lb. per sq. in. Entry of this oil to the inboard side of the propeller dome is permitted when the pilot valve opens the pressure port, moving the piston forward and thus increasing blade angle and decreasing engine rpm.

Underspeed—An underspeed condition indicates that the engine is running slower than the selected rpm. To correct this, the pilot valve is forced downward, opening the drain port. Oil drains from the inboard side of the piston in the propeller dome. The centrifugal twisting moment of the blades, plus engine oil pressure on the outboard side of the piston, moves the blades to a lower angle, thus increasing engine rpm to the selected setting.

Feathering

You feather a propeller by actuating the feathering control button on the pilot's pedestal. An electric feathering pump supplies oil at 400 lb. sq. in. through a transfer valve. Through

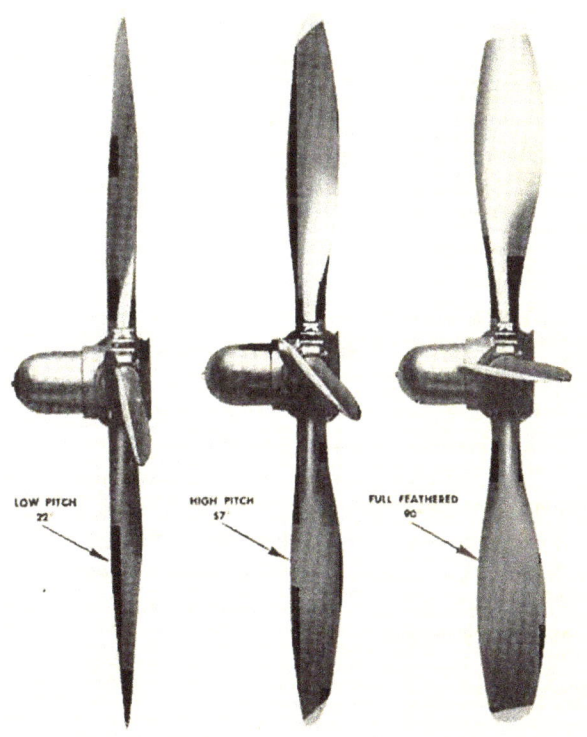

this valve the oil bypasses the governor to the propeller dome. Pressure is then built up on the inboard side of the piston, twisting the blades to the full-feathered position (90°.) When the blades are at this angle, pressure increases sufficiently to operate a cut-out switch, disengaging the feathering pump.

Unfeathering

To unfeather a propeller hold the control button down. This operates the feathering pump, applying pressure through the same passages used for feathering. Since further travel of the piston is no longer possible, oil pressure at 600 lb. sq. in. shifts a distributor valve to its outboard limit, which reverses the oil passages to the propeller dome. The pressure is now applied to the outboard side of the piston and moves it inboard, decreasing the blade angle. Hold control button down until the propeller is windmilling at 800 rpm. Then resume control in a normal manner.

HYDRAULIC SYSTEM

The hydraulic system provides quick and easy operation of the following equipment on the B-25:

Tricycle Landing Gear
Brakes
Wing Flaps
Cowl Flaps
Bomb Bay Doors
Automatic Pilot
Gun Chargers

The reservoir which contains the hydraulic fluid has a capacity of 5.9 gallons. A standpipe in the reservoir retains a reserve of 2.33 gallons for the emergency hand pump.

This reservoir, made of aluminum alloy, has a sight gage which shows the level of the fluid. The gage has only 2 markings—"FULL" and "REFILL." There is a removable screen in the filler neck which must be cleaned whenever the reservoir is re-serviced.

Two lines lead from the reservoir to a foam tank, built into the system to allow for expansion of the fluid caused by temperature changes. A vent line maintains constant atmospheric pressure in the system, allowing excess fluid or pressure bubbles to escape.

There is an engine-driven, gear-type, positive displacement pump in the accessory section below the right magneto of each engine. These pumps supply fluid pressure to the accumulators. They are connected in parallel. If one pump fails, the other will supply sufficient pressure to the system.

An emergency double-action, single-impulse hand pump, on the floor between pilot's and copilot's seats, supplies pressure to the system if both engine-driven pumps fail.

Two accumulators, located in the forward right corner of the navigator's compartment, store fluid under air pressure for the brakes and main hydraulic system. The accumulators also provide an air cushion in the system to absorb sudden changes in fluid flow.

These accumulators consist of a tubular steel housing into which is fitted a neoprene rubber boot. The boot is filled with air to a pressure of 400 lb. sq. in. The steel housing contains hydraulic fluid. When the fluid pressure exceeds 400 lb. sq. in. it compresses the air in the boot.

Fluid is pumped into the accumulators until the pressure is 1050 lb. sq. in. in the main system and 1150 lb. sq. in. in the brake system, sufficient for normal operation.

In late-series aircraft, pistons replace the rubber boots in the accumulators. The action is unchanged, however.

There are actuating cylinders at all points of the equipment where hydraulic pressure is converted into mechanical action.

This does not apply to the brakes, where toe pressure on the rudder pedals is converted into hydraulic pressure, which in turn supplies braking action through the power brake valve.

There is an emergency air brake system for use if the hydraulic brake system fails.

HYDRAULIC SYSTEM

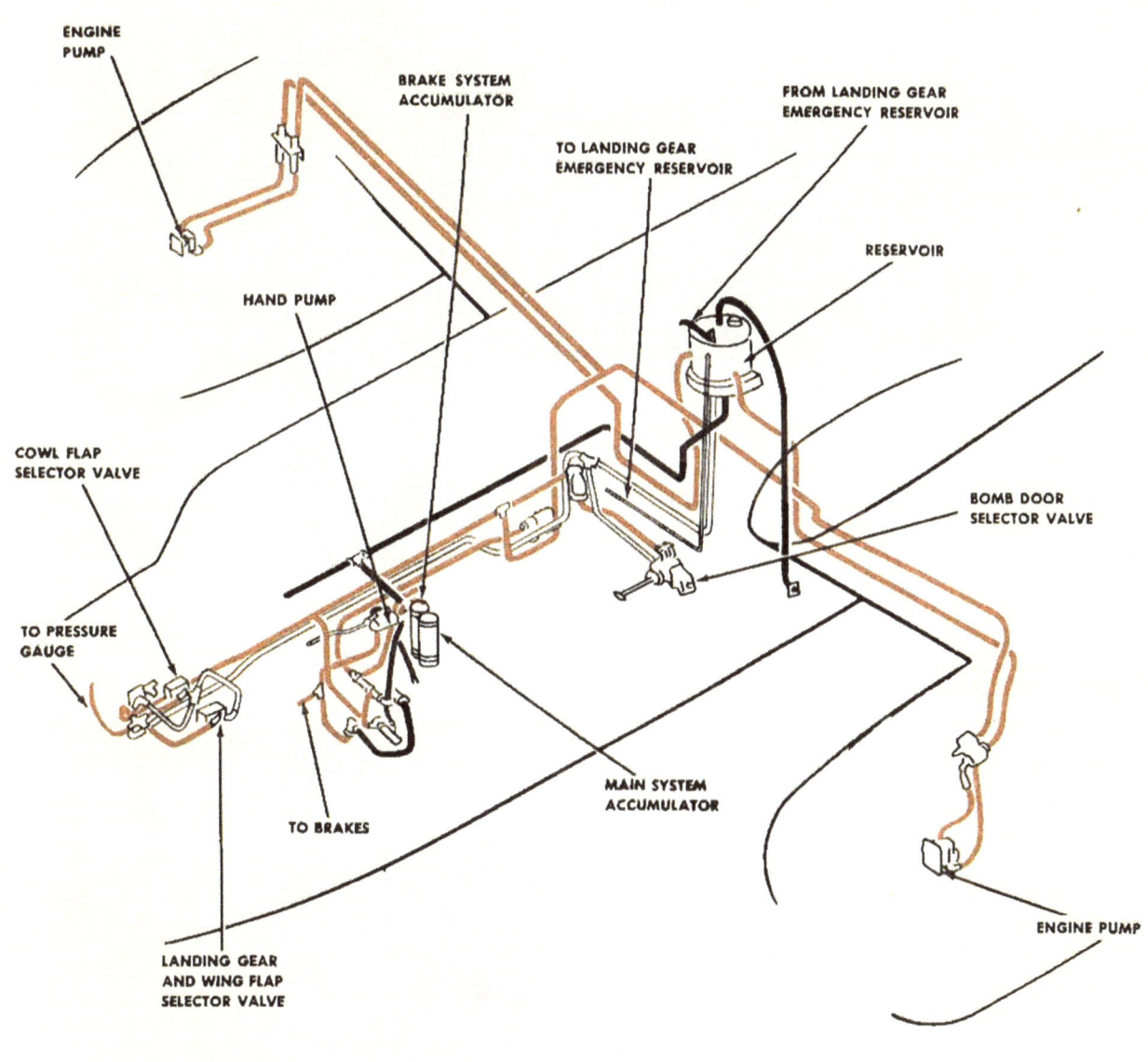

Landing Gear

The B-25 has retractable, tricycle landing gear, hydraulically operated. The landing gear retracts aft, the main gear into the engine nacelles, the nose gear into the fuselage. Doors cover the gear openings in both the retracted and extended positions.

The landing gear control handle is on the lower section of the pilot's control pedestal. Three distinct safety devices prevent accidental movement of the control handle:

1. A latch on the pedestal that must be set in the correct position before you can move the handle.

2. A wire hook fastened to the pedestal which is placed over the control handle whenever the handle is in the "DOWN" position.

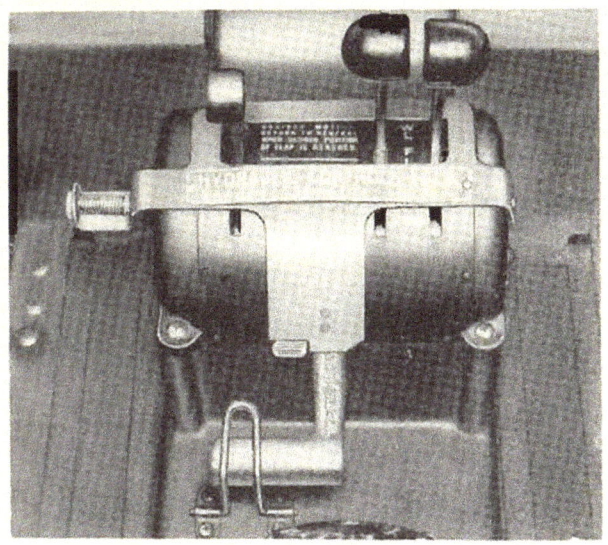

3. A locking plate that the pilot attaches to the pedestal whenever he leaves the airplane.

The swivel-type nose gear strut incorporates a centering device. It functions when weight is removed from the nosewheel. There is a shimmy damper on the nosewheel strut to absorb the vibrations created in taxiing. The nosewheel may be released from the shimmy damper for towing purposes. A static ground wire is attached to the nosewheel.

There is a position indicator for the landing gear on the instrument panel. A warning horn, replaced on later models by a warning light, indicates whether landing gear is down and locked when throttles are retarded.

You can check the position of the main wheels visually from the cockpit. Check the position of the nosewheel visually by use of the drift meter or by removing the inspection plate from the floor in front of the copilot.

The landing gear has smooth-contour wheels and tires. The nosewheel tire has a dual-seal tube, but the main wheel tires use regular tubes.

The main wheels have hydraulically operated, multiple-disc brakes. Varying pressures on the toe pedals produce braking action.

Conventional parking brakes permit setting the brakes in a locked position.

For emergency operation of landing gear and brakes, see Emergency Section.

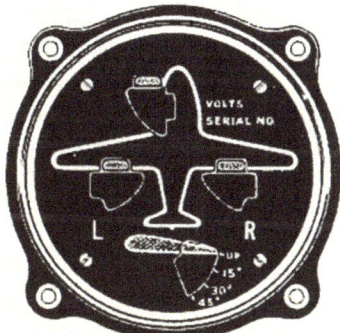

LANDING GEAR UP AND LOCKED. FLAPS UP

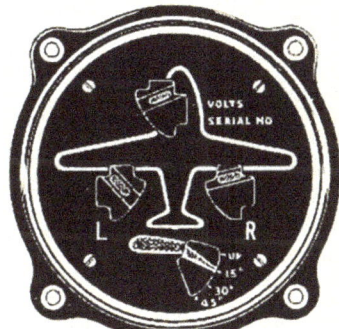

LANDING GEAR PARTIALLY DOWN. FLAPS 15°

LANDING GEAR DOWN NOT LOCKED. FLAPS 15°

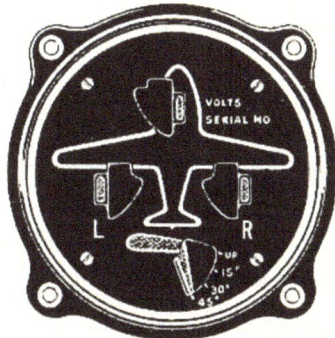

LANDING GEAR DOWN AND LOCKED. FLAPS 45°

INSTRUMENTS

The following instruments are installed on the B-25. You need no special instructions for their operation, as they are basically the same as those on any 2-engine bombardment or training airplane.

Flight Instruments

Pitot Static Instruments
1. Airspeed indicator
2. Sensitive altimeter
3. Rate-of-climb indicator

A static pressure selector valve on the instrument panel allows the pilot to use an alternate source of static pressure from inside the airplane. Use this when the static side of the pitot tube fails because of damage or unusual air conditions, such as might be encountered during a thunderstorm.

Vacuum Instruments

Vacuum pumps, one on each engine, supply the pressure to operate these instruments and also the autopilot and the de-icer boots.
1. Artificial horizon
2. Directional gyro
3. Bank-and-turn indicator

A bank-and-turn needle-valve control on the instrument panel allows adjustment of the suction pressures operating the gyro of the bank-and-turn indicator. Flight tests on this instrument should give a standard-rate turn (90° in 30 seconds) at one needle-width deflection. Adjust the suction pressures until this deflection is accurate.

Engine Instruments

1. Cylinder-head temperature gage
2. Oil temperature gage
3. Oil pressure gage
4. Fuel pressure gage
5. Tachometer
6. Manifold pressure gage
7. Carburetor air temperature gage

Miscellaneous Instruments

1. Suction gage
2. Clock
3. Magnetic compass
4. Remote compass indicator
5. Radio compass indicator
6. Hydraulic and brake pressure indicators
7. Fuel gages
8. Free air temperature gages
9. Air pressure gages—for the emergency air brake system and the hydraulic accumulators.
10. Oxygen regulators
11. Nosewheel warning lights
12. Landing gear and flap position indicator—this is a resistance-type indicator.

A contact, linked to the landing gear and flaps, moves across the arc of a resistor as you operate the gear and flaps. Thus the resistance varies and is converted to an indication of position on the instrument dial.

Autosyn Instruments

Autosyn instruments are electrically operated. Each instrument consists of two motors, one of which is a transmitter and the other an indicator. The transmitter is located at the source of mechanical energy, the indicator on the instrument panel. The two motors are synchronized so that the speed of the motor at the source governs the speed of the motor at the indicator, and gives an accurate reading.

The most common autosyn installations are:
Fuel pressure
Oil pressure
Manifold pressure
Tachometer
Remote reading compass

On late series aircraft, pressure transmitting instruments replace all autosyn instruments, except the remote reading compass.

Pressure Transmitting Instruments

Pressure forces in the pressure transmitting instruments actuate a diaphragm. This diaphragm transmits the pressure through a line filled with compass fluid to an indicator on the instrument panel, where it is converted to the desired reading.

The pressure transmitting instruments on the B-25 are fuel pressure and oil pressure.

Aircraft with these instruments have direct reading manifold pressure gages and electric tachometers.

AUTOMATIC PILOT

Most B-25's have A-3 or A-3A autopilots which operate on a pneumatic-hydraulic principle. They fly the airplane automatically in straight and level flight and make the necessary corrections for holding a given course or altitude. They do this by utilizing the indications of the directional gyro control unit and the bank and climb control unit.

The difference between the human pilot and the autopilot is that the autopilot acts instantaneously and with a precision not possible for a human pilot.

The reaction time of the human pilot is always governed by such factors as fatigue, muscle coordination and a failure to detect errors the instant they occur.

The autopilot however, corrects instantaneously for any deviation from the set course. Properly adjusted, it will neither overcontrol nor undercontrol the airplane, but will keep it flying straight and level with all controls operating in complete coordination.

How It Works

The principle of operation of the autopilot is the same for correcting all off-movements.

Suppose that an airplane is in straight and level flight and that the autopilot is operating. So long as the airplane continues to fly straight and level, equal amounts of air pass through two channels around the spinning wheel of the bank-and-climb control unit.

the volume of flow. You can also overpower the automatic pilot by applying increased pressure to the controls. Spring-loaded relief valves in the hydraulic cylinders permit this overpowering action if it becomes desirable.

An automatic follow-up mechanism is part of the automatic pilot. It eases the pressure on the controls as the airplane starts to recover. When the plane is again in level flight, the action of the follow-up mechanism equalizes the pressure in the air relay chamber and cuts off the oil supply.

You can disengage the automatic pilot quickly, if necessary, by a control on the pilot's pedestal. This control is connected by a cable to a bypass valve in the hydraulic cylinder.

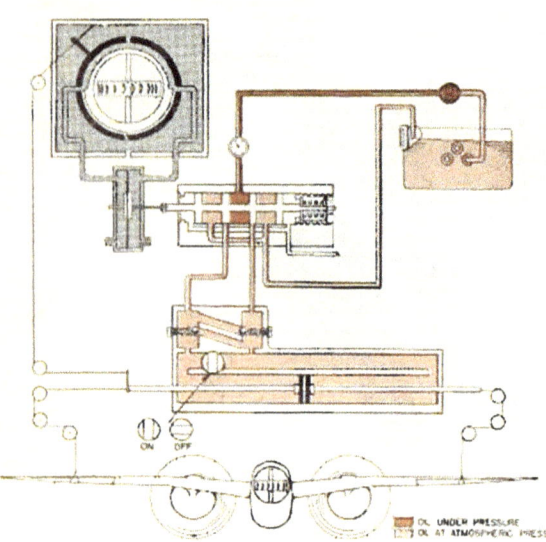

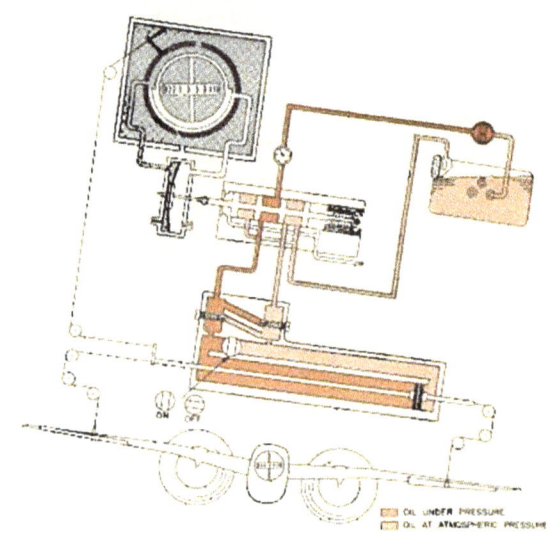

Suddenly rough air causes one wing to drop. Immediately, a ring around the spinning wheel shuts air off from one of the channels. This unequalizes the air in the relay chamber of the bank-and-climb control unit, depressing the diaphragm which divides the relay chamber. When the diaphragm is depressed, a balanced oil valve opens and permits oil to flow to the hydraulic control cylinders. The pressure of this oil actuates a piston connected to the aileron cables. The piston moves forward or backward until the plane is righted.

The flow of oil from the hydraulic cylinder is regulated by speed adjustment knobs on the automatic pilot assembly. You can vary the speed of correction by increasing or decreasing

COMMUNICATION EQUIPMENT

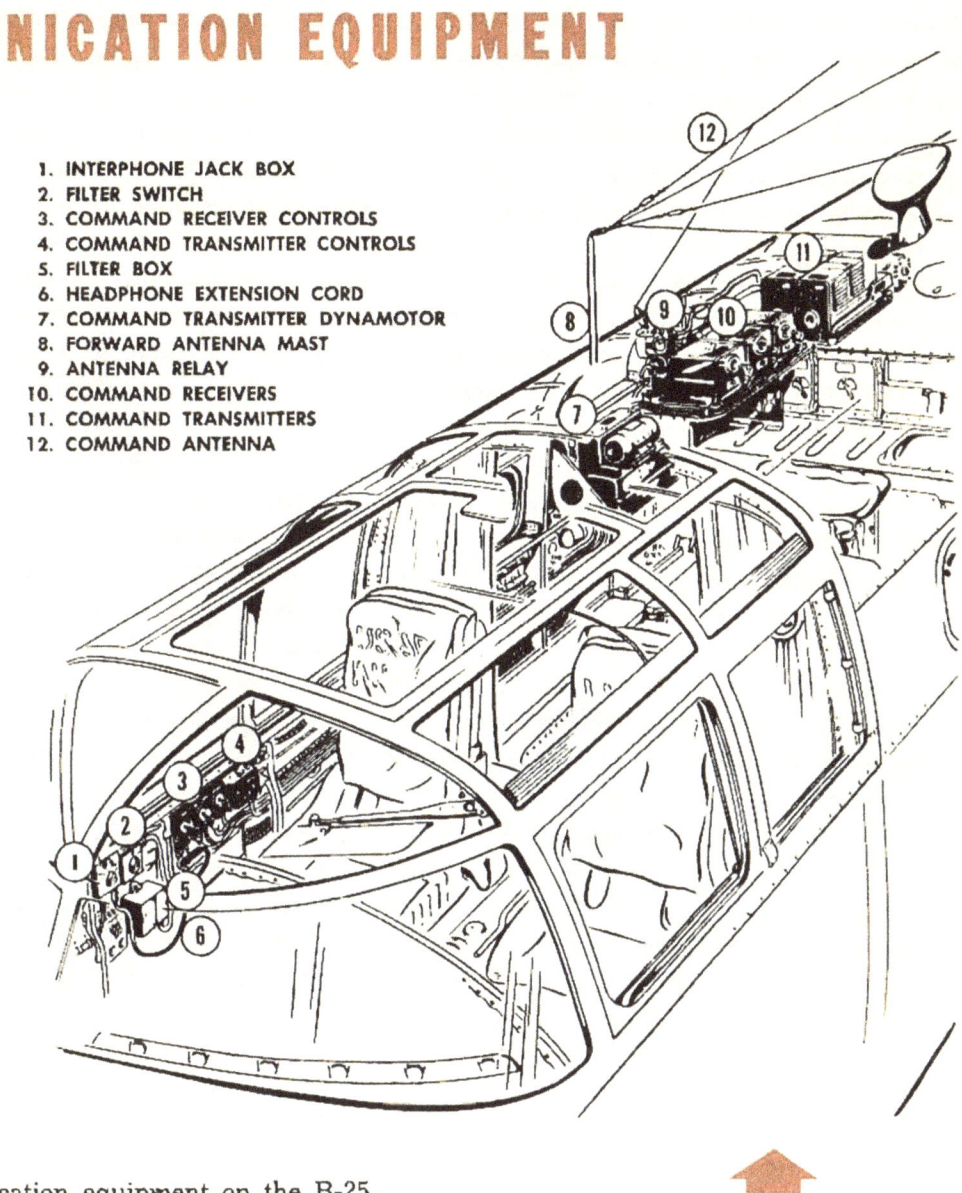

1. INTERPHONE JACK BOX
2. FILTER SWITCH
3. COMMAND RECEIVER CONTROLS
4. COMMAND TRANSMITTER CONTROLS
5. FILTER BOX
6. HEADPHONE EXTENSION CORD
7. COMMAND TRANSMITTER DYNAMOTOR
8. FORWARD ANTENNA MAST
9. ANTENNA RELAY
10. COMMAND RECEIVERS
11. COMMAND TRANSMITTERS
12. COMMAND ANTENNA

The communication equipment on the B-25 is basically the same as that on all Army bombardment airplanes.

The following radio sets are installed:
Command set
Liaison set
Radio compass receiver
Marker beacon receiver
Interphone system

On some models the tactical use of the airplane requires the installation of VHF and IFF equipment. Special training in this equipment will be given when missions require its use.

Command Set

The command set has 2 transmitters with a range of 4 to 5.3 Mc on one transmitter and a range of 7 to 9.1 Mc on the other.

Three receivers cover ranges of 190 to 550 Kc, 3 to 6 Mc, and 6 to 9.1 Mc. Selective use of these ranges is made by switching one or all of the receivers "ON."

The command set allows transmission and reception by voice and code for air-to-air and air-to-ground stations over short ranges.

Liaison Set

The liaison set has one transmitter with 7 interchangeable tuning units, covering frequency ranges of 150 to 600 Kc and from 1500 Kc to 12,500 Kc.

The set has one receiver capable of reception of voice, tone, or CW signals over a range of 150 to 18,000 Kc.

A radio operator uses this set for long-range air-to-ground communication. In emergencies the pilot, copilot, and navigator, by using the interphone circuits, can transmit voice messages to the ground.

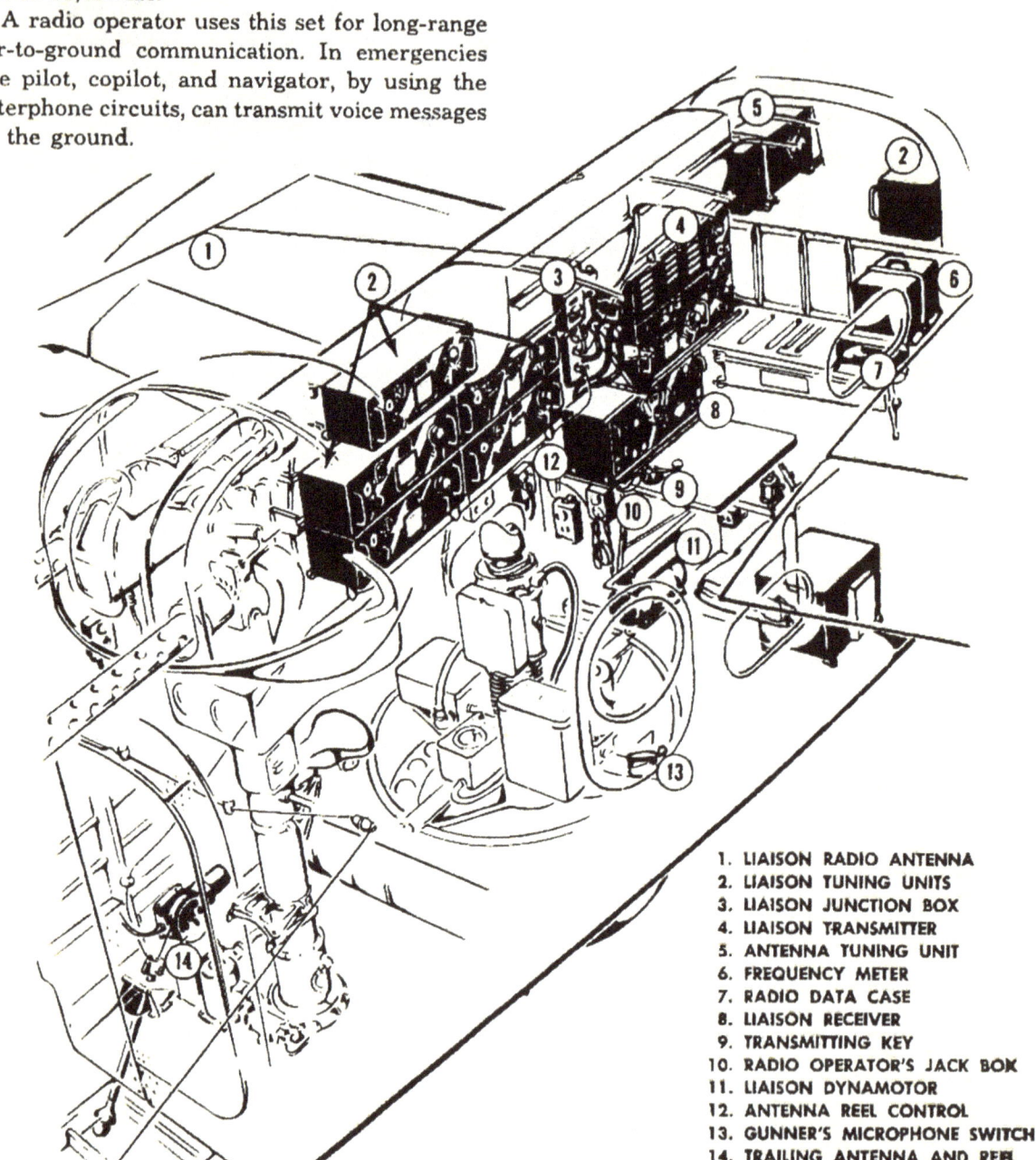

1. LIAISON RADIO ANTENNA
2. LIAISON TUNING UNITS
3. LIAISON JUNCTION BOX
4. LIAISON TRANSMITTER
5. ANTENNA TUNING UNIT
6. FREQUENCY METER
7. RADIO DATA CASE
8. LIAISON RECEIVER
9. TRANSMITTING KEY
10. RADIO OPERATOR'S JACK BOX
11. LIAISON DYNAMOTOR
12. ANTENNA REEL CONTROL
13. GUNNER'S MICROPHONE SWITCH
14. TRAILING ANTENNA AND REEL
15. UPPER TURRET JACK BOX

1. RADIO COMPASS LOOP
2. RADIO COMPASS RECEIVER
3. RADIO COMPASS AND RELAY JUNCTION BOX
4. NAVIGATOR'S AZIMUTH INDICATOR
5. NAVIGATOR'S INTERPHONE JACK BOX
6. NAVIGATOR'S HEADPHONE EXTENSION CORD
7. NAVIGATOR'S RADIO COMPASS CONTROL BOX
8. INTERPHONE DYNAMOTOR
9. FILTER BOX
10. PILOT'S INTERPHONE JACK BOX
11. PILOT'S HEADPHONE EXTENSION CORD
12. PILOT'S RADIO COMPASS CONTROL BOX
13. PILOT'S AZIMUTH INDICATOR

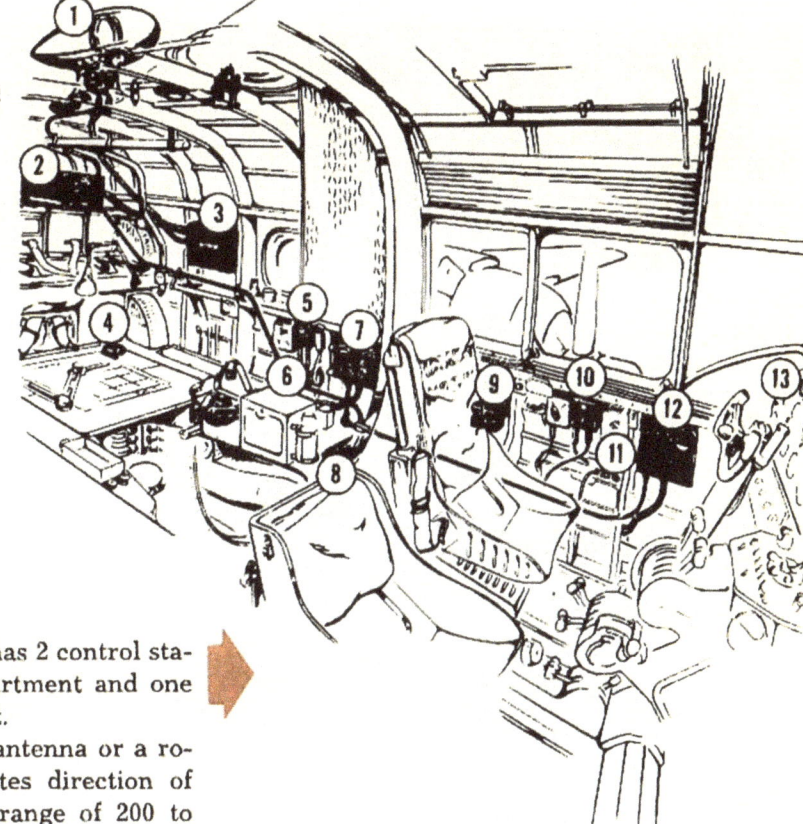

Radio Compass Receiver

The radio compass receiver has 2 control stations, one in the pilot's compartment and one in the navigator's compartment.

Operating on either a fixed antenna or a rotating loop antenna, it indicates direction of incoming signals. It covers a range of 200 to 1750 Kc.

For detailed instructions in the use of this equipment see T.O. 30-100 series.

Marker Beacon Receiver

The marker beacon receiver is a specialist. It performs only one job. Operating on a frequency of 75 Mc, it detects signals transmitted by fan marker beacons, and by Z marker beacons operating in the cones of silence. A blinking light on the instrument panel is connected to the receiver, blinking on when the airplane passes a 75 Mc transmitter.

Interphone

The interphone system of the B-25 is a standard installation. It operates whenever the battery-disconnect switches are "ON." It is used by every crew member to communicate with all other crew members.

The interphone plays a vital part in crew coordination. Used effectively in combat, it serves as the eyes of the entire crew.

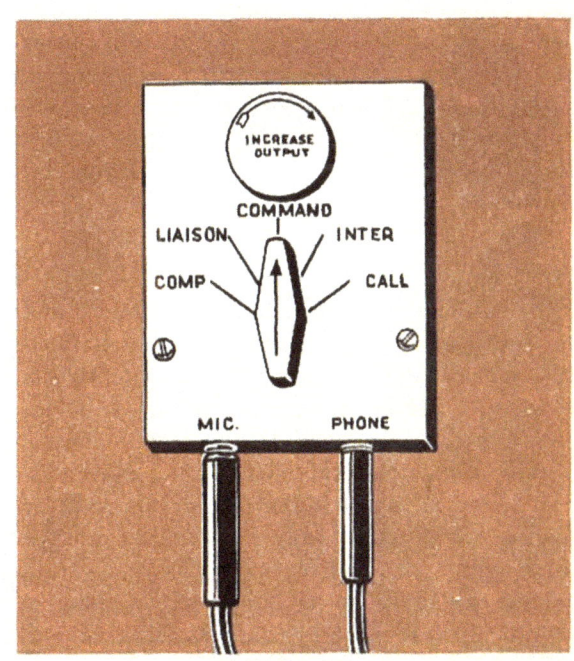

INTERPHONE JACK BOX

ARMAMENT

The armament of the B-25 follows basically the same pattern found in any AAF bombardment airplane. The detailed installation varies greatly according to the tactical uses intended.

Safe handling and operation require thorough knowledge and practice on this equipment, under the supervision of a competent instructor.

Bombing

The bomb bay, between the navigator's and the radio operator's compartments, has fixed ladder bomb racks which accommodate 100-lb. to 1600-lb. bombs. A special rack may be installed to carry one 2000-lb. bomb. The control system is electric and most of the system is dual wired as a precaution against damage by gunfire. Wing racks may be installed on the outer wing panels to carry 8 bombs of from 100 lb. to 300 lb., or 6 325-lb. depth charges.

Controls for operating the bomb bay doors and bomb releases are in the bombardier's compartment.

On the B-25 G and H, the bomb bay and bombing controls are in the pilot's compartment.

On the B-25 J, the bombardment controls are in both the bombardier's and pilot's compartments.

Controls in the pilot's compartment will salvo both bomb load and bomb bay tanks. (See Emergency Procedures.)

Provision is made for carrying a torpedo as an alternate bomb load. Use of the torpedo precludes bomb loads in the bomb bay, but does not limit the use of external wing racks.

Chemical spray tanks may be carried in the bomb bay and on the wing racks when necessary.

Gunnery

Gunnery equipment varies greatly in different series airplanes. They are as follows: **B-25 C and D.**

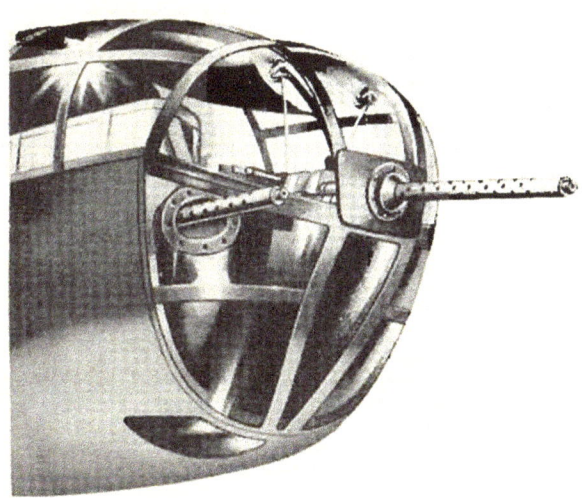

One fixed .50-cal. nose gun is mounted on the right side of the bombardier's compartment. The pilot fires this gun and the bombardier charges it. There is a type N-3B optical gunsight on the upper left side of the instrument panel.

One flexible .50-cal. nose gun, in a ball-and-socket mount, is directly above the bombsight window. The bombardier fires this gun, which has a ring-and-post sight.

There is an electrically powered Bendix upper turret in the radio gunner's compartment. This turret carries two .50-cal. guns fired by either the radio operator or the gunner, and has a type N-6A optical gunsight.

B-25 G

One 75-mm. cannon (type M-4) is in the tunnel beneath the left side of the pilot's compartment and fires through the nose. The pilot fires the cannon and the cannoneer loads it. There is a type N-3B optical gunsight on the left side of the pilot's instrument panel for the forward-firing guns.

Two forward-firing, .50-cal. fixed guns are in the nose. The pilot charges and fires these guns.

There is a Bendix upper turret in the radio gunner's compartment. It carries two .50-cal. guns, fired by either the radio operator or the gunner, and has a type N-6A optical gunsight.

A few modified G's carry flexible .50-cal. waist guns, blister guns, and one flexible .50-cal. tail gun.

B-25 H

One 75-mm. cannon (type T-13) is in the tunnel beneath the left side of the pilot's compartment and fires through the nose. The pilot fires the cannon and the cannoneer loads it. A type N-3B optical gunsight for the forward-firing guns is on the left side of the pilot's instrument panel.

Four forward-firing, .50-cal. fixed guns are in the nose section. The pilot fires these guns, which are charged in the navigator-cannoneer's compartment.

Two or four fixed .50-cal. guns are mounted in blisters on each side of the plane. The cannoneer charges these guns and the pilot fires them.

A Bendix upper turret, in the aft portion of the cannoneer's compartment, carries two .50-cal. guns, fired by the engineer, and has an N-6A gunsight.

Two flexible .50-cal. guns in Plexiglas windows, one at each side of the fuselage aft of the bomb bay, are fired by the radio operator. They have ring-and-post sights.

A Bell model M-7 electric-hydraulic turret with two .50-cal. guns and a type N-8 gunsight is in the tail. A tail gunner operates this turret.

B-25 J

There is one or two forward-firing, fixed .50-cal. nose gun. The bombardier charges this gun and the pilot fires it. The bombardier fires one flexible .50-cal. gun in the nose.

Four fixed .50-cal. guns are installed in blisters, two on each side of the fuselage. The cannoneer charges these guns and the pilot fires them.

A type N-3B optical gunsight governs the forward-firing guns.

A Bendix upper turret, in the aft portion of the cannoneer's compartment, carries two .50-cal. guns, fired by the engineer, and has an N-6A gunsight.

Two flexible .50-cal. guns in Plexiglas windows, one at each side of the fuselage aft of the bomb bay, are fired by the radio operator. They have ring-and-bead or optical sights.

A Bell model M-7 electric-hydraulic turret with two .50-cal. guns and a type N-8 gunsight is in the tail and is operated by a tail gunner.

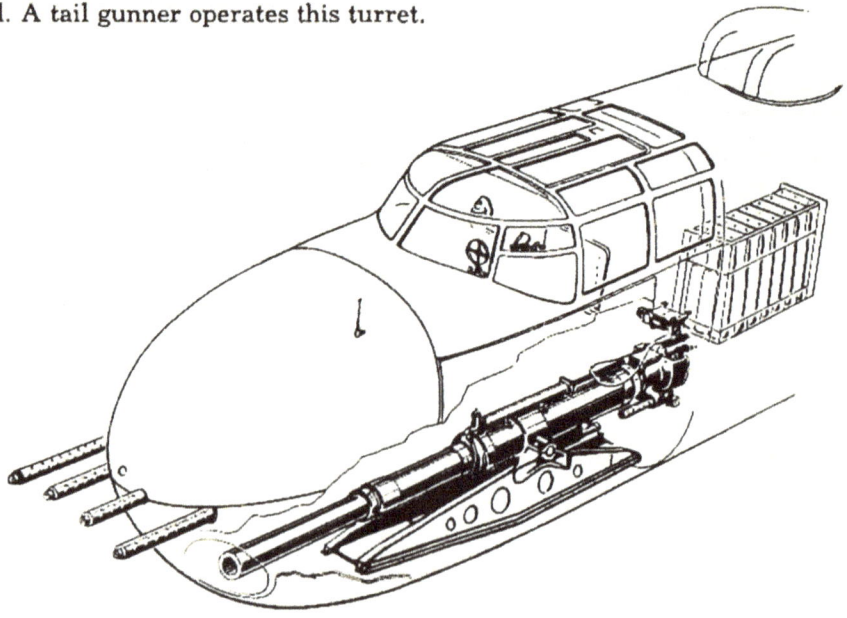

B-25 H CANNON AND NOSE GUNS

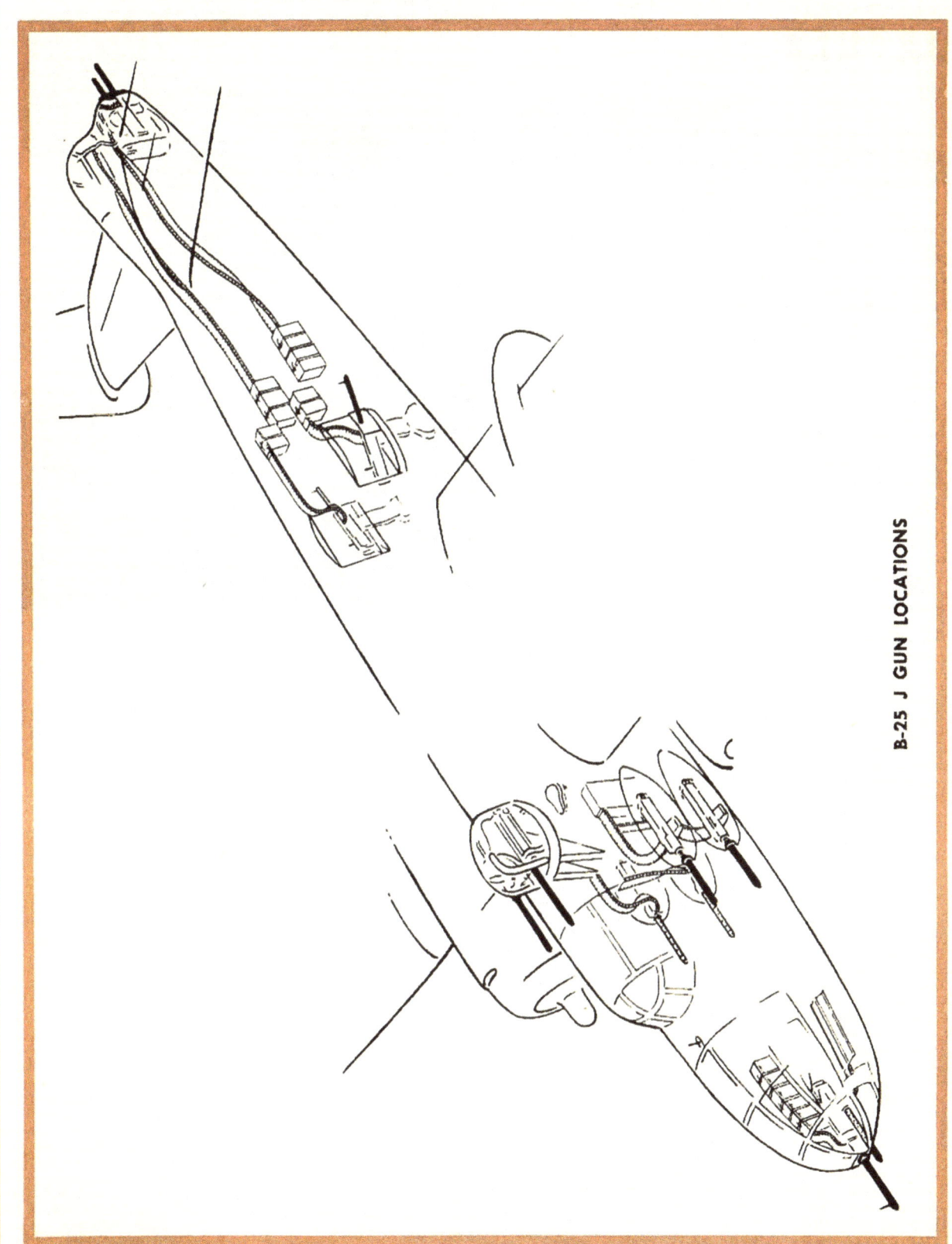

B-25 J GUN LOCATIONS

OXYGEN

The B-25 has two systems of oxygen supply. The first is a permanent installation in the early-series aircraft, the second a portable system in later-series B-25's.

The permanent oxygen system is of the low-pressure type, operating at an average starting pressure of 400 lb. sq. in. There are three low-pressure oxygen cylinders in each nacelle, two at the front and one at the rear. The cylinders, held in place by padded metal straps, are removable.

One filler valve in each nacelle allows servicing of the system. A relief valve in the bomb bay relieves overload pressure on the oxygen system caused by overfilling of oxygen cylinders or thermal expansion.

The oxygen system has eight low-pressure regulators. A pressure gage in each regulator shows the pressure of the entire system. The valve, operated by turning a knob on the lower part of the regulator, adjusts the amount of oxygen flow. A dial on the face of the regulator

A-14 Demand Oxygen Mask

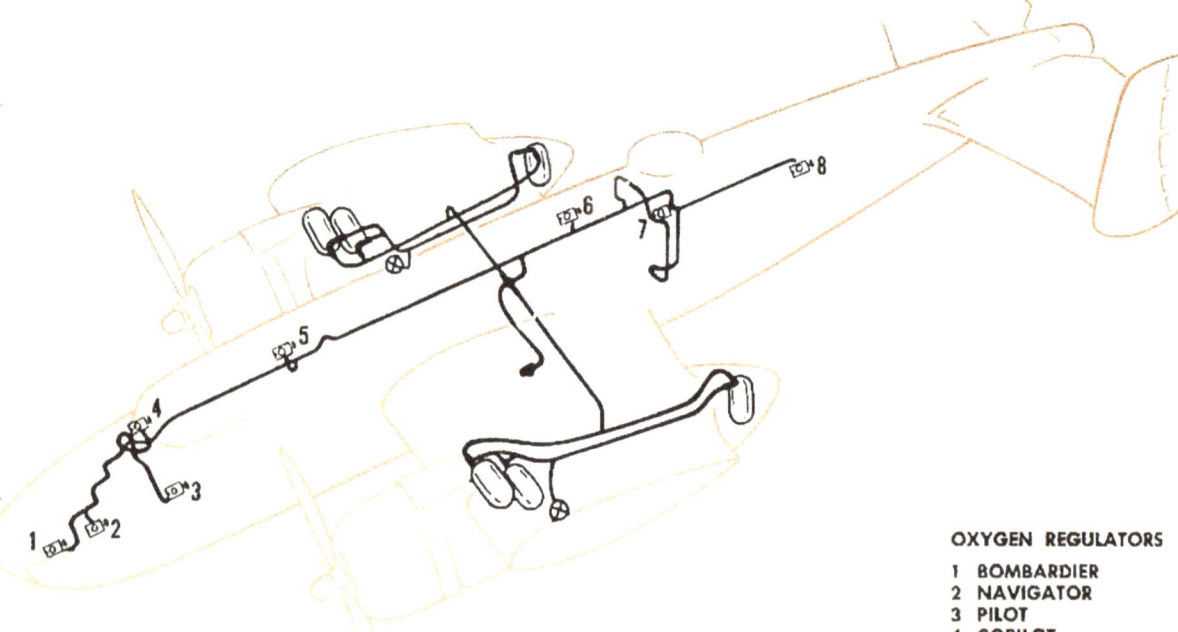

OXYGEN REGULATORS
1. BOMBARDIER
2. NAVIGATOR
3. PILOT
4. COPILOT
5. ENGINEER-GUNNER
6. RADIO OPERATOR
7. TURRET GUNNER
8. PHOTOGRAPHER

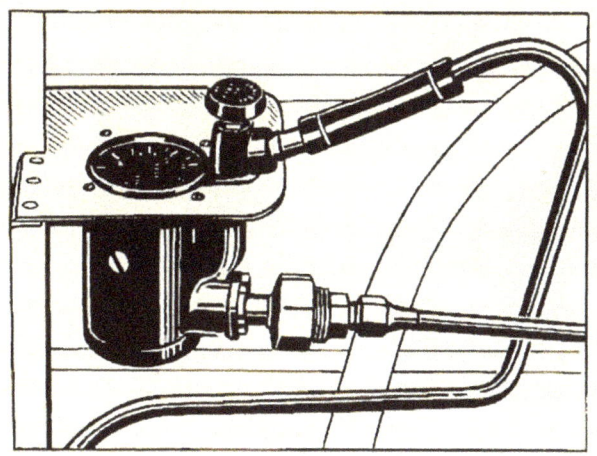

Oxygen Regulator

indicates the oxygen flow in thousands of feet of altitude, thereby simplifying regulator adjustment.

An outlet tube extends outward from the bottom of each regulator, and the hose from the oxygen mask slips over this tube. The outlet tube of the upper turret operator's regulator is on the upper turret support column.

When oxygen is not being drawn from a regulator, be sure that the valve is completely closed to prevent leakage.

Type A-8B masks are used with this system and permit breathing through either the mouth or the nose. The small valve at the bottom of the re-breather bag is for draining off any water collecting in the bag. A low-pressure rubber tube connects the mask to the regulator. Use a weak solution of creosol to clean and sterilize the mask parts.

The portable oxygen system consists of two or more low-pressure units. Each unit, comprising cylinder, regulator, pressure gage, filler valve, and the necessary fittings, lines, and supports, is complete and independent. Each portable oxygen unit employs one F-1 type cylinder having a working pressure rating of 400 lb. sq. in. The regulator gages, lines, and fittings are on one end of the cylinder and the drain is in the port at the opposite end.

A demand-type regulator feeds oxygen to the mask. It automatically admits into the system the proper amount of air from the cabin, the quantity depending on the altitude, and releases the mixture as the user inhales.

The tube assembly which conducts the mixture to the mask is clamped to the regulator elbow. Adjust the position of the elbow by loosening the nose coupling which attaches the elbow to the regulator, moving the elbow to the proper position, and tightening the nose coupling. It is important that the coupling and all other connections be tight at all times.

If the regulator fails, it may be bypassed by turning the red emergency knob in a counter-clockwise direction to "ON." A lever controls the automatic mixture feature of the regulator. When the auto-mix is turned "OFF," the regulator releases pure oxygen to the mask.

An A-10 revised or A-14 type mask may be used with the portable oxygen unit. Before any flight on which you expect to use oxygen, see that the mask is of the proper type and is the correct size and shape for your face.

Portable Oxygen Unit

KEEP ALL OXYGEN EQUIPMENT FREE FROM CONTACT WITH OIL OR GREASE

FAILURE TO DO THIS MAY RESULT IN AN EXPLOSION

RESTRICTED

PHOTOGRAPHIC EQUIPMENT

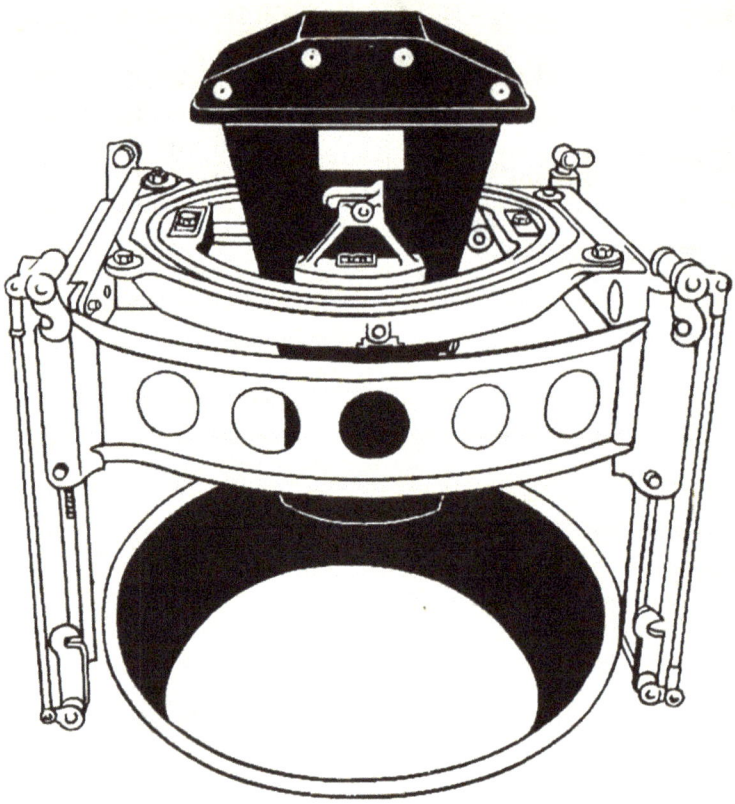

There is a photography station in the fuselage rear section on early-model airplanes. On late-model airplanes it is immediately aft of the bomb bay. Vertical photographs are made through a camera opening in the fuselage floor. A vertical viewfinder mounting plate and openings are in the fuselage floor just aft of the camera opening. There is a window on each side of the fuselage for taking oblique photographs. Orientation photographs may be made with the use of additional controls located in the bombardier's compartment.

The photographic station has storage space for a shutter induction coil and an extra film magazine.

The camera support is above the camera opening and is mounted on 4 spring-loaded support tubes. When the camera is installed and the camera door is removed, the support is lowered to the operating position.

Install the mount for the particular camera to be used on the camera support by placing the mount so that the bolts beneath the corner of the mount will go into the keyhole slots pro-

Warning

Do not raise the camera support from the operating position to the up position when the inner door of the rear entrance hatch is in the stowed position; this door interferes with the travel of the camera support and damage to both may result.

vided for them at the top of the camera support frame.

The mount acts as a gimbal ring for leveling the camera during flight. Orient the camera by means of the horizontal vernier scale on the mount.

The camera power junction box is on the left side of the compartment, convenient to the operator. The panel of the box contains a camera power socket, an intervalometer socket, a camera heater socket, and a camera power switch.

A vacuum valve, a suction gage, and a regulator to control the vacuum pressure to the camera are mounted to the left of the box. Suction holds films flat to the camera back.

The camera operator must keep in direct interphone contact with the pilot whenever photographs are being made so that the pilot may correct the attitude and course of the airplane as necessary.

There is a great variety of cameras and installations for various types of photography. The crew of the plane rarely has to use this equipment. At all other times a trained photographer uses it. The responsibility of the air crew is simply to collaborate in every way possible to make this photography a success.

Models and Changes

Combat problems in several theaters of war found the A, B, C, and D models of the B-25 unsuited for certain tactical operations. A series of modifications were necessary to overcome these problems.

The B-25 was originally designed for medium-altitude bombing, but combat theaters found it maneuverable and fast, making it suitable for low-altitude bombing and strafing missions. Additional firepower, armor plating, and re-arrangement of equipment were necessary to equip the B-25 for this type mission.

The B-25G, basically a modified C or D, has a 75-mm. cannon and additional forward-firing .50-cal. guns. The B-25G carries no bombardier; therefore the pilot operates bombing mechanisms and all forward-firing guns. Later models of the B-25G have additional firepower. Waist guns and a tail stinger, with more armor plating for the crew, make the B-25G a 4-fisted menace to enemy shipping and ground installation.

The B-25H, which followed the B-25G, underwent several changes to make it an even more formidable weapon. With the 75-mm. cannon still part of the equipment, four .50-cal. forward-firing guns were installed in the nose, and four .50-cal. blister guns, two on each side of the fuselage, were added.

With no bombardier aboard, the pilot does all the bombing and fires all forward-firing guns. The upper turret has been moved from the rear of the plane to the navigator's compartment, giving it a more effective arc of fire. Two .50-cal. waist guns, one on each side of the fuselage just aft of the bomb bay, are operated by the radio gunner. A tail turret provides two more .50-cal. guns. The B-25H, primarily used for low-altitude attack, has fourteen .50-cal. machine guns and one 75-mm. cannon in addition to its complete bombardment equipment.

The B-25J is designed to operate as a medium altitude bomber and at the same time to provide sufficient firepower for low-altitude strafing missions. With no cannon aboard, the nose is reconverted into a bombardier's compartment with the addition of two forward-firing .50-cal. guns. One fixed .50-cal. gun and one flexible .50-cal. gun in the bombardier's compartment—plus the four forward-firing blister guns—give the pilot highly effective firepower. The rest of the firepower is identical with that of the B-25H. One excellent feature of the B-25J is the dual bombing controls, giving the pilot or the bombardier individual control of all bombing equipment. With twelve .50-cal. guns, it is one of the deadliest medium bombers in operation.

Comparison Equipment Chart

EQUIPMENT	C & D	G	H	J
NOSE COMPARTMENT				
One .50-cal. fixed gun	★			★
Two .50-cal. fixed guns		★		★
Four .50-cal. fixed guns			★	
One .50-cal. flexible gun	★			★
Bombing controls & equipment	★			★
PILOT'S COMPARTMENT				
Pilot's and copilot's controls	★	★		★
Bombardier's tunnel	★			★
75-mm cannon & mount		★	★	
Driftmeter			★	★
Bombing controls & equipment		★	★	★
Astrocompass & mount			★	★
NAVIGATOR'S COMPARTMENT				
Navigator's table & equipment	★	★		
75-mm. cannon storage		★	★	
50-cal. supply for blister guns			★	★
Four .50-cal. blister guns			★	★
Upper turret (two .50-cal. guns)			★	★
Drift meter	★	★		
Astrocompass & mount	★	★		
RADIO COMPARTMENT				
Upper turret (two .50-cal. guns)	★	★		
Waist guns (two .50-cal. guns)			★	★
Camera & mounting brackets	★	★		
Liaison Radio	★	★		★
CAMERA & AMMUNITION COMPARTMENT				
Camera & mounting brackets	★	★		
50-cal. supply for tail guns			★	★
Chemical toilet	★	★		
TAIL TURRET OR OBSERVATION COMPARTMENT				
Two .50-cal. gun turret			★	★
Observation floor	★	★		

★ — In Airplane

AAF PILOT'S CHECKLIST

B25 OR TB25

PREFLIGHT

1. All switches "OFF"
2. Check Forms 1 and 1A
3. Controls "LOCKED"
4. Trim tabs at "O"
5. Props pulled through 15 blades if standing more than 30 minutes.

OUTSIDE VISUAL INSPECTION

1. **NOSE SECTION**
   a. Bombardier's escape hatch "unlocked"
   b. Bombardier's compartment for proper stowage
   c. Shimmy damper ($3/8$-inch extension)
   d. Nosewheel towing pin engaged (acorn nut tight)
   e. Nosewheel oleo strut for proper clearance
   f. Nosewheel ground wire for contact
   g. Tire for cuts, blisters, slippage, wear, and proper inflation
   h. Nosewheel door for proper fitting and tension (40 lb.); nosewheel door locknut
   i. Nose hood "locked" and safetied. (B-25 G, H, and TB-25)
   j. Engine fire extinguisher fuse if installed

2. **RIGHT ENGINE SECTION**
   a. Carburetor air scoop cover removed
   b. Prop for nicks, prop dome and governor for leaks
   c. Pulleys, cables and safety wires
   d. Cowls, cowl flaps and Dzus fasteners secure
   e. Exhaust stacks, fingers, gaskets and studs for looseness and cracks.
   f. Oil sump magnetic plugs safetied
   g. Oleo strut (extension $2\frac{7}{8}$ inches), brake lines for leaks
   h. Tire for cuts, bruises, excessive wear, slippage, and proper inflation
   i. Battery jar in nacelle for proper servicing
   j. Wheel chocks in place
   k. Gasoline drain plugs properly safetied

3. **RIGHT WING SECTION**
   a. De-icer boots for cuts, tears, worn spots, and proper installation
   b. Pitot head cover removed
   c. Wing surfaces for wrinkles, dents, or loose rivets, and evidence of gasoline leaks
   d. Control surfaces for general condition
   e. Trim tabs neutral at "O" setting

4. **EMPENNAGE**
   a. Checks for wrinkles, dents, loose rivets, de-icer installation
   b. Trim tabs neutral at "O" setting

5. **REAR COMPARTMENT**
   a. Loading and stowage
   b. Emergency escape hatches unlocked
   c. Emergency landing gear and flap lowering mechanism stowed
   d. Trailing antenna fully retracted
   e. Entrance hatch closed and latched

6. **LEFT WING SECTION**
   a. Repeat the right wing section inspection

7. **LEFT ENGINE SECTION**
   a. Repeat the right engine section inspection
   b. Hand energizer stowed

8. BOMB BAY
   a. Bomb bay doors for looseness
   b. Gasoline lines and plugs for leaks
   c. Check for strong gasoline odors. (Turn booster pumps "ON" before making this check.)

9. GENERAL
   a. Check visually amount of fuel in each tank
   b. Fuel caps for proper installation
   c. Check visually amount of oil in each tank
   d. Caps and Dzus fasteners
   e. Life raft storage compartment release handle locked
   f. Crew briefing: Location and operation of escape hatches; proper use of parachutes; abandon-ship procedure and signals
   g. Testing and operation of oxygen equipment
   h. Interphone operation

NAVIGATOR'S COMPARTMENT

1. Emergency air brake pressure 550-600 lb.
2. Nosewheel pawl "OFF"—handle stowed (or emergency handle safetied)
3. Brake accumulator pressure 400 lb.
4. Hydraulic accumulator pressure 400 lb.
5. Oxygen pressure
6. Crossfeed "OFF"
7. Fuel transfer valve and switches "OFF"
8. Fuel cut-off valves "ON"
9. Generators and inverters "ON" (inverters on after engines are started if plane's batteries are used)
10. Level of hydraulic fluid in reservoir, and spare fluid
11. Cabin heaters "OFF"
12. Load and balance

COCKPIT

1. Adjust seat and belt
2. Escape hatch unlocked—hatch secure
3. Controls unlocked—free and proper movement
4. Parking brakes set—Brake Pressure 500 lbs.
5. Hydraulic selector "NORMAL"
6. Air brake handle down and safetied

7. Landing gear handle "DOWN" and locked
8. Wing flaps up, control neutral
9. Cowl flaps open—Control neutral
10. Automatic pilot "OFF" and locked
11. Supercharger "LOW" and locked
12. Oil shutters as required
13. Carburetor heat "NORMAL"
14. Throttles cracked
15. Props "INC. RPM"
16. Mixture "IDLE CUT-OFF"
17. Radios "OFF"
18. De-icers "OFF"
19. Airspeed selector static position
20. Altimeter set (station elevation)
21. Gyros "UNCAGED"
22. Battery—disconnect switches "ON" (unless external power is used)
23. Light switches as required
24. Anti-icing "OFF"
25. Check fuel levels

STARTING ENGINES

1. Fire guard posted
2. Props clear
3. Ignition switches "ON" (One at a time)
4. Booster pumps "ON"
5. Start right engine
6. Oil pressure 40 lb. in 30 seconds
7. Start left engine
8. Booster pumps "OFF" (Fuel pressure 6-7 lb.)
9. Warm up at approximately 1200 rpm
10. Battery-disconnect switches "ON" (if external power is used)
11. Hydraulic pressure (800-1100 lb.)
12. Brake pressure (1000-1200 lb.)
13. Suction 3.75-4.25" Hg. (Right and left engine)
14. Radio "ON"

BEFORE TAKEOFF

1. C.—CONTROLS for free movement

2. I.—INSTRUMENTS
   a. Altimeter
   b. Directional gyro set
   c. Artificial horizon set

    d. Suction 3.75–4.25" Hg. (right and left engine)
    e. Oil pressure 75–90 lb.
    f. Oil temperature 50–85°
    g. Cylinder-head temperature 100°-205°
    h. Other instruments and switches as desired

3. G.—GAS
    a. Fuel pressure 6–7 lb.
    b. Fuel levels
    c. Booster pumps "OFF"
    d. Transfer pumps "OFF"
    e. Mixture "FULL RICH"
    f. Carburetor heat "NORMAL"
    g. Shut-off valves "ON"
    h. Crossfeed "OFF"

4. F.—FLAPS
    a. Flaps set for takeoff

5. T.—TRIM
    a. Trim tabs set for takeoff

6. P.—PROPS
    a. Full forward

7. R.—RUN-UP
    a. Run up coolest engine to 2000 rpm. Maximum manifold pressure 28.5" Hg. Check mags
    b. Run up second engine to 2000 rpm. Maximum manifold pressure 28.5" Hg. Check mags
    c. Run engines singly to 30" Hg. Check for 2400 rpm

8. Friction Brake snug—Booster pumps "ON"—Bomb bay doors closed

CLIMB

1. Wheels up
2. Reduce power for initial climb (after CSE speed is obtained)
3. Flaps up
4. Reduce power for continuous climb
5. Adjust temperature

6. Booster pumps "OFF" above 1000 feet
6a. Booster pumps "ON" above 10,000 feet

BEFORE LANDING

1. Trailing antenna retracted
2. Wing de-icers "OFF"
3. Heaters "OFF"
4. Automatic pilot "OFF"
5. Superchargers "LOW" and locked
6. Fuel pressure 6–7 lb.
7. Fuel levels
8. Booster pumps "ON"
9. Transfer pumps "OFF"
10. Mixture "FULL RICH"
11. Carburetor heat "NORMAL"
12. Props 2400 rpm
13. Landing gear "DOWN," locked and safetied below 170 mph (Visually and orally checked)
14. Brake and hydraulic pressure

APPROACH

1. Landing gear "DOWN"
2. Hydraulic and brake pressure checked

AFTER LANDING

1. Props "INC. RPM"
2. Booster pumps "OFF"
3. Cowl flaps "OPEN"
4. Wing flaps "UP"

STOPPING ENGINES

1. Bomb bay doors open
2. Set engine rpm at 1200
3. Mixture "IDLE CUT-OFF"
4. Electrical switches "OFF" (After props have stopped turning)
5. Chocks placed
6. Brakes "OFF"
7. Controls locked. Trim tabs "O"
8. Carburetor air scoop covers "ON"

AAF PILOT'S ABBREVIATED CHECKLIST B-25

(To be used only after thorough familiarization with Amplified Checklist)

PREFLIGHT

1. Switches "OFF"
2. Forms 1 and 1A
3. Controls locked
4. Tabs "O"
5. Props pulled through

OUTSIDE VISUAL INSPECTION

1. Nose section
2. Right engine and wing section
3. Empennage rear compartment
4. Left engine and wing section
5. Bomb bay

NAVIGATOR'S COMPARTMENT

1. Emergency brake pressure
2. Accumulator pressures
3. Generators and inverters
4. Fuel valves and switches
5. Heater "OFF"
6. Load and balance

COCKPIT

1. Parachutes on, seat and belt adjusted
2. Controls
3. Brakes and pressure
4. Hydraulic selector
5. Air brake handle
6. Landing gear
7. Wing flaps
8. Cowl flaps
9. Autopilot
10. Supercharger
11. Oil shutters
12. Carburetor heat
13. Throttles
14. Props
15. Mixture
16. Radios
17. De-icers "OFF"
18. Airspeed selector static
19. Altimeter set
20. Gyros
21. Battery switches
22. Light switches
23. Anti-icing "OFF"
24. Fuel levels

BEFORE TAKEOFF

1. Controls
2. Instruments
3. Gas
4. Flaps
5. Trim tabs
6. Props
7. Run-up
8. Booster pumps
9. Throttle brake

C-I-G-F-T-P-R—Booster pumps-Throttle brake-Bomb bay doors

BEFORE LANDING

1. De-icers and trailing antenna
2. Heater
3. Autopilot
4. Superchargers
5. Gas checks
6. Mixture
7. Props
8. Landing gear

FINAL CHECK BEFORE LANDING

1. Gas
2. Undercarriage and pressures
3. Mixture
4. Props

G-U-M-P

AFTER LANDING

1. Props
2. Boosters
3. Cowl flaps
4. Oil shutters
5. Wing flaps

INSPECTIONS AND CHECKS

You have a very personal reason for wanting to know that your airplane is in the best possible condition for a flight. That reason is you. If anything happens to the plane, it also happens to **you** and your crew.

Use your checklists. You are entrusted with the lives of a highly trained crew and valuable equipment. The plane and its crew are your only business while you are its pilot.

There are too many controls which must be set properly, too many instruments and indicators to be checked, to allow for any but the most definite procedures, always systematically planned and executed.

Check and Inspect Before You Fly!

These checks and inspections will not take a lot of your time. When proficient, you can check and inspect the whole plane thoroughly in the time you usually waste for lack of a definite procedure.

Consult the crew chief about the status of the plane. You will pick up many of valuable tips from him.

Preflight

Enter cockpit and check that all switches are "OFF."

Check Form 1A for status of the airplane.

Surface controls locked.

Trim tabs set at "O."

Pull props through 12 to 15 blades if the airplane has been standing for more than 30 minutes. This will work the oil from the lower cylinders.

If you start the engine with excess oil present in the cylinders this oil will form a pressure block, cracking the cylinder heads and bending the connecting rods.

Always pull the props through in the direction of rotation. Otherwise fuel and oil will be forced back into the intake section. This will cause an unknown and possibly dangerous fuel-air ratio and make starting difficult.

Nose Section

Bombardier's escape hatch unlocked.

Check bombardier's compartment for proper stowage.

Shimmy damper pin (⅜-inch extension).

Nosewheel towing lockpin engaged—Red acorn-nut covering this pin must be in place and secure. Rotate clockwise until hand-tight. The towing lockpin locks the nosewheel into position. (The cover will not engage if this pin is unlocked.)

Nosewheel oleo strut for proper clearance.

Tires for cuts, wear, blisters, slippage, and proper inflation.

Ground wire on nosewheel for contact with ground.

Nosewheel door for proper fitting and tension (40 lb.). Spring tension closes this door when the airplane is in flight. If it closes improperly the slip-stream forces it open, and the resulting air blast may tear it off and damage other parts of the airplane.

Nose hood locked and safetied (B-25 G, H, and TB-25).

Check engine fire extinguisher fuse if installed.

Right Engine Section

Carburetor air scoop cover removed.

Propeller for nicks, propeller dome and governor for leaks.

Check pulleys, cables, and safety wires.

Cowls, cowl flaps, and Dzus fasteners secure—a loose cowl section can be a serious hazard in flight.

Exhaust stacks, fingers, gaskets and studs, for looseness and cracks.

Oil sump magnetic plugs safetied.

Oleo strut (extension 2⅞ inches), brake lines for leaks, torque arm scissors, main wheel down-lock engaged.

Tire for cuts, bruises, excessive wear, slippage, and proper inflation.

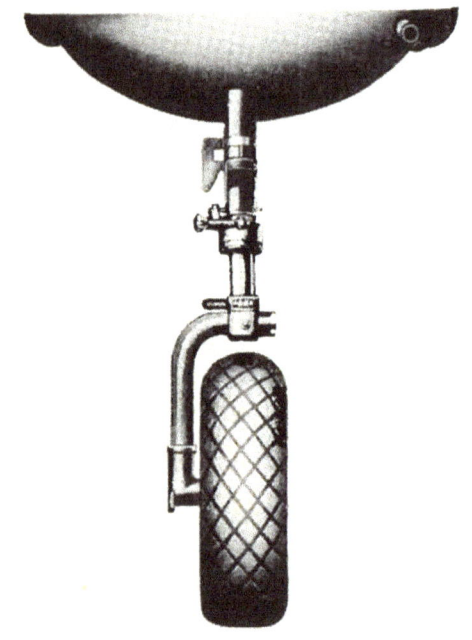

Battery jar in nacelle for proper servicing.
Wheel chocks in place.
Gasoline drain plugs properly safetied.

Right Wing Section

De-icer boots for cuts, tears, worn spots, and proper installation.
Pitot head cover removed.

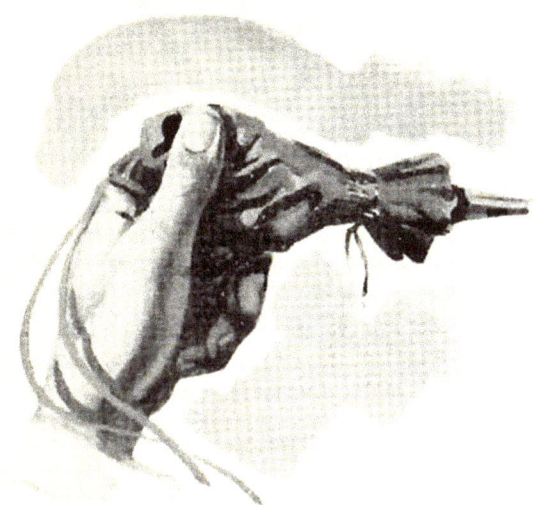

Wing surfaces for wrinkles, dents, or loose rivets. This is an important check. Wrinkles in the metal surface indicate excessive strain.
Control surfaces for general condition.
Trim tabs neutral at "O" settings.

Empennage

Check for wrinkles, dents, loose rivets, de-icer installation.
Trim tabs neutral at "0" settings.

Rear Compartment

Loading and stowage—In the photographer's compartment sections of the control cables are exposed on the sidewalls of the fuselage. Check the stowage carefully at this point; a loose cord, parachute buckle, or any loose equipment entangled in the controls may cause them to freeze.
Emergency escape hatches unlocked.
Emergency landing-gear and flap lowering mechanisms stowed.
Trailing antenna fully retracted.
Entrance hatch closed and latched.

Left Wing Section

Repeat the right wing section inspection.

Left Engine Section

Repeat the right engine section inspection.
Check left nacelle for stowage of the hand energizer.

Bomb Bay

Check doors for looseness.
Check gasoline lines and plugs for leaks.
Check bomb bay for strong gasoline odors.
Note: Turn booster pumps "ON" before making this check.

General

Check visually the amount of fuel in each tank.
Check fuel caps for proper installation.
Check visually the amount of oil in tanks and see that caps and Dzus fasteners are secure.
Check life raft storage compartment release handle "LOCKED."
Crew briefing—Location and operation of escape hatches.
Proper use of parachutes.
Abandon-ship procedure and signals.
Escape hatches—Emergency operation. Check with crew chief to determine the time of the last check on the emergency operation of the escape hatches.
Testing and operation of oxygen equipment—check crew on knowledge of proper usage. (Consult your Pilots' Information File.)
Interphone operation.

Navigator's Compartment

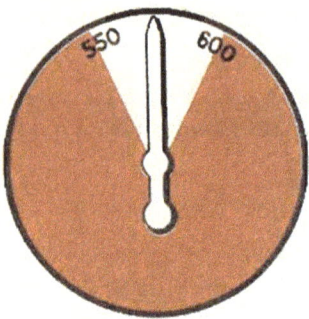

Emergency air brake pressure (550-600 lb. sq. in.).

Nosewheel pawl "OFF," handle stowed. The cable on this system moves as the nosewheel is raised and lowered. If the engaging pawl is "ON" the movement of the nosewheel will tear the cable out of the system. (On later-series aircraft, hydraulic emergency systems replace this type. When you operate ships with these installed, safety the handle "UP.")

Brake accumulator pressure 400 lb. sq. in. minimum.

Hydraulic accumulator pressure 400 lb. sq. in. minimum.

Oxygen pressure (where applicable).

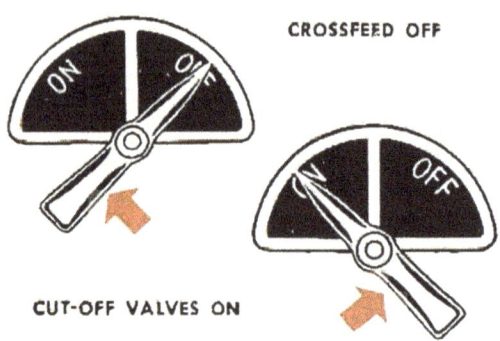

Crossfeed "OFF."

Fuel transfer valve and switches "OFF."

Right and left engine fuel cut-off valves "ON."

Generators and inverters "ON"—External power should be used whenever possible. If external power is not available for starting, keep inverters "OFF" until engine is operating.

Level of Hydraulic fluid reservoir (spare fluid aboard).

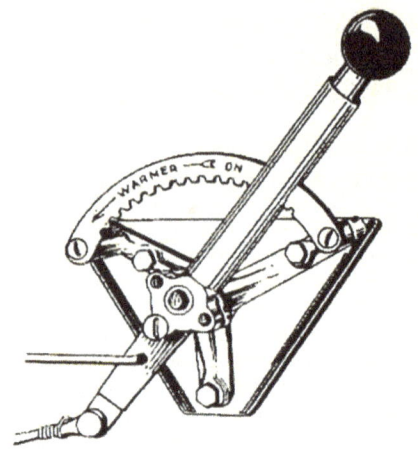

Cabin heaters "OFF."

Check the load and balance of the ship. Check Form F with the load adjuster. The B-25 carries great loads and is unstable and dangerous if the weight is not properly distributed. (For detailed information, see the PIF and the Weights and Balance section of this manual.)

Cockpit

Have your parachute fitted to your body and always wear it.

An improperly fitted chute will cause serious physical injury—protect yourself.

Adjust seat and belt—If the seat is not locked the acceleration of takeoff will force the seat away from the controls. You cannot reach the controls properly even for taxiing if the seat is not forward and locked.

Escape hatch unlocked, hatch secure.

Controls unlocked, check for free and proper movement. This insures the release of the lock, and reveals the presence of obstructions to free movement of the controls.

Parking brakes "SET." Brake pressure 500 lb. sq. in. minimum.

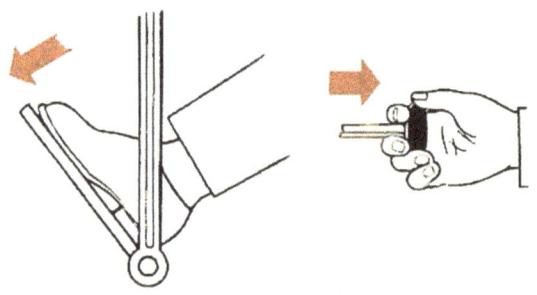

CHECK CONTROLS FOR FREE AND PROPER MOVEMENT

Hydraulic selector "NORMAL."
Air brake handle down and safetied.
Landing gear handle "DOWN" and locked.
Wing flaps up, controls neutral.
Cowl flaps open, controls neutral.

Set all hydraulic controls except landing gear at neutral when they are not in use; this prevents loss of fluid and pressure in the entire system if part of it fails.

Automatic pilot "OFF" and locked.
Supercharger "LOW BLOWER" and locked—All takeoffs must be made in "LOW BLOWER." Any attempt to do otherwise robs the engines of power.
Oil shutters as required.
Carburetor heat "NORMAL."

Gyros "UNCAGED."

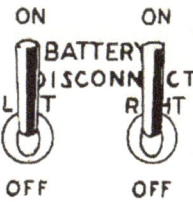

Battery-disconnect switches "ON" (unless external power is used).
Light switches as required.

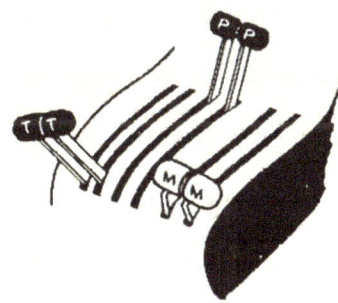

Throttles cracked (½ inch to 1 inch).
Propellers "INC. RPM."
Mixture "IDLE CUT-OFF."
Radios "OFF."
De-icers "OFF."
Airspeed selector "STATIC."
Altimeter set (station elevation). This setting will enable you to check the radioed altimeter setting and detect any scale error in your altimeter.

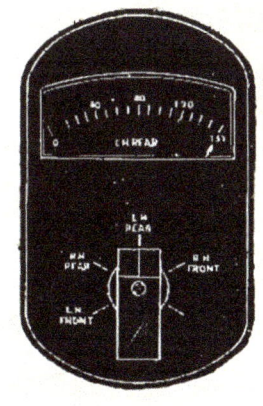 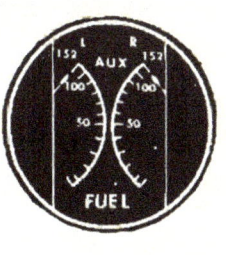

Check fuel levels—the visual preflight check acts as a check on the instrument reading.

Starting Engines

USE THE CHECKLIST FOR STARTING

Fire guard posted.
Props clear.

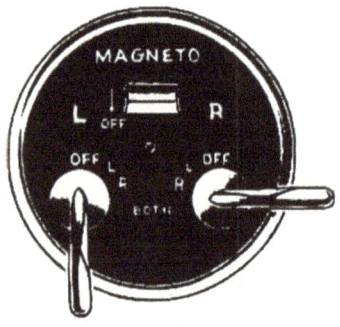

Ignition switches "ON," one at a time

Booster pumps "ON"—operate only the switch on the engine you are starting.

Energize 10 seconds when using an external power source, 20 seconds when using the plane's batteries.

Prime—Use primer for 2 seconds while energizing. This is not a priming action; it merely fills the primer lines with fluid and allows instant priming when the engine is engaged.

Engage—Hold down energizer, primer and engaging switch until the engine starts. Mesh for reasonable time. If engine does not fire, repeat starting procedure.

Move mixture control to "FULL RICH" when engine starts.

Check oil pressure—(40 lb. in 30 seconds).

If the oil pressure does not reach 40 lb. in 30 seconds stop the engine and investigate.

Repeat procedure on the left engine.

Booster pumps "OFF"—check fuel pressure. There must be 6-7 lb. sq. in.

Warm up at approximately 1200 rpm.

Battery-disconnect switches **"ON"** (if external power is used).

Hydraulic pressure—(800-1100 lb. sq. in.).
Brake pressure—(1000-1200 lb. sq. in.).
Suction—(3.75-4.25" Hg.).
Radio "ON."

If the engine backfires and excess fuel in the intake section catches fire, move the mixture control to "IDLE CUT-OFF" and advance the throttles to full open.

Keep the engine turning over with the starter if the fire is small. Keep the throttles open wide and the mixture in "IDLE CUT-OFF" until the fire burns out.

If the fire continues to burn, flaring out of the air scoop and the cowl flaps, **turn the engine fuel cut-off valve "OFF" and use the**

hand extinguisher (CO_2) on the base of the flame. Always keep the throttles open wide to exhaust all the fuel that can reach the engine.

If this fails, use the Lux system if it is installed in the airplane. When you encounter fires of this type and have used the Lux system, **do not attempt to restart the engine.** If in attempting to restart the engine you start another fire, you will have no positive means of extinguishing the flames.

Don't try to rush the warming of the engines during the warm-up period. The R-2600 engines have a great mass of metal in them, and the warm-up must be thorough. Some parts of the engines will warm up while other parts are still cold.

Many engines have been ruined by improper warm-up.

Watch cylinder-head temperatures closely during warm-up, as the engine temperature rises more quickly in operation at idling settings on the ground than at high power settings in the air.

There are pressure baffles on this plane, and very little air can flow around the cylinder heads when the plane has no forward speed.

Taxiing the B-25, with its tricycle landing gear, may seem strange after handling the conventional type.

The primary controls for taxiing are the throttles, rudders, and the brakes when necessary. A secondary aid is the aileron.

Proper coordination of these controls gives you effortless taxiing.

Carburetors should be adjusted to idle at 650 rpm. The scavenger pumps lose their prime and the plugs foul at a lower rpm.

Operate the throttles as smoothly as possible, and when you stop the plane for any reason set the rpm at 1000. This prevents fouling and creates enough propeller blast to help cool the engines.

UNLOCK THE PARKING BRAKE AND ALLOW THE PLANE TO ROLL STRAIGHT AHEAD

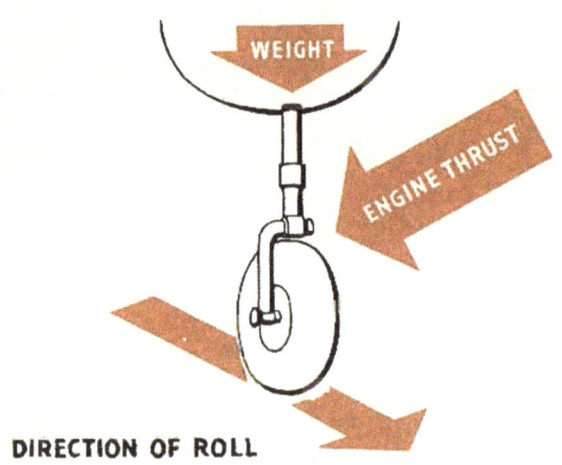

DIRECTION OF ROLL

Don't try to guide the plane for the first few feet of its roll. If you do a great side load is exerted on the nosewheel strut if the nosewheel is not pointing in the direction you are trying to guide the plane. Never use force; you will shear or snap the nosewheel strut under the pressures applied by the brakes and engines.

This airplane has conventional-type toe brakes on the rudder pedal. After the airplane is moving, apply the brakes evenly and firmly to check for adequate braking action. **Never allow the taxi speed to build up without making a brake check.**

When the direction of roll is established, make corrections by coordinating the rudder and the throttle and using the brakes only when necessary. Use the brakes lightly, working to achieve accurate control with minimum pressure.

You will never need hard, rough braking action if you use the brakes properly.

Use the throttles to aid in taxiing, always keeping in mind that you must anticipate the reaction of the thrust. Lead the turn. Lead the corrective action needed to stop the turn.

Do not use excessive power. When one throttle is advanced, retard the opposite throttle. Don't let power accumulate by jockeying first one throttle and then the other.

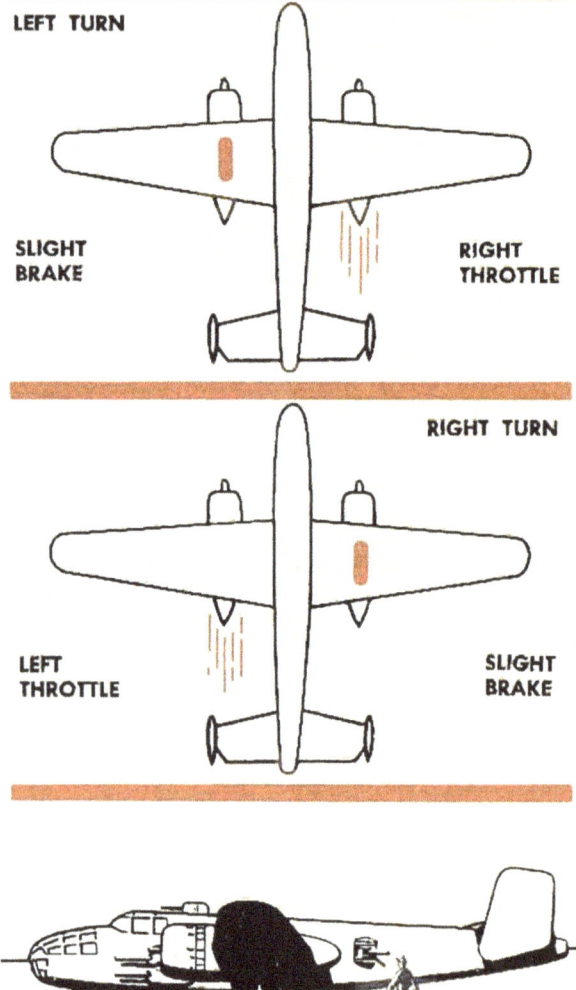

IN THE VICINITY OF OTHER PLANES AND EQUIPMENT, KEEP THE SPEED DOWN TO THAT OF A WALKING MAN.

On straight-away taxiing let the plane roll free and maintain directional control with the rudders. The twin tail assembly of the B-25 gives ample rudder control even at relatively low taxiing speeds, although even when full rudder is applied there is a slight delayed-action effect.

Never ride the brakes; this causes them to heat up rapidly.

Apply the brakes by feel, not by the position of the pedals.

Never allow the inside wheel to stop during a turn. To turn sharply, slow the airplane to a low speed and coordinate the brake and throttle to keep the inside wheel turning on an approximate 10-foot circle.

Any attempt to twist the plane on the inside wheel damages the wheel, tire, and strut. Turning in this manner on soft ground, sand, or thin paved runways causes the wheel to dig into the runway, sometimes rupturing the runway surface.

This turning action may twist the wheel and strut off the airplane. What is worse, the damage may not be apparent but the gear may be damaged so badly that it will fold up under the strain of a landing.

Park a safe distance off the end of the runway you intend to use for the takeoff. Turn into the wind to provide maximum cooling for the engine run-up. The engine installations cool efficiently only when the airplane is in flight. Sufficient air for cooling is never available during ground operation. Take advantage of every opportunity to aid the engines in cooling.

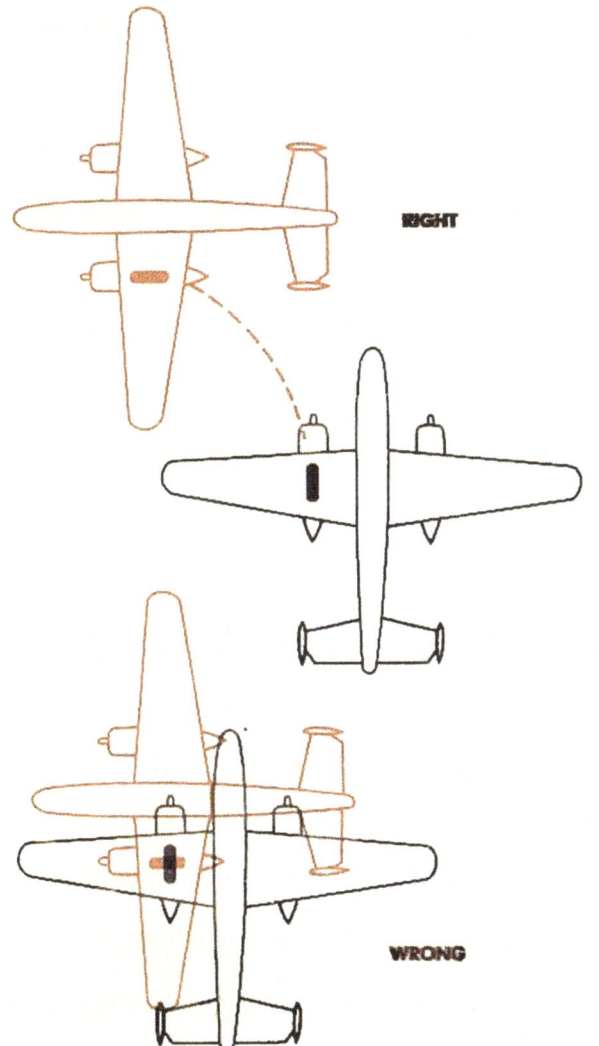

Nosewheel Position Indicator

A nosewheel position indicator is on the lower center section of the pilot's instrument panel. It warns you of the position of the nosewheel by flashing on one of two lights when the nosewheel turns past 15° in either direction.

You can adjust the brilliancy of these lights by turning the jeweled cap to "DAY" or "NIGHT." Check this indicator constantly when taxiing under abnormal conditions and when recovering from sharp turns.

Crosswind Taxiing

The windvane effect so noticeable in lighter airplanes will still be with you in the B-25, but not to the same extent. The airplane tends to turn into the wind.

To prevent this streamlining, use the engines, rudder and downwind brake. Advance the upwind throttle and use strong rudder pressures. This gives ample control in all but the most violent winds. Use a small amount of downwind brake when necessary. Don't let this become a habit, however, as in all ordinary conditions the throttles and rudders provide good directional control.

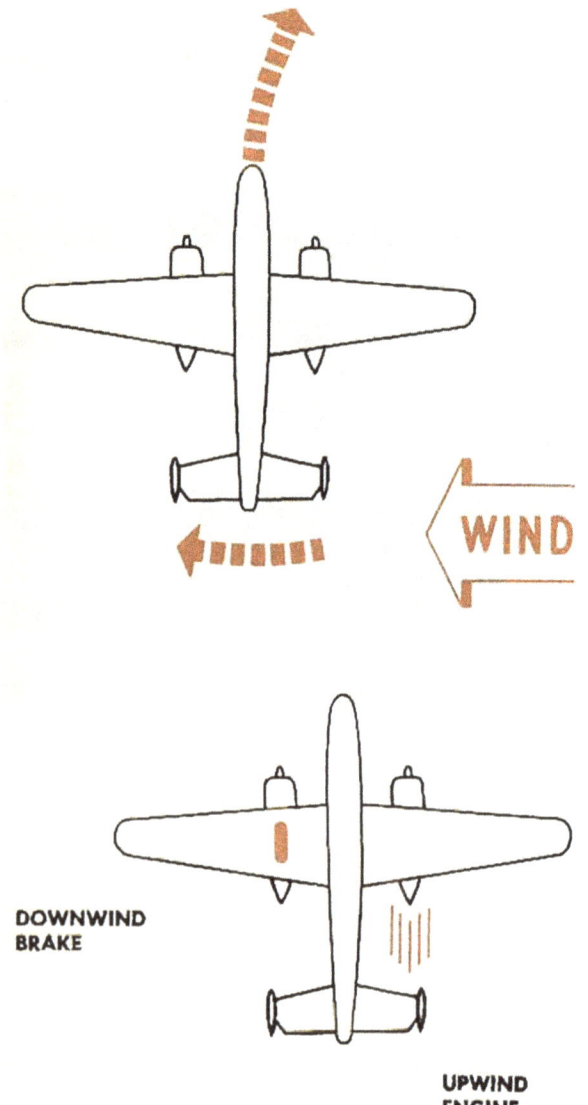

DOWNWIND BRAKE

UPWIND ENGINE

Taxiing in Mud or Sand

The only new element added to taxiing by the presence of mud or sand on an airfield is the greater resistance to the passage of the nosewheel. This resistance tries to force the nosewheel from its normal trailing action to a reversed position.

Because of this new factor observe these additional precautions:

1. **Once the airplane is moving, keep it moving.**
2. **Avoid sharp turns unless absolutely necessary.**
3. **Avoid using the brakes unless absolutely necessary.**

The following procedure is best in mud or sand:

While taxiing, control the turns with throttle, using brakes only when necessary. The minimum radius of turn on the inside wheel is 10 feet.

When the airplane straightens out of a turn the nosewheel loses the tendency to trail properly as the depth of the tire sink increases.

When abnormal power must be used to move the airplane, the tire sink is too great. One of the crew must walk ahead of the plane and warn you when the nosewheel attempts to reverse its direction.

If the airplane is allowed to pivot on one wheel the nosewheel assumes a short angle toward the rear and the pivot wheel mires itself. To correct this:

1. Cut the engines
2. Remove the towing lockpin
3. Insert the tow bar or a piece of iron pipe and manually turn the nosewheel in line with the airplane fuselage.

If either of the main wheels is deeply mired, dig a shallow trench, with a slight upslope, in front of the wheel. Check to see that the nosewheel is lined up in the direction of roll.

Start the engines and run them up with brakes set. Lower the flaps, pull back on the wheel, and release the brakes.

Caution—If the wheels are mired too deeply the propeller tips will strike the ground. When there is danger of this, the airplane must be moved by a tractor.

GET THE NOSEWHEEL UP QUICK ON TAKEOFF IN MUD OR SAND

Don't try to move the airplane over soft ground with the nosewheel towbar alone. This will break the nosewheel strut and pull it from under the nose of the plane. Attach chains to the main wheel struts for towing. Guide the nosewheel with the tow bar.

To take off from mud, sand, or a rough field, raise the nosewheel quickly to relieve the weight during the run.

Land normally on mud or sand. Make every effort to hold the airplane straight without using the brakes. This prevents skidding on a slick surface. Great side loads are applied to the gear in skids of this type and must be avoided.

Common Taxiing Errors

Riding the brakes. Depress the toe pedals only when necessary.

Rough braking action. Avoid this by anticipating the need for brakes.

Rough or no use of the throttles.

Improper use of the rudders. There is a common tendency to forget that there are rudders. When the runway and taxi strip are clear, let the plane roll free and control with rudders.

Failure to clear the area. This is the cause of most taxi accidents. There is no excuse for taxi accidents.

Fast taxiing in congested areas.

Turning with the inside wheel not moving.

TAXIING TIPS

Never pivot on the inside wheel during a turn.

Never turn sharply at high speeds.

Do not use more power than necessary when taxiing.

Be extremely careful when taxiing on a strange airfield.

In the immediate vicinity of other planes, never taxi faster than is necessary to maintain control. Always proceed under guidance from the ground.

When taxiing over soft smooth terrain and there is a tendency of the wheels to dig in, don't stop. Keep the plane moving unless the situation is dangerous. If in doubt, stop. Get out and look. Have a crew member walk ahead of the plane until you are out of trouble.

Do not turn sharply into the parking area. Come up behind the parking position and move the airplane ahead slowly.

Never cut the engines with the idea of rolling to a stop. Lack of hydraulic pressure may cause brake failure.

Do not run up engines if light planes are behind you.

Before Takeoff

C.I.G.F.T.P.R.— FRICTION BRAKE

Controls for free movement

Instruments
1. Altimeter
2. Directional gyro set and uncaged
3. Artificial horizon set and uncaged
4. Suction 3.75-4.25" Hg.
5. Oil pressure 75 to 90 lb. sq. in.
6. Oil temperature 50°C to 85°C
7. Cylinder-head temperature 100° to 205°C

Gas
1. Fuel pressure 6-7 lb sq. in.
2. Fuel levels
3. Booster Pumps "OFF"
4. Transfer Pumps "OFF"
5. Mixture "FULL RICH"
6. Carburetor heat "NORMAL"
7. Shut-off valves "ON"
8. Crossfeed "OFF"

Flaps set for takeoff (normal 20°). Run the flaps full down and then raise them to 20°.

Trim tabs set for takeoff.

Props "INC. RPM."

Run-up.

Friction brake snug, booster pumps "ON," bomb bay doors closed

RUN-UP

1. Advance the throttles to 1600 rpm.
2. Pull back prop controls until a reduction in rpm of 350-400 is indicated.
3. Re-set prop controls to "INC. RPM." (Manipulation of prop controls circulates warm oil in the prop dome and gives smoother governing action.
4. At 1600 rpm, check generators' output: voltage at 28 to 28.5, amperes 20 to 60.
5. Advance the throttle on your coolest engine until the rpm is set at 2000. Maximum manifold pressure 28.5" Hg. Check the right and left mags. For a thorough check, the time on one mag is 2 to 3 seconds. Between checks on "L" and "R" settings return the switch to "BOTH" and allow the engine to regain speed. A loss of 75 to 100 rpm does not necessarily mean that the plane is unsafe for flight. If the engine does not vibrate excessively during the check, and if it will put out rated power, a drop of 75 to 100 rpm is considered safe for takeoff. However, be on the lookout for a drop in rpm. If the drop is sudden, or if backfiring occurs, do not fly the plane until it has been re-checked. A drop of 100 rpm is the maximum permissible for takeoff.

Repeat this procedure on the other engine.

Following the mag check, run the engines up singly to 30" Hg. At this manifold pressure you will get an approximate reading of 2400 rpm, which means that the plane should give you sufficient power for takeoff.

DO NOT HURRY A TAKEOFF

TAKEOFF

Takeoff in the B-25, with its tricycle gear, varies from that with conventional gear only during the initial part of the roll. You will find it much easier. The principal difference is in attaining the proper angle of attack of the wing. On the conventional type you start from a stall attitude and reduce the angle to permit flight. In the B-25 you start from a negative angle of attack and increase the angle of attack by raising the nosewheel.

Several factors affect the takeoff technique. Chief of these are gross weight, wind velocity, type of runway, and the height and distance of the nearest obstacles. Plan your takeoff according to these variables. The following takeoff is normal.

When you get permission to take off, taxi out and line up properly. Advance the throttles slowly, using them to obtain directional control. As soon as the plane is rolling straight, equalize the throttles and advance them smoothly to takeoff power. **Check the engine instruments for maximum power indications and for irregular operation—if in doubt cut off the power.** Don't load up the engines with a sudden blast of power. You are operating powerful engines; treat them with care and respect.

Be prepared to make power adjustments during the takeoff. If an engine fails before you gain critical single engine speed, you must reduce power quickly to prevent loss of control.

After you start the takeoff run, use the

START TAKEOFF RUN WITH 20° FLAPS

RAISE NOSEWHEEL OFF GROUND

RAISE THE GEAR AS SOON AS PLANE IS DEFINITELY AIRBORNE

brakes only in an emergency. Maintain directional control with the throttles and rudders.

Raise the nosewheel off the ground slightly as soon as you have good control. The angle of attack and the weight of the B-25 tend to keep the plane on the ground during the takeoff roll. The takeoff becomes conventional when a positive angle of attack, with resulting lift, is developed.

The B-25 flies itself off the ground. Allow it to do so, for smoother, easily controlled takeoffs. If the plane attempts to skip and bounce in slight crosswinds, help it lift off the runway, thus smoothing out the takeoff.

When the airplane is definitely airborne, raise the wheels. **Be sure there is no possibility of further contact with the ground.** Good airplanes have been lost through carelessness.

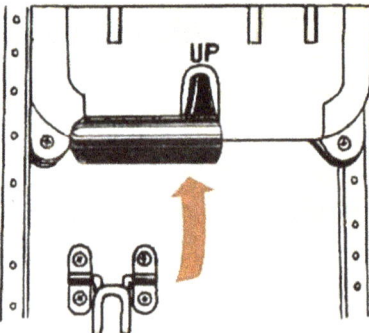

1. Lift the safety lock holding the control handle "DOWN" and locked.
2. Move the mechanical lock up.
3. Move the landing gear handle to "UP."

Level off and allow the plane to gain CSE flying speed (140 mph).

Reduce power to maximum climbing power settings. (See chart of Grade 91 and Grade 100 power settings.) Don't base this power reduction on distance from the field. The particular situation, load, speed, terrain features, and altitude determine the proper place for this reduction.

Reduce power as soon as possible, however, to relieve the strain on the engines. Let the plane climb slowly, gaining speed as it climbs. Reduce the power to normal climb settings as soon as you establish a constant climb. Load conditions cause the climb settings to vary slightly.

Maintain a climbing speed between 160 and 170 mph for these reasons:

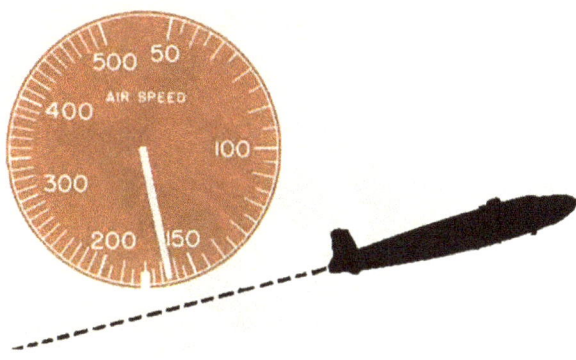

1. Speed is developed quickly and maintained to allow single engine operation if necessary.
2. Excessively slow climbs prevent proper cooling of the engines at high power settings.
3. You obtain good forward visibility by keeping the nose relatively low.

Raise the wing flaps when you have sufficient altitude. This will normally be about 300 feet above the terrain and between 150 mph and 170 mph. Apply back pressure to the control column as the flaps come up, increasing the angle of attack of the wings. This defeats any tendency to settle and lose altitude.

Close cowl flaps as soon as possible after takeoff, but leave them open if the cylinder-head temperature approaches 200°C.

NOTES ON TAKEOFF

Do not dive the airplane after lifting it at the end of the takeoff run. When you level out to pick up CSE speed after takeoff release the stick pressure as the speed picks up.

Gain critical single engine speed immediately after takeoff. This is the slowest speed at which the rudder has a safe margin of control over the unbalanced thrust of the live engine at full power. In the B-25, **it is 140 mph.**

Don't be an instrument pilot on takeoff. Fly the airplane by feel and by visual reference to the ground. An occasional check of the instruments is a necessity, but make instrument takeoffs only when contact flight is impossible. Attention to the panel should be concentrated on the engine instruments.

Common Takeoff Errors

Failure to keep the airplane straight ahead. Unfamiliarity with the airplane and uneven power application cause this. **Remember,** there are 2 large rudders. It takes considerable foot pressure to control them on takeoff.

Jockeying or blasting the throttles to maintain directional control.

Using brakes to steer the plane

Excessive manifold pressure

Instrument flying instead of contact flying

Excessive airspeed on the ground

Retracting landing gear too soon

Failure to level off after takeoff

Failure to correct properly for drift

Skidding immediately after takeoff

Tenseness and overcontrolling

POWER CHANGES

Always make power changes smoothly and evenly. This engine will not absorb a sudden blast of power without acting up.

Move the controls slowly and smoothly to the desired settings rather than attempting to **make one swift** movement and pick up the proper settings.

TO REDUCE POWER

1. Reduce manifold pressure

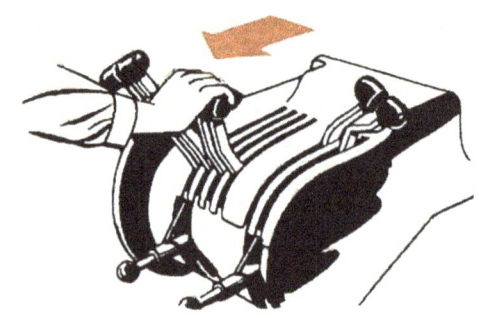

2. Reduce rpm

If the rpm is reduced first, you get a jump in manifold pressures. This causes detonation if the relation of the rpm to manifold pressure is altered greatly.

An engine running at constant power settings uses a constant amount of fuel and air. If the rpm is reduced, this fuel-air supply remains almost constant, and an engine running at reduced speed cannot absorb this fuel-air charge. Pressures in the impeller and cylinder heads rise as a result and cause detonation.

TO INCREASE POWER

1. Increase rpm

2. Advance throttles

As engines pick up speed the manifold pressures drop; this is a normal and desired reaction. Adjust the throttles and synchronize the engines.

For the proper relation of manifold pressure to rpm see the power control chart.

Remember

MAKE POWER CHANGES SMOOTHLY AND EVENLY

Climb

TURN AS YOU CLIMB

How do you climb the B-25? Simple, you say—just pull her nose up. That is a definite part of the procedure, but unless a little more thought and a little less muscle accompanies the pulling you will ruin a good airplane.

The minimum safe climbing speed for proper cooling is 155 mph. Climbing at lower speeds overheats and ruins the engines.

Establish a normal climb at 160 to 170 mph using correct power settings. Trim the plane for hands-off flight. This allows you to concentrate on your surroundings. Turn as you climb so that you can spot approaching air traffic.

Turn the booster pumps "OFF" above 1000 feet. Set your power at the desired cruising settings when you reach your desired cruising altitude. Move the mixture control to "CRUISING LEAN" if long-range cruise settings are used. Level off and make any necessary adjustments in power and trim.

LET-DOWN

A let-down is a simple procedure either in instrument or contact flight.

Reduce manifold pressure slightly. Trim for hands-off flight and allow the plane to descend at a steady rate.

Adjust the throttles to avoid using excess manifold pressure during the descent. Never allow the engines to cool off rapidly in the let-down; if you do the engines will not run properly when power is applied because they will have become too cold. Lower the wheels, lower partial flaps and increase the power settings to prevent rapid cooling.

Level off at the desired altitude and adjust power and trim.

KEEP ENGINE WARM

IF IT COOLS OFF IT MAY COUGH

AT THE WRONG TIME

TRIMMING

When properly trimmed the B-25 flies with an ease that belies its weight and size. Watch an old instructor pilot at the controls and you will see that he practically flies the plane with the trim tabs.

Learning to trim a plane properly and to detect quickly when it is out of trim boosts your ability as a pilot.

Every change of attitude, airspeed, and power settings, causes a corresponding change in pressures on the controls. If the trim tabs are not adjusted for the varying pressures, the resulting physical strain tires the strongest man in a surprisingly short time.

Always Keep the B-25 in Trim

To execute any maneuver properly, you must keep the airplane in trim. Exercise particular care in setting the trim tabs on takeoff.

Improperly set tabs make control difficult as the speed and lift increase during the take-off run.

To Trim the Airplane Properly

1. Keep the wings level by visual reference or by instruments.

2. Trim rudder until ball is centered or until directional gyro stops turning.

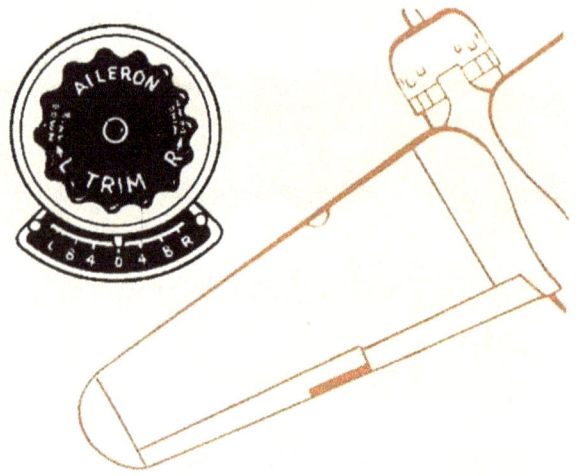

3. Trim aileron.

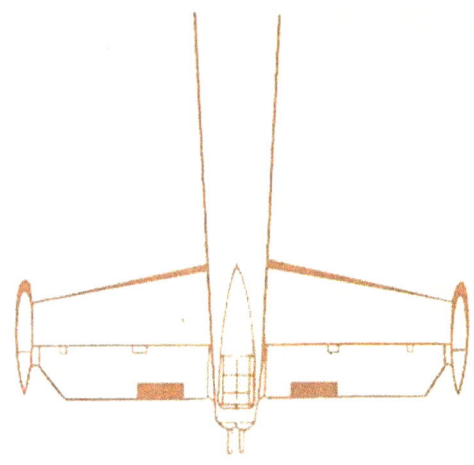

4. Trim elevator.

Check the trim by releasing all controls, allowing the plane to fly for a short time without guidance. Properly trimmed it holds course, altitude, and heading for some time.

Some planes are difficult to trim properly. This is a result of improper rigging and you cannot correct it while in the air. If you encounter this difficulty, check the trim and the weight and balance of the plane to see that it is properly loaded. After assuring yourself that it is the plane and not the pilot, report this condition on the Form 1A.

The engineering officer will run a check flight on the plane. His findings may result in the re-rigging of the plane and subsequent improvement in its flying characteristics.

LANDING

"The easiest plane to land I have ever flown."

Thus the old-timer will start his answer to your query on how to land the B-25. After a few landings you, too, will decide that the Mitchell is indeed an easy plane to land.

Always land as close to the stalling speed as possible, to reduce the wear and tear caused by excessive speed. However, if tricky wind conditions, faulty instruments, or other abnormal conditions require a fast landing, the B-25 will let you land in a speed range of from 85 to 125 mph.

You can use power on the approach to shallow the glide. By using power you also get a greater spread of stalling speed, greater safety and more accurate landings. You also keep the engines from loading up, thus insuring power when you need it.

There are two types of power-on landings. In the first you use the power only on the approach, then cut the power for the roundout and landing; in the second you use power all the way through the roundout and to the desired point of contact with the ground. The first is the normal type of landing. The second is generally used for night landings, under abnormal surface wind conditions, or when flying heavily loaded planes.

The approach is the secret of a good landing. The approach is affected by these four variables:

1. Distance from the field
2. Altitude above the field
3. Gliding speed and gliding angle
4. Wind

Wind is the only one of these variables you can't control. Master the other three quickly, since it is difficult to make an accurate judgment of more than one variable at a time.

Set your base leg at the proper distance and altitude, roll out of the turn and set your gliding speed and angle of glide quickly. A good landing is then assured.

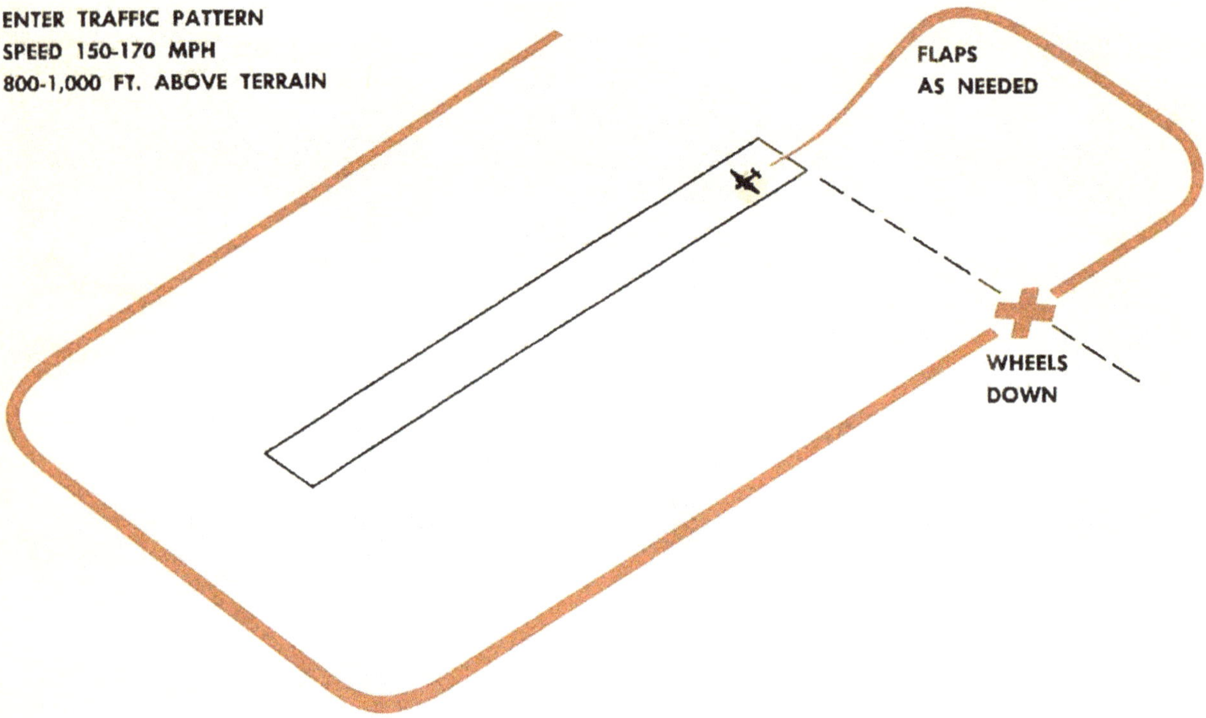

ENTER TRAFFIC PATTERN
SPEED 150-170 MPH
800-1,000 FT. ABOVE TERRAIN

FLAPS AS NEEDED

WHEELS DOWN

In making the roundout, the wingloading is greater than at any other time in the landing cycle. The flight path changes rapidly from the vertical to the horizontal plane, and centrifugal force adds to the wingloading. There is no danger in this increased wingloading at normal gliding speeds if the roundout is smooth and gradual. Abrupt roundouts and rough handling of the controls during the roundout increase the wingloading to the point where a stall may occur at speeds considerably higher than normal stalling speeds.

On any landing, enter traffic as instructed by field regulations or as instructed by the control tower. Adjust the power settings to bring the speed below 170 mph but not below 150 mph. Prior to landing, make this landing check:

Trailing antenna "RETRACTED"
Wing de-icers "OFF"
Heaters "OFF"
Autopilot "OFF"
Fuel pressure
Fuel levels
Booster pumps "ON"
Transfer pumps "OFF"

Mixture "FULL RICH"
Carburetor heat "NORMAL" except in severe icing conditions
Propellers 2400 rpm—This permits the use of maximum climbing power in the event of a go-around. (See power control charts.)
Landing gear "DOWN"—locked and safetied, visually and orally checked.
Brake and hydraulic pressure.

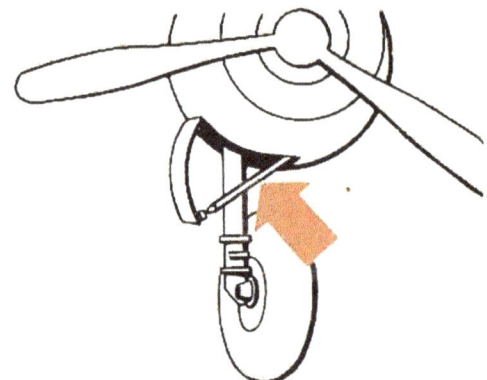

You can check the main gear visually and the nose gear on the selsyn indicator, and, if the prop hub is polished, you can check it by its reflection in the hub. There is a warning horn in some aircraft and a warning light in later models. This warning system operates when the throttles are retarded.

Optional with local regulations, you may use 15° of flaps on the downwind leg to improve visibility and to improve handling characteristics at low speeds.

Do not allow the speed to drop below 150 mph until you are on the approach.

FINAL CHECK BEFORE LANDING

G Gas
U Undercarriage and Pressures
M Mixture
P Props

POWER—ON LANDINGS

Before turning onto the base leg, one landing is much like another. The variations in procedure start as you leave the downwind leg.

The first of the techniques discussed is a normal landing procedure.

Turn onto the base leg and make your final radio check unless the tower has given other instructions. Play the turn into the runway from the base leg to allow a straight approach.

When you are lined up, lower the flaps full down and drop the nose to a point short of the runway. Adjust the power and glide angle to keep the nose traveling along a line that would, if not corrected, put the nose of your plane squarely on the point you have selected. Maintain a predetermined speed all through the approach and to the point at which your roundout starts. This gliding speed varies with the load, but on most planes it is from 120 to 130 mph.

Adjust the trim tabs to ease the load on the controls. Keep the speed constant and the nose on the point, thus setting up a constant glide path. As you approach the runway, flare off and reduce the power and speed. When over the runway, hold the throttles completely closed to prevent them from creeping open and stretching the glide.

Land in a tail-low attitude. Make contact with the main wheels touching down at the same time. The landing gear is designed to absorb great loads if they are applied straight ahead. Tremendous thrust is generated in landing, and if it is applied in a side thrust it can easily collapse the gear.

The landing speed depends on your skill and on weight conditions.

**SPEED CONSTANT
NOSE ON THE POINT**

NEVER MAKE A LANDING IF THE PLANE IS NOT ON THE GROUND WITHIN THE FIRST ⅓ OF THE RUNWAY.

LOWER NOSEWHEEL SLOWLY

Hold the nosewheel in the air with the elevators, thus reducing the length of the landing roll. The increased angle of attack of the wings, plus the 45° of flaps, acts as an air brake.

Lower the nosewheel slowly with elevator control as you lose airspeed on the landing roll. Do not allow the nosewheel to drop heavily onto the runway. It was not designed to absorb this type of load.

Never use the brakes when the nosewheel is off the ground. This throws the nosewheel to the ground suddenly and will collapse it, seriously damaging the airplane. Keep your heels on the floor to avoid unintentional braking.

On the runway, move the prop control to "INC. RPM." When the plane has slowed, complete this landing check.

1. Booster Pumps "OFF."
2. Cowl Flaps "OPEN."
3. Wing Flaps "UP."

Clear the runway quickly, freeing it for the next plane to land.

The second technique for power-on landing is a procedure for use at night, under strong wind conditions, or whenever you want more positive control. In this you fly the airplane all the way to the ground.

Set the approach in exactly the same manner as for the first technique.

As you approach the runway, reduce the power at a point farther out from the end of the runway. Reduce power gradually, slowing the plane as you come in. The use of power lowers your stall speed and the speed must be low to prevent overshooting the runway.

As you reach the end of the runway your speed should be slightly above the power-off stalling speed, with the plane in a landing attitude. Now reduce power slowly until the plane settles onto the ground. Close the throttles completely only when the plane is on the ground.

Don't make a dragging approach in this type of landing.

This is not a short-field landing—there is no place in it for slow flying. The plane is never below power-off stall speed until it is over the runway. The maneuver is designed to give you maximum control of the airplane. You lose this advantage if you do not execute it properly.

The remainder of the ground roll and landing check are identical with the first procedure.

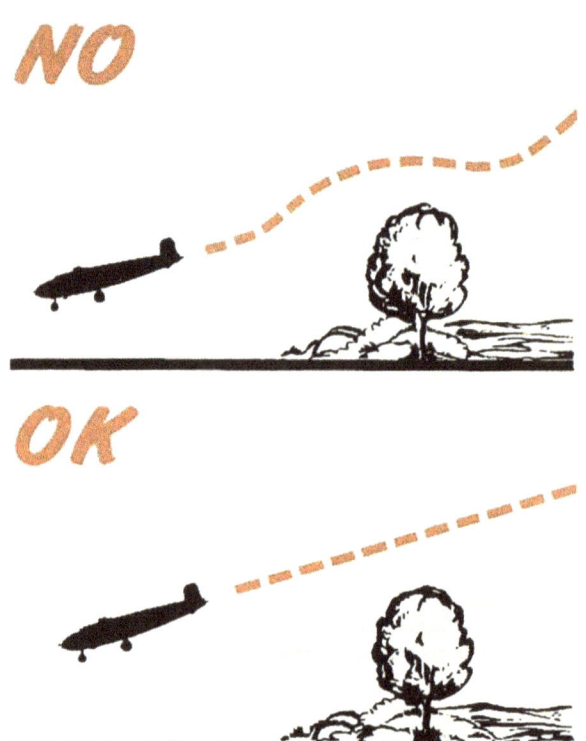

The third technique is commonly called a combat landing. It is the product of combat theatres, where the difference between life and death is often the amount of time it takes you to get out of the traffic pattern and onto the ground.

A slow-flying bomber with wheels and flaps down is a setup for any fighter which spots it.

This is a precision maneuver requiring a lot of skill and judgment.

Fly the downwind leg in the same way as the two other power-on landing techniques. The rest of the procedure is entirely different.

When you are opposite the end of the runway on your downwind leg, start a turn into the field.

Play your speed and altitude in a constantly descending turn. Lower your flaps in the turn so that they will be full down as you roll out above the runway.

Properly executed, you can complete this roll-out just above the end of the runway at a speed that permits the minimum amount of float above the runway before touching down.

If you visualize a chandelle and then reverse it so that you picture a diving turn through 180°, you have an accurate picture of this landing.

Caution

This maneuver requires the touch and skill of an experienced pilot. Have an instructor pilot demonstrate it to you and practice it when he is present.

The rest of the landing procedure is identical with the others.

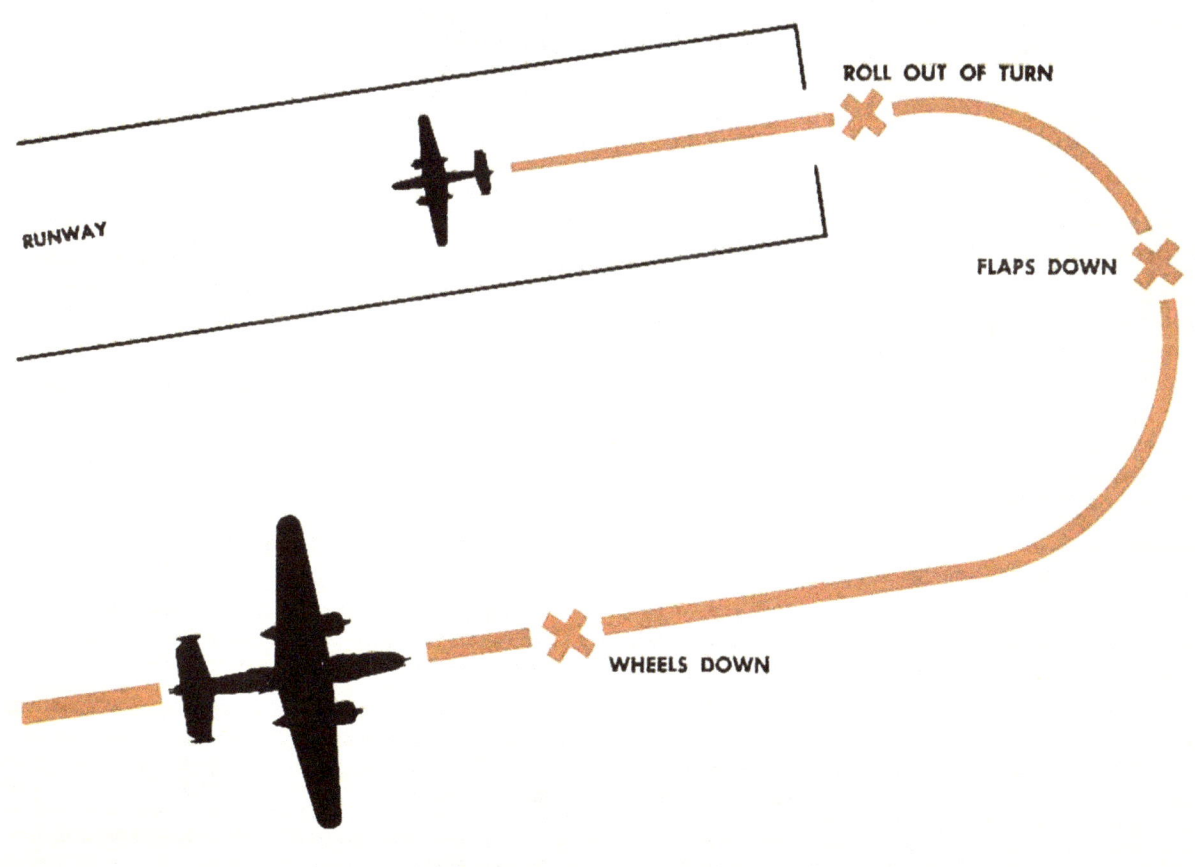

POWER-OFF LANDING

Diagram labels: POWER OFF FLAPS DOWN; RUNWAY; WHEELS DOWN

The B-25 is too large and heavy to practice the prescribed forced-landing procedures used in lighter planes. The power-off approach allows the pilot to become familiar with all the factors involved in a forced landing without the hazards involved in actually practicing them.

The power-off approach duplicates exactly the conditions of a forced landing with these exceptions:

1. You make the landing with wheels down instead of up.
2. You make the landing on a known field.

These landings acquaint the pilot with the power-off gliding characteristics of the B-25 and improve his judgment for an actual forced landing. Make a power-off approach and landing as follows:

1. Fly a normal traffic pattern and hold your altitude through the last turn into the field.
2. Hold your altitude until you are in position to make a glide to the end of the runway.
3. Reduce the power and establish a normal glide short of the end of the runway.
4. Lower the desired amount of flaps.
5. Make a normal roundout and landing.

Caution

In an actual emergency make the landing with wheels up unless you are over a known airfield. This increases the gliding distance of the plane. Make allowances for the increased gliding distance.

In an emergency use the prop to vary the glide of the airplane.

To increase drag, move the prop control to "INC. RPM."

To decrease drag, move the prop control to "DEC. RPM."

NO-FLAP LANDING

Occasionally both in combat and normal operations your plane may be damaged to the extent that flaps cannot be lowered for landing. The use of full flaps reduces your landing speed approximately 20 mph; therefore, a slightly different technique is required for landing when using no flaps.

You must be familiar with this technique:

1. Add approximately 10 mph to your normal gliding speed.
2. Keep the plane's attitude almost level on the approach.
3. Use less elevator control and more power than normal in the roundout. (In some instances, it may be necessary to use considerable power to decrease your rate of descent.)

When making no-flap landings **always** land on the first few feet of the runway. Your landing speed is greater and your landing roll much longer.

Don't let the nosewheel touch the ground before or with the main wheels.

TIPS ON LANDING

Don't let the nosewheel strike immediately after landing.

You can easily control the position of the nosewheel with the elevator.

Hold the nose well up after landing. This reduces the length of the roll considerably.

Excessive use of brakes is not necessary—the rudders give ample control.

Use the brakes in accordance with the amount of runway available.

The speed decreases considerably during the roll. Therefore, emergency operations with the brakes can be delayed to prevent damage to the airplane.

On slick runways the B-25 is exceedingly difficult to control. Land short, and slow the plane as much as possible without brakes.

Guard the throttles on all landings to prevent creeping.

Never apply the brakes until the nosewheel is on the runway.

Go-Around Procedure

There is a common reluctance among pilots to go around. They feel it implies a lack of ability to meet an unusual situation.

A pilot admires a buddy who has sufficient moral courage to go around when the situation seems to call for it. Yet he believes his fellow pilots will censure him for the very thing he admires in another.

Don't be a dope! Go around when you must.

The go-around procedure is an important emergency maneuver. It is not difficult, but it requires practice.

Since the go-around procedure may begin at extremely low altitudes and airspeeds, with wheels and flaps down, its relation to slow flying and full-flap maneuvering is obvious. Practice these maneuvers before practicing the go-around.

Practice full-flap turns at safe altitudes to experience the feel of the lower airspeeds at which these turns may be made.

It is not true that the flaps will blank out the tail surfaces at a certain degree of bank.

Do not make abrupt steep turns, however, as the stalling speed increases with the degree of bank, and abrupt control movements might precipitate a stall.

The most important part of the go-around procedure is determining its necessity and starting it soon enough. When it is necessary to go around, the sooner you start the procedure the easier it is.

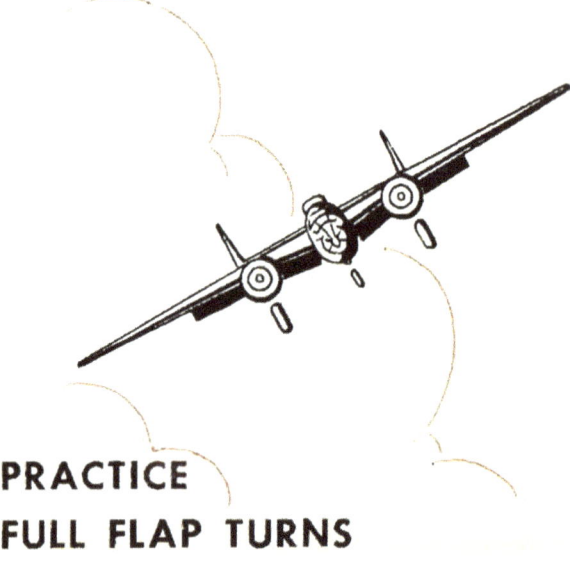

PRACTICE FULL FLAP TURNS

GO-AROUND PROCEDURE IS AS FOLLOWS:

ADVANCE THROTTLES—RAISE WHEELS

RAISE THE FLAPS TO 15°

CLEAR THE RUNWAY AREA

1. Keep the prop set at 2400 rpm.
2. Advance the power smoothly to climbing power.
3. **Keep the nose of the plane down.**
4. Raise landing gear.
5. Raise the flaps to 15°.
6. Allow the plane to settle to a slightly lower altitude, if necessary, to maintain or increase the airspeed.

With the plane trimmed for landing there is a strong tendency for the nose to lift when power is applied. This will throw the plane into a stall if it is not counteracted.

When the plane has gained sufficient airspeed to lift and gain altitude, pull over to one side of the runway, thus clearing the runway for any plane attempting to take off or land.

Keep an eye on all planes near you! The pilot taking off under you may not know that you are there.

As soon as you gain sufficient speed, raise the balance of your flaps. Establish a normal climb, break traffic, re-enter traffic as before and make a normal landing.

Don't hesitate to go around. Any doubt that the plane is under perfect control is sufficient cause to go around. If you have made a poor approach and know that the landing will be too long, or too rough—go around.

Common Errors

1. A reluctance to go around or failure to anticipate the necessity.
2. Waiting until the airplane is too low and moving too slowly before deciding to go around.
3. Failure to add sufficient power or adding power too slowly, thus losing altitude.
4. Raising the wheels before applying power.
5. Starting climb without a safe airspeed.
6. Raising the last 15° of flaps without increasing the angle of attack of the wings, causing an uncontrolled sinking.
7. Tenseness, causing a hurried procedure. Learn the procedure thoroughly, use it with confidence, perform each step calmly and deliberately as needed.

PARKING

When you park your plane after a flight, just remember that the Colonel may make the next flight in that particular airplane.

As you approach the parking ramp stay alert and plan your taxiing so that you can pull into position straight ahead.

Never make a sharp turn into the parking position. This leaves the nosewheel angled across the direction of roll you use in leaving. Furthermore, a buddy may snuggle up on each side of you, locking you in position just as securely as if they used a chain.

The nosewheel position indicator warns you when the nosewheel is more than 15° from straight ahead. Release the brakes and allow the plane to roll forward. Correct the alignment of the nosewheel, and re-park. Set the parking brakes and prepare to stop the engines.

1. Open bomb bay door.
   a. Set engine at 1200 rpm.
2. Mixture control to "IDLE CUT-OFF."
3. Throttle full "OPEN" as rpm starts to drop. This prevents a tendency of the engines to backfire as the last of the fuel is running through the cylinder heads.
4. Ignition switches "OFF" when the props have stopped turning. **Don't be careless about this.** An engine with a cylinder loaded is like a stick of dynamite with a fuse attached. Just a little carelessness will set either one off with a bang. A pilot climbing into his seat may nudge the ignition switch and an unlucky mechanic may lose the top of his head.
5. Turn all switches "OFF."

Note: Whenever necessary, dilute the oil before the engines are stopped. (See cold weather section.)

After the wheels have been chocked, release the parking brakes. Never keep the parking brakes set after you return to the line. The multiple-disc brakes get extremely hot when you taxi for long periods, and if sufficiently hot, they lock, necessitating removal of the wheels and brakes, and extensive repairs.

Make a complete check of the plane to see that trim tabs are set on "O," switches and radios are "OFF," controls "LOCKED," etc. It is only common courtesy to leave the plane clean and neat for the next crew. See that carburetor air scoop covers are on to exclude dust from the engines. Complete the necessary local forms, gas forms, squadron reports, combat crew training reports, etc. Talk to the crew chief and tell him of the plane's performance. Give him any ideas you have for improvements.

PARKING COMPLETE – NOSEWHEEL PROPERLY LINED UP

Fuel System Operation

Every man on your crew must know the fuel system so thoroughly that a mistake in its operation is impossible.

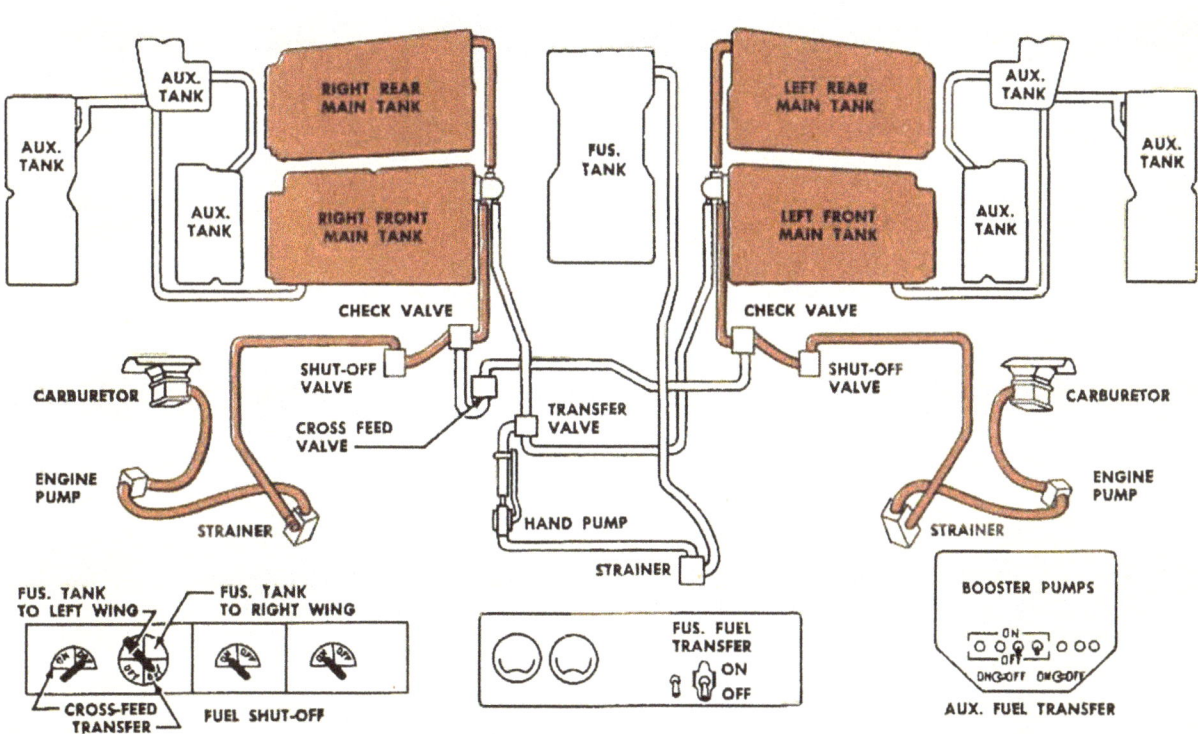

NORMAL OPERATION

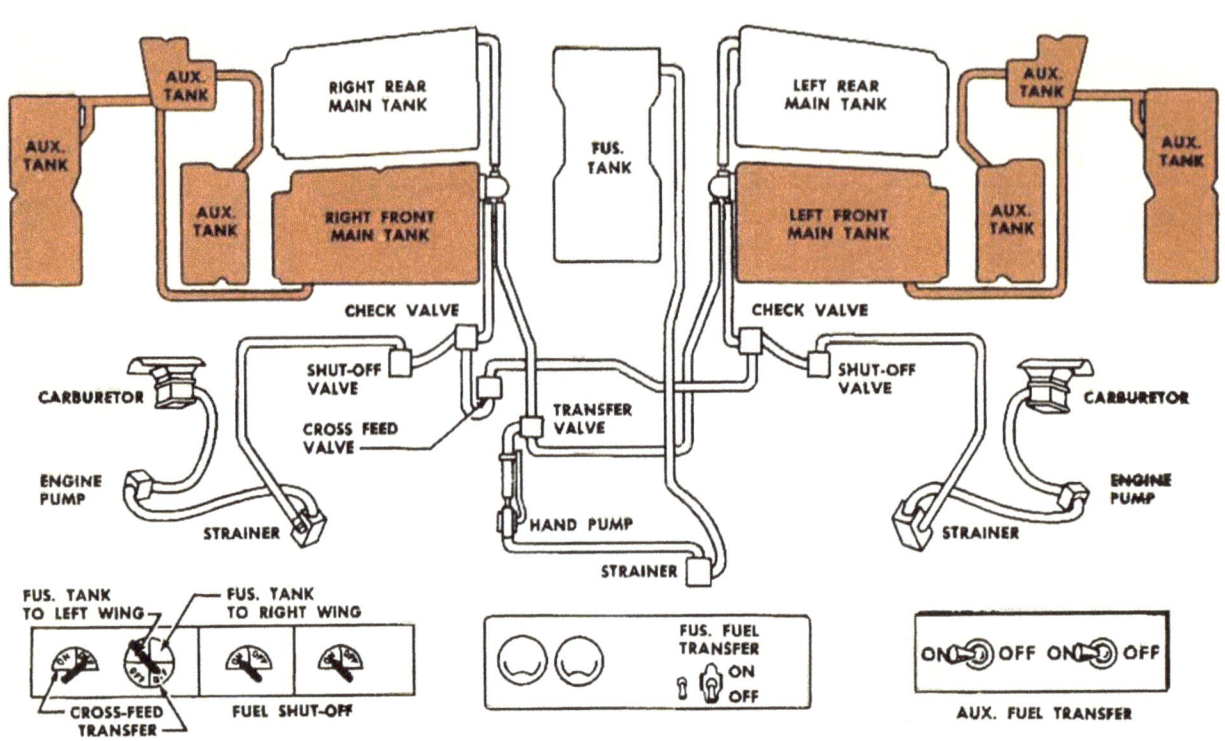

AUXILIARY FUEL TRANSFER

To use auxiliary fuel you must first get it into the front main cells.

To transfer fuel from the auxiliary wing cells;
1. Check fuel levels in front cells to see that space is available for transfer.
2. Turn auxiliary fuel transfer switches "ON." (On pilot's pedestal.)
3. Turn liquidometer to the front cell receiving fuel.
4. After front cell is full turn transfer switch "OFF."
5. Repeat on opposite side.

There are no valves to open and close during this transfer. When transferring fuel, time the operation to give equal distribution to right and left cells.

Warning

Don't leave switches "ON" after front cell is full. Fuel may be pumped overboard through a loose filler cap.

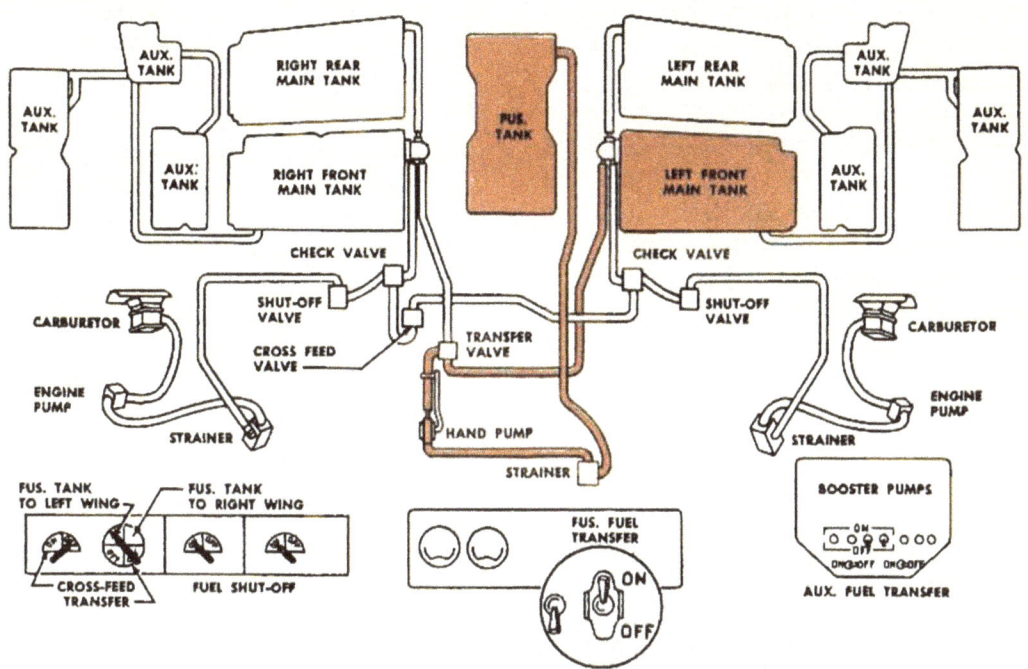

FUSELAGE TANK TO LEFT FRONT MAIN

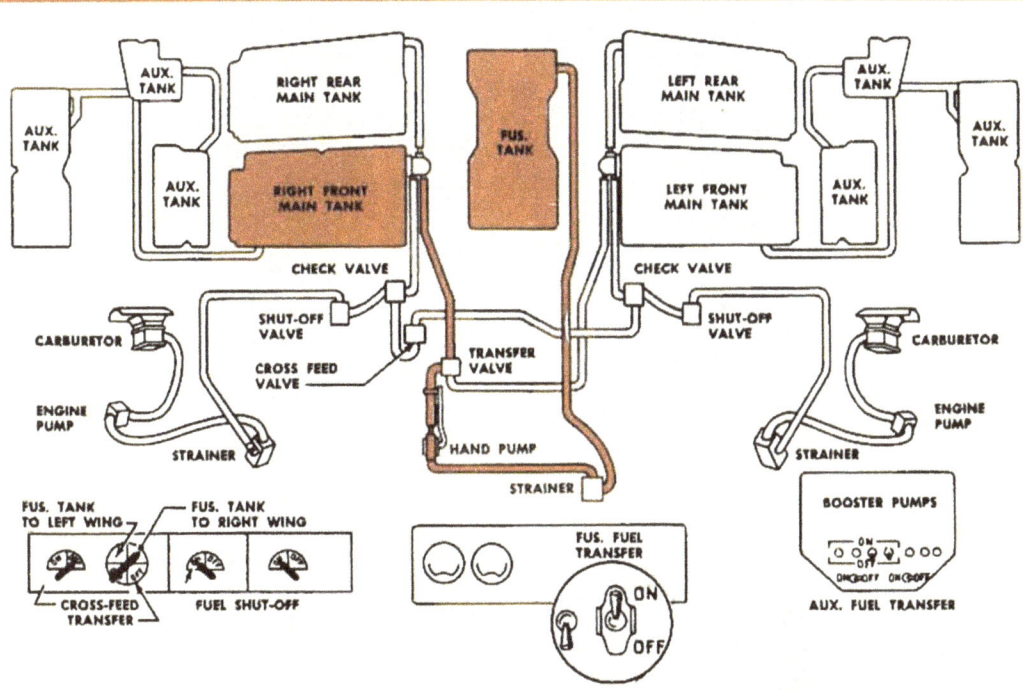

FUSELAGE TANK TO RIGHT FRONT MAIN

Fuselage Tank Fuel

Before you can use fuel from any fuselage tank you must transfer it to either the right or left front main fuel cells.

Transfer fuel as follows:

1. Turn fuel transfer valve from "OFF" to either "FUS. TANK TO LEFT WING" or "FUS. TANK TO RIGHT WING."
2. Turn transfer pump switch "ON." (On generator control panel.)
3. Turn liquidometer to front cell receiving fuel.
4. When transfer operations are finished turn transfer switch "OFF" and place fuel transfer valve at "OFF."

Keep the main fuel cells as nearly full as possible. Transfer fuel at frequent intervals.

It may become necessary to salvo the bomb bay tank. In that case you will want as much fuel as possible in the front main cells.

Emergency Fuel Transfer

If fuselage transfer pump fails:

1. Set transfer valve to desired position.
2. Unstrap hand transfer pump handle.
3. Operate pump until desired fuel transfer is complete.
4. Return handle to stowed position and turn transfer valve "OFF."

Crossfeed Operation

The fuel crossfeed is installed for emergency use only. Keep the crossfeed valve "OFF" unless an engine-driven fuel pump fails. The crossfeed system allows you to operate either or both engines from either or both tanks.

EMERGENCY FUEL TRANSFER HAND PUMP

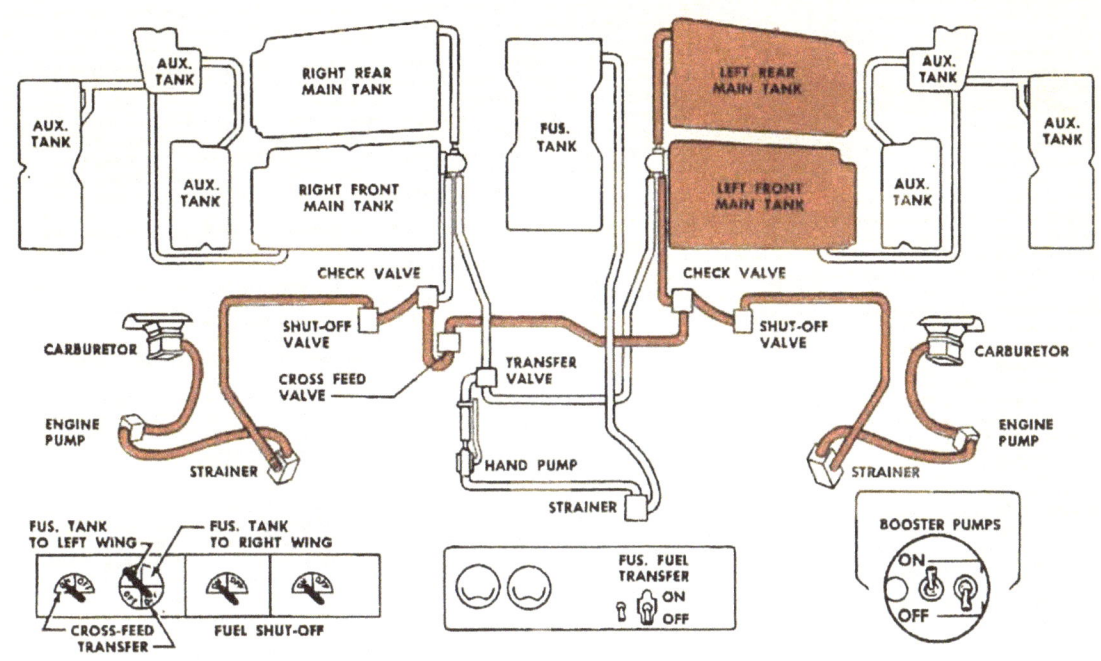

FUEL TANKS ON ONE SIDE TO BOTH ENGINES

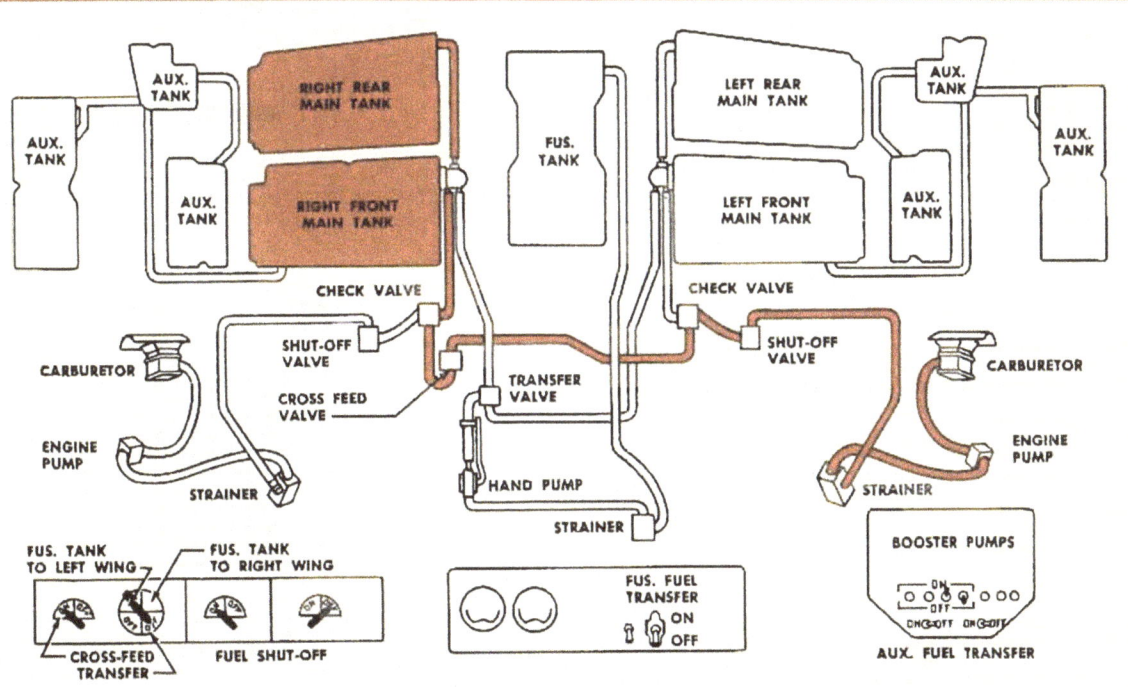

FUEL TANKS ON ONE SIDE TO OPPOSITE ENGINE

OPERATING INSTRUCTIONS FOR THE
Supercharger

The supercharger is an integral part of your engine **at all altitudes**. Don't fall into the trap of assuming that because you are operating at medium and low altitudes, your supercharger is not important. Your supercharger must have proper care all the time, regardless of whether you intend to use high blower.

Flight Instructions

1. Except where airfields are at extremely high altitudes, always take off in "LOW" blower. (There are no fields in the continental U.S. where "HIGH" blower take-offs are necessary.) While in "LOW" blower, operate the engine as a single-speed supercharged engine.

2. Never operate in "HIGH" blower below 9,000 feet. The power gained by operating in "HIGH" blower below this altitude is offset by the power required to operate in "HIGH" blower. Make the shift from "LOW" to "HIGH" blower between 11,000 and 13,000 feet, depending on the need for additional power.

Operation

Shift From Low Blower To High Blower:
1. Mixture control "FULL RICH."
2. Reduce manifold pressure. (Reduce throttles sufficiently to prevent the surge in manifold pressure exceeding the prescribed power setting when the shift is made.)
3. Set rpm at 1700.
4. Shift the controls rapidly and evenly from "LOW" to "HIGH," and lock. Make this a quick, positive action.
5. Re-set the desired power setting.

Warning

Never operate in "HIGH" blower below 1500 rpm. During prolonged operation in "HIGH" blower, change to "LOW" blower for 15 minutes every 2 hours. (This removes sludge from the clutch.)

Shift From High Blower To Low Blower.
1. Mixture control "FULL RICH."
2. Reduce throttles. (Your manifold pressure must not exceed the setting for 1700 rpm.)
3. Set rpm at 1700.
4. Shift the controls from "HIGH" to "LOW" in a quick, positive action.
5. Re-set the desired power setting.

Note: For maximum performance above 12,000 ft. reduce rpm to 2400. This adds 5 to 8 mph. to the maximum speed.

LOW BLOWER TO HIGH BLOWER

HIGH BLOWER TO LOW BLOWER

CARBURETOR AIR HEAT

The carburetor air heater on the B-25 is a 2-position gate in the air induction system.

Manual controls directly connect this gate to the position handles in the pilot's cockpit. It cannot be set in an intermediate position and it is spring loaded to return to "NORMAL" if the controls are shot away.

Keep controls at "NORMAL" setting unless carburetor icing conditions are suspected, as a loss of horsepower results with the controls in "ICING." This effect increases as power is increased.

Whenever you observe a gradual loss of manifold pressure without a change in throttles or attitude, or the engine runs rough without apparent cause, move the control to "ICING."

In this position the air scoop entrance is closed off, and ice free and heated air enters the carburetor from behind the cylinders.

Operation in "ICING" will not harm the engines. Even in warm weather the carburetor air temperature rise is small. The engines lose efficiency, however, since fuel vaporization is impeded.

Takeoffs are made with the controls at "NORMAL" to obtain maximum power and prevent detonation at high power settings.

Resistance-type carburetor air thermometers are installed in the intake air stream on each carburetor. They are electrically connected to a dual indicator on the right side of the instrument panel.

Keep the air inlet temperature above 15°C during any conditions where you suspect carburetor ice.

A temperature between 15°C and 30°C is desirable. If, with the carburetor air control at "ICING," a temperature of 15°C cannot be maintained, move the control to "NORMAL" to provide air to the carburetor at so low a temperature that icing will not occur. If, with the carburetor air control at "ICING," ice that is already formed is not eliminated, use the alcohol anti-icing system (if installed).

CARBURETOR AIR FILTER

The false impression exists among some pilots and mechanics that the carburetor air filter affects airplane performance. Installation of a filter is merely equivalent to closing the throttles slightly. This means that for all altitudes less than critical, where manifold pressure limits prevent full throttle opening, the filter has no effect at all on engine power output or airplane performance.

Manifold pressure gives the best indication of engine power output, and at a given pressure the engine develops the same power regardless of whether a filter is installed. The only time that removal of the filter benefits performance is when the throttle is full open and still more manifold pressure is permissible.

When the filter is installed, it affects only cold ram air. Heated air does not pass through the filter element.

PRIMING

Priming is necessary to supply a sufficiently rich fuel air mixture to the cylinder heads to facilitate starting of a cold motor.

Prime by operating the 3-position spring-loaded toggle switch on the pilot's pedestal. This actuates the 2 primary active solenoids on the carburetors.

For manual priming, press the small pin next to the solenoid on the carburetor.

The primer allows fuel under pressure to pass through a valve and enter the adapter section at 3 different points. On some late-model carburetors no provision is made for manual priming.

OPERATING THE AUTOPILOT

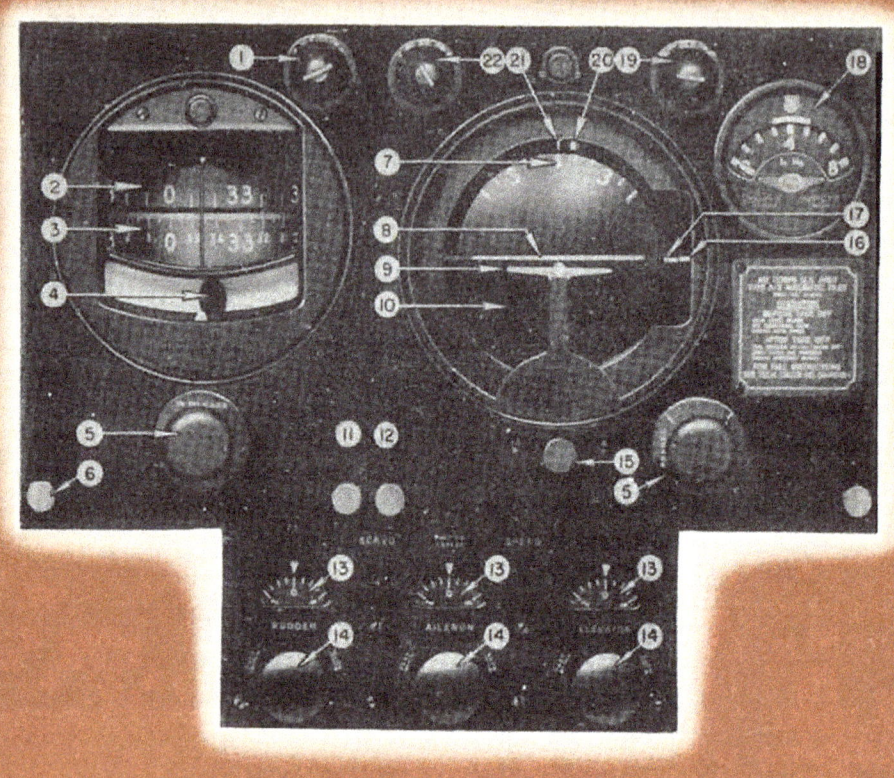

1. Rudder Control Knob
2. Rudder Follow-up Card
3. Directional Gyro Card
4. Ball Bank Indicator
5. Caging Knobs
6. Installation Bolts
7. Banking Scale
8. Horizon Bar
9. Miniature Airplane
10. Horizon Dial
11. Directional Gyro Unit
12. Bank and Climb Gyro Unit
13. Valve Adjustment Reference Dials
14. Valve Adjustment Knobs
15. Miniature Airplane Adjusting Knob
16. Elevator Alignment Index
17. Elevator Follow-up Index
18. Suction Gage
19. Elevator Control Knob
20. Aileron Follow-up Index
21. Bank Index
22. Aileron Control Knob

It's okay to let Elmer take over and do some of your flying for you, particularly to relieve you of the strain caused by long over-water flights. Or, if you are cruising over the top and need to be very accurate in your cross country courses, let Elmer fly.

Remember, though, that the autopilot is a machine. It cannot do your thinking for you. Use it as an aid to flight, not to do your flying and particularly not your thinking.

Experience has demonstrated that the instantaneous control responses of the autopilot under flight conditions which might cause sideslip or stall, may result in a spin. Because of this, the following restrictions are placed on its use.

Do not use it in extremely turbulent air. You can, if you choose, use it to aid you but you must be on the controls also.

Do not use it when the de-icer system is in operation.

Do not use it if both engines are not delivering normal power.

Do not turn it on until you are sure that flight conditions permit safe control by the autopilot.

Maintain at least minimum cruise power settings. The B-25 is too sluggish at low speeds to permit safe operation on autopilot.

Never operate the autopilot unless one rated pilot is on watch in the cockpit. You must constantly check the instruments, and the trim of the plane must be accurate.

Never engage the autopilot unless the indices are lined up properly.

Never make course and altitude changes rapidly with the autopilot.

When the autopilot is engaged, never turn the speed valves to "O" setting. This will lock the corresponding surface controls in their position.

Ground Checklist

Check suction—3.75" to 4.25" Hg.
Check oil pressure—75 to 90 lb. sq. in.
Check bank-and-climb unit uncaged.
Check directional unit uncaged.

Engage autopilot and check operation by moving each control knob. Watch the surface controls for corresponding movements.

Check for air in the Servo units by moving the normal surface controls. A springy reaction shows the presence of air in the system.

Disengage autopilot, leave gyros uncaged.

In Flight

Trim the plane hands-off.
Set Servo controls at No. 4.
Set rudder follow-up card to match directional gyro card.
Set aileron follow-up card to match bank index.

Operating Limits

CLIMBING OR GLIDING

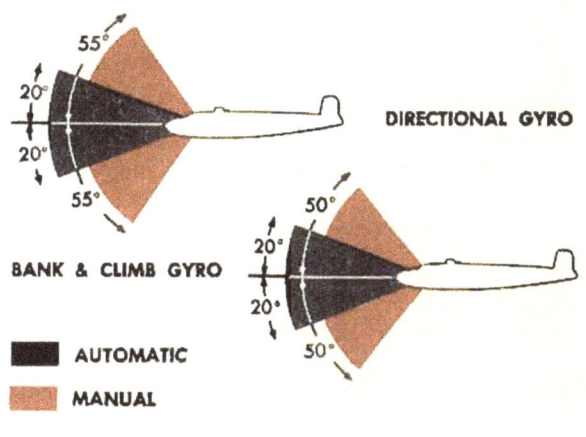

BANKING

Set elevator follow-up card to match elevator alignment index.

Caution—Do not set the elevator follow-up card to match the horizon bar. Their relative movement is in opposite directions.

Move the "ON-OFF" control to the "ON" position slowly.

Adjust the Servo speed controls as needed.

These controls are calibrated from 0 to 8, the speed range of operation is 0 (locked) to 8 (high speed reaction). If the instrument is in good condition, the proper setting for the B-25 is between 2 and 4. These need not read the same for all controls.

Set fore and aft attitude with the elevator knob.

Set directional control with the rudder knob.

Set in bank when you wish to turn more than 5°.

Always keep the gyros uncaged except during maneuvers which exceed the operating limits of the autopilot. These are 50° from the vertical for the bank-and-climb unit and 55° for the directional gyro unit.

Warning

During flight do not overcontrol the autopilot more than 15°. This causes the autopilot to attempt an abrupt return to the original position, with possible damage to the control surfaces and the autopilot.

The autopilot gives accurate control with a plus or minus tolerance of 1°. It flies a far better course than a human pilot.

When the autopilot is in use for extended periods, be sure to disengage it at least once every half hour to check the trim manually. This instrument will not give efficient performance if it is operating against the pressures of the trim tabs.

If the Servo speed controls are improperly set, the plane oscillates or hunts for a stable position. If this happens, open the Servo speed controls and slowly turn them toward the closed position. Do not close them completely, but find the point at which the oscillation stops. Adjust the controls slowly back and forth at this point until you obtain the desired setting.

Warning

ALWAYS BE SURE YOU CAN OVER POWER THE AUTOPILOT MANUALLY. TRY IT ON THE GROUND BEFORE YOU FLY.

ADVANCED AIR WORK

Many of the maneuvers described here are prohibited in this airplane. However, knowing the reactions of the airplane to these maneuvers is important.

Do not take these instructions as a license to abuse your airplane. It is better to stay away from trouble than invite it.

THE PROHIBITED MANEUVERS IN THIS AIRPLANE ARE:

LOOPS • SPINS • ROLLS • VERTICAL DIVES
IMMELMANNS • INVERTED FLIGHT • VERTICAL BANKS

These maneuvers are not prohibited because of the flying characteristics of the airplane, but because they impose severe structural stresses on it. The B-25 is a bomber, not a pursuit plane. Those pilots who try to make a pursuit plane out of a bomber succeed only in making a wreck of the bomber.

The maximum safe wingloading on the B-25 when pulling out of a dive is 3.67 G's, and then only at normal weight loadings or below. The designed gross weight of the plane is 26,620 lb. The maximum possible overload is 35,500 lb. Remember, however, that in present-day military operations you seldom fly a mission under normal load conditions. Almost all bombardment missions are overload flights.

The maximum diving speed of the B-25 is 340 mph with normal load weights. When the weight is 35,500 lb. the maximum speed is only 281 mph.

Know your airplane. The total flying time on the plane you are flying may have reduced the safety factor the manufacturer built into it. Some small trouble not found on the periodic inspections may show up in violent maneuvers.

The pilot who flew the plane the previous day may have abused the airplane, so conquer that urge to show off.

SPINS

No pilot should ever knowingly allow the airplane to get into a spin. If you accidentally get into a spin, however, the recovery is normal.

Cut power completely and use conventional control movement to recover. You need a lot of muscle to make positive rudder and elevator actions.

In violent spins and stalls, airplanes with 30° of rudder travel have a tendency to throw the rudder full into the spin and the elevator control full back in the pilot's lap. You and your copilot may have to use your combined strength to effect a recovery.

The airplane is clean aerodynamically and picks up tremendous speeds if left in a steep dive. Be careful in making the recovery to prevent structural damage to the airplane.

The best advice possible is—stay out of spins. If you do get into a spin and there is doubt that you can recover safely, don't stay with the airplane too long. It is bad enough to lose the airplane—**don't ride it down.**

If you are still out of control when you reach 5000 feet—Get out!

DIVES

The diving characteristics of the B-25, like all its flight characteristics, are exceptionally good. The first thing for you to remember, as a new pilot in the B-25, is this: the plane is not a dive bomber.

It was designed and built to carry a load of bombs to a target and return to its base. The fact that the plane can exceed these minimum requirements is no excuse to abuse it.

The red-lined diving speed on the B-25 is 340 mph. This maximum speed is possible only under definite weight limits.

Recover from a dive gradually. The structural load on the airplane increases in direct relation to the abruptness of the pullout.

Be careful if you dive the plane in rough air, because the roughness increases the load and shock forces the plane must carry.

Combat requirements may force you to dive the plane when the gross weight is excessive. The plane will carry you through some tight spots in an emergency, but treat it gently. Don't place unnecessary loads on the plane by rough and careless handling.

MAXIMUM DIVING SPEED

Gross Weight Lbs.	Normal Up to 26,620	Overload				
		28,000	30,000	32,000	34,000	35,000
Maximum allowable pull-out and push-over acceleration "g"	+3.67 −2.00	+2.67 −1.67	+2.67 −1.67	+2.67 −1.67	+2.67 −1.67	+2.67 −1.67
Maximum allowable diving speed (indicated) MPH	340	340	340	332	303	281
Maximum permissible landing load factor	3.33	2.67	2.67	2.67		

NIGHT FLYING

The technique of night flying is closely akin to instrument flying. A few tips on night flying:

1. Know the location of your controls.
2. Always carry a flashlight.
3. Use extra care in taxiing.
4. Use landing lights **alternately** for taxiing, except in very congested areas.
5. Use the extension light rather than the dome light for reading maps and charts.
6. Check all lighting equipment and fluorescent lighting of instrument panel before leaving the ground.
7. Make an accurate check of your flight instruments.
8. Switch on the dome light if your eyes feel strained during prolonged instrument flight at night. This creates the illusion of flying under a hood and relieves strain.

Important **IN NIGHT FLYING, A TURN MAY SUDDENLY CHANGE CONTACT FLIGHT TO INSTRUMENT FLIGHT BE READY TO FLY INSTRUMENTS AT ANY MOMENT.**

INSTRUMENT FLYING

Every pilot must have in his possession a copy of T. O. series 30-100. You must know these Technical Orders for the mastery of instrument flight. Study them frequently. Your path through the overcast will be a lot easier.

Formation

"You just gotta stay in there." Thus returning combat pilots pass on to you the most important thing they learned in the battle zones.

"You just don't come back from a mission if you straggle from a formation. Even if you are hit and hurt badly, if the plane can stay in the air, stay in formation."

This is not an obsession; it is a lesson so well learned that it is instinct. Combat pilots know, as no other men on earth can know, that mutual protection alone makes possible the operations over enemy territory today.

As a trainee pilot it is a lesson you can learn from the experiences of other men. Prepare yourself for the job to come by mastering the elements of formation flying.

Why Fly in Formation?

Bombardment units fly in formation for many reasons, and mutual defense is only one of them. Other reasons are:

1. Concentrate the power of the attack.
2. Concentrate the power of the defense.
3. Maintain the element of surprise in attack.
4. Observation against surprise attack.
5. Unity of command.
6. Maneuverability for attack and defense.
7. Control of navigation.

The basic formation procedures you have learned remain the same. The difference in tactical training is slight; it is primarily in the accuracy of your technique, and the limitations of your airplane.

The B-25 is easy to fly in formation. You need good instruction and plenty of practice, however, to become competent in the technique.

Your main problem is learning the difference between handling the B-25 and a light training plane. Weight and momentum are your chief concerns.

The B-25 does not respond instantly to changes in power settings.

You have more than 26,000 lb. to control, and the momentum of this weight must be overcome before the plane responds to changes in power. When applying power, give the plane a chance to respond. Don't be a throttle juggler—it is not necessary, and you cannot fly good formation by blasting the power on and then cutting it off. Tease your plane into its position by small, accurate corrections. You can fly accurate, well-controlled formation and seldom need a great change in power setting.

Learn to anticipate. This is the hardest part of formation flying in the B-25. The ideal formation is one in which each man so anticipates his power needs that he never has to make any but the slightest corrections in his power settings.

Tactical formation places a high premium on a pilot's ability to move accurately from one type of formation to another. You must be able to move quickly from a relatively loose route formation to a tight defensive formation. If you are in proper position above and well up on the lead plane, you can close accurately and quickly by nosing down, thus converting altitude to the speed required.

You may fly in a formation of hundreds of airplanes, but these huge formations break down into the familiar 3-plane combinations. Learn these fundamentals well and you will feel at home and be in position in any formation.

Air Discipline

A formation in the air is no place for a difference of opinion. You are in a formation to enable the formation leader to exercise his right of command.

He is the boss of the formation as a captain is boss of his ship at sea; there is no question of his orders and no recourse. Once you have landed, you—like a sailor—can take your complaint to a higher authority.

In the air—Obey.

Types of Formations

There are many types of formations; for simplicity, the three basic groupings are sufficient to give you the primary elements of all formations.

These formations are illustrated as squadron formations to allow you to see their integration into larger groups.

JAVELIN UP

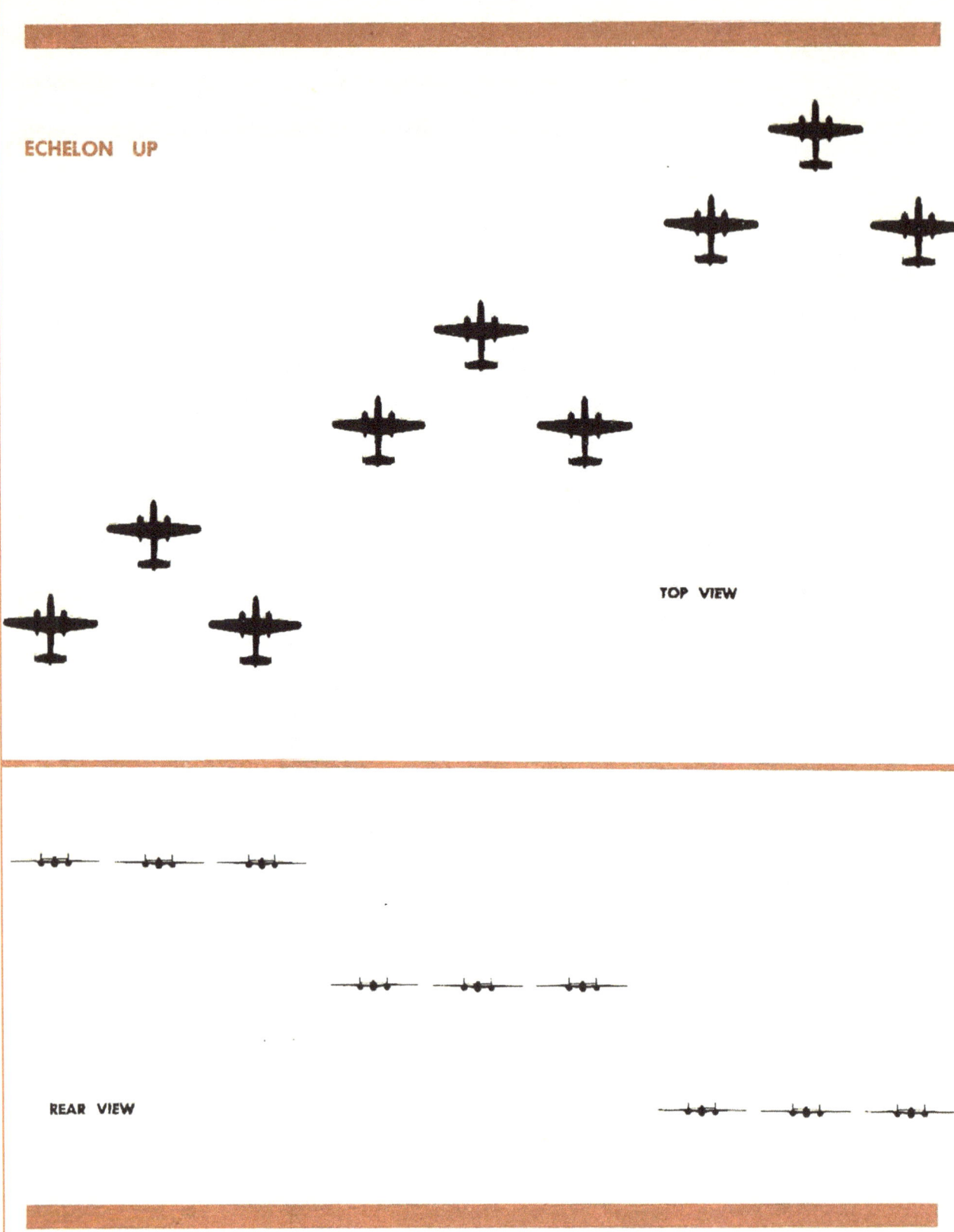

Takeoff and Landing

Many variations of takeoff and landing procedures are used in the different Air Forces. The fundamentals are the same wherever you go.

A time interval is set between takeoffs for each plane; on the basis of this time interval, the formation leader flies straight out from the end of the runway at a predetermined rate of climb and a set airspeed. When the time interval shows that his immediate flight is in the air, he starts a constant-rate turn, allowing the rear planes to turn inside him and close in to pick up position.

Each plane takes an alternate side of the runway at takeoff to avoid the prop wash of the preceding plane.

Warning—Watch wind direction closely to determine where you will encounter the heaviest prop wash, and try to fly above or below it at that point.

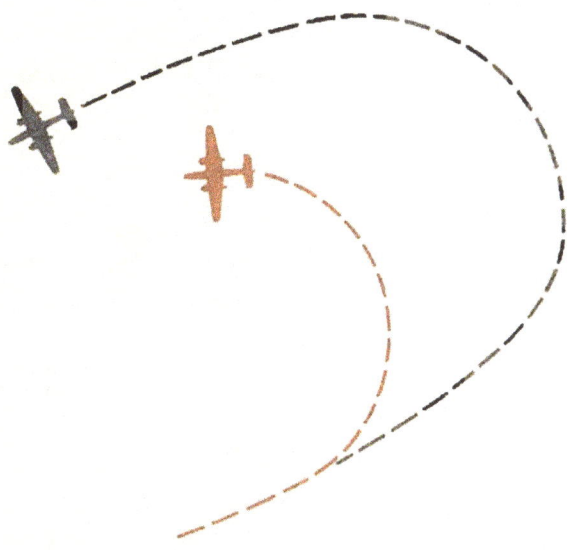

Keep your nose inside the nose of the lead plane. You will delay the entire joining procedure if you turn with the lead plane instead of inside him.

To land in formation you must land accurately at varying distances on the runway. Land on the side away from the plane ahead of you, and give the man behind you a little room to get down. Don't blast your throttles on the approach. You only create unnecessary prop wash. Plan your landing to get in without increasing power.

Don't be afraid to go around if you mess up a formation landing. **Remember, there is a man coming in right behind you.** If you can't land accurately, go around.

Watch the plane ahead of you. If you see him make a low, dragging approach, you will eat a lot of his prop wash as you land. Try to plan your landing to come in over his prop wash, and let down to the runway where his power has been cut, thereby missing the worst turbulence.

Leading a Formation

Leading a formation requires accurate, precise flying and excellent judgment. It is similar to instrument flying. A definite planned procedure is the secret of leading a formation properly.

Remember—your wingmen trust you implicitly for leadership and direction. Neither you, they, nor anyone else will trust a leader who bounces around like a Yo-Yo. Make each maneuver smooth and slow enough so that your poorest wingman can follow you without difficulty.

Make your signals distinct, but not violent. Remember that the size of the formation following you governs the arc of turn. If you pour on the coal and turn tight you play crack-the-whip with the man on the tail of the formation. Tomorrow he may be the guy whose gunners could save your neck if he was in position.

Fly at reduced power. Your wingmen must have a margin of power available to maintain position.

Follow the instructions given on the ground. Many combat reports show that formation leaders have caused casualties by ignoring the planned attack to try a makeshift at the last moment.

Remember the size of your formation.

Fly accurately.

Plan your work well in advance.

Fly at reduced power—compact defensive power is more potent than a little extra speed.

Use the best judgment you are able to exercise.

Tips for a Wingman

Trust your leader. Stay in formation.

These two simple things will do more than anything else to bring you home safely from the toughest missions. If you disagree with the formation leader, wait until you are on the ground to say so.

Watch the lead plane constantly.

Make power changes smoothly, waiting for the plane's reaction.

Keep your head out of the cockpit. Train your copilot or engineer to make rpm adjustments to compensate for your changing throttle settings. Don't change them constantly, but stay out of the detonation range.

When changing position, keep all other planes in your field of vision.

Coordinate the controls. You don't have to kick your plane around; fly it through the necessary corrections.

Be ready in advance of takeoff time. Don't be so late that you have no time for a good pre-takeoff check of your plane.

Caution

When operating on Grade 91 fuel, for additional safety, formation leaders should reduce manifold pressure 2″ Hg. and wingmen should increase rpm settings by 100 rpm.

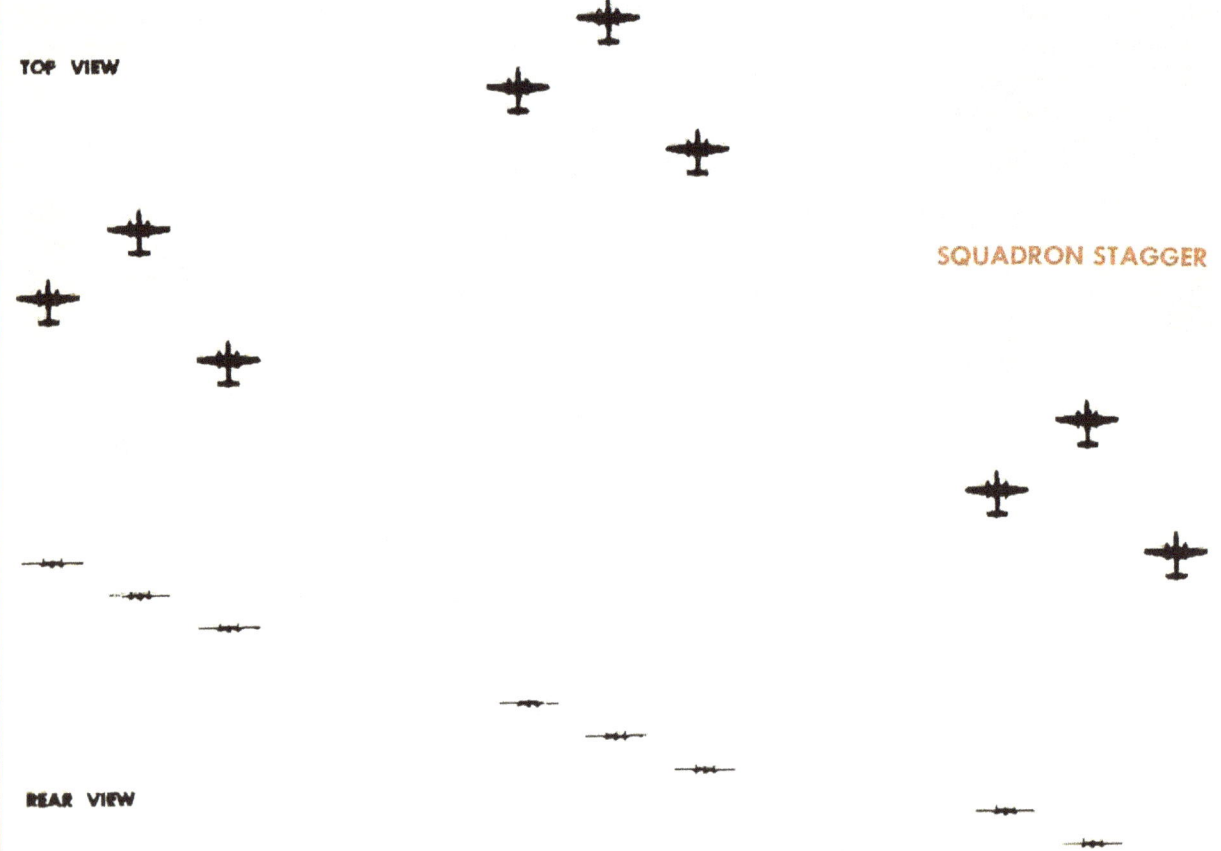

SQUADRON STAGGER

TOP VIEW

REAR VIEW

TRUST YOUR LEADER

STAY IN FORMATION

STRANGE FIELD LANDINGS

**LOOK IT OVER
BEFORE YOU DECIDE TO LAND**

Flying above your home base you instinctively use familiar features of landscape to orient yourself. Your judgment of distance, altitude, speed, and depth are sharpened. You have probably walked into the familiar front room at home, neatly sidestepped the lamp, and continued on your way in total darkness. This same perception of familiar objects operates in every flight you make.

When away from familiar terrain, however, you may have trouble in setting the base leg at the proper place, judging the approach leg, and even regulating your speed properly.

There is a tendency toward poor depth perception when coming down from a higher altitude. All these things, while small, increase in unfamiliar surroundings.

Let down to the traffic altitude gradually and give your eyes a chance to become adjusted. Watch your speed. Because you have been flying at higher speeds you may have a tendency to fly the traffic pattern too fast and mismanage the landing.

While the local pattern is well understood, it is harder to set up the same pattern or to conform to local regulations at another field. Plan your way clearly and confidently; use your head and your eyes; take things calmly.

In landing at a strange field, come in over the field and circle once above it in the direction of traffic. Check carefully the altitude of the field and get the traffic altitude from the tower. If you cannot get specific instructions, fly the traffic pattern 1000 feet above the terrain. Obtain wind direction and velocity, line up the proper runway, visualizing exactly what you intend to do, and then drop down and enter the traffic pattern.

Get a normal base leg, establish your glide at the proper angle and airspeed, and make a power approach landing.

The power approach is important in handling the B-25. The longer you maintain the power and the closer to the ground you cut it off, the more exact is your judgment of where the airplane will land. Use the power, however, only as an aid, and not to make a low dragging approach.

After landing, call the control tower for taxiing and parking instructions.

Common Errors

1. Low dragging approach with no clear conception of the field altitude. This is the result of poor planning.

2. A fast approach, the result of tenseness. Trust your plane and fly it calmly and confidently. Don't get excited.

3. Poor radio procedure, usually caused by poor tuning. Be accurate—learn procedures perfectly and use them as you have learned them. This isn't book flying; it is just plain common sense.

CROSSWIND TAKEOFF

Modern flying, with its heavy airplanes, demands a runway for safe operation. The days when you taxied out, lined up parallel to the wind tee, and took off are gone forever. Instead of 360° of airfield available for takeoff, the modern airfield has three runways, usually set to take advantage of the six cardinal points of the prevailing winds. Using these runways, you encounter crosswinds of varying degrees and intensities.

The aids to a crosswind takeoff are the rudders, the throttles, the aileron, and, as a last resort, the brakes.

The technique is:

1. Make the usual takeoff checks.

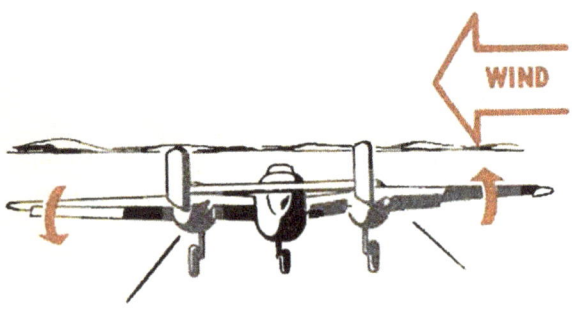

2. Advance the throttles, leading with the upwind throttle. The strength of the wind will determine the amount of lead.

3. As the speed increases and the rudders become effective, equalize the throttles.

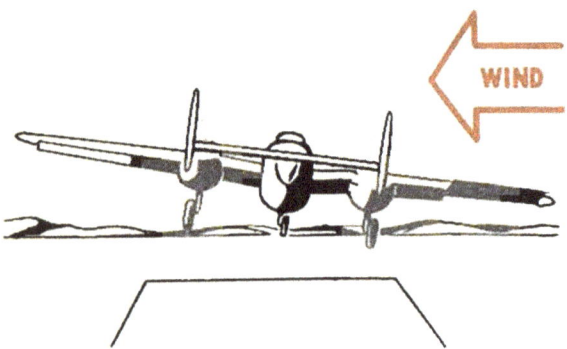

4. Leave the ground with the throttles evenly set and use just enough rudder and aileron to make a coordinated turn into the wind, thus counteracting any drift.

The plane may skip as the speed increases toward the end of the takeoff roll. This is an indication that it is ready to fly. Help it along to prevent skipping and to keep the consequent side thrust from injuring the landing gear.

DON'T JUGGLE THE THROTTLES

Common Errors

1. Failure to recognize the drift.

2. Trying to correct the drift by skidding instead of turning into the wind. This increases the stalling speed and if violent enough it will put the plane back on the ground. The bounce will be made with the drift applying a side thrust to the gear.

3. Juggling the throttles, giving uneven control. Lead the upwind throttle, constantly reducing the lead. As the speed increases the rudder control is great enough to take off cleanly.

CROSSWIND LANDING

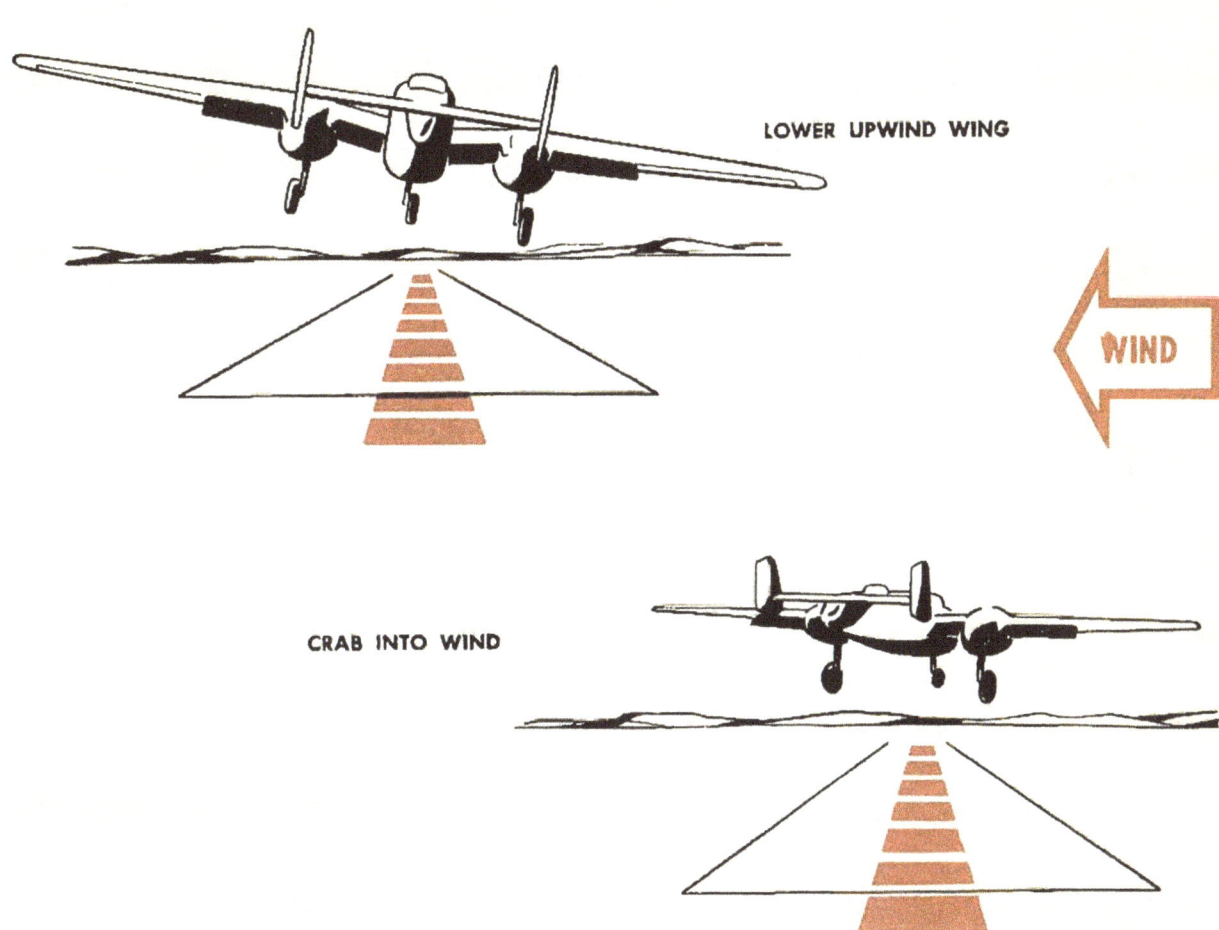

Crosswind landing in the B-25 requires accurate flying, to save the plane from unnecessary structural stresses. You must land the airplane smoothly to prevent blowing a tire, collapsing a strut, or exerting side loads on the gear.

There are three possible ways to land crosswind:

1. Hold the airplane straight and level toward the landing strip and drop one wing into the wind to counteract drift.
2. Crab into the wind to keep a straight ground path.
3. A combination of the two methods.

The third method is the best. Crab into the wind, then lower a wing. This prevents you from dropping a wing too low or crabbing too much, and it makes it easier to straighten out.

Any uncoordinated movement such as a slip raises the stalling speed. At the speeds you must fly, a slip and the consequent stall spell disaster.

Once again, the secret of the landing lies in the approach. Allow for drift on the turn into the approach, and do not overshoot or undershoot the approach leg. Correct for drift as soon as possible on the approach, making a straight path to the landing strip.

If there is only a moderate wind, use full flaps; with a stronger wind, use less flaps. If no flaps are used, a long ground roll will result. As you begin to roundout for landing, bring up the low wing and straighten the airplane so that there is no side load on the gear as it touches the ground.

You may have to use fairly hard rudder pressure just before contact to straighten the airplane properly.

After the plane is on the ground and has reached a three-point position, there will be a tendency to weathervane into the wind. Hold a straight course by lowering the downwind aileron and using the drag on that aileron to counteract the weathervaning tendencies. The stronger the crosswind, the greater the force exerted on the downwind aileron.

Use full rudder if necessary. As a last resort, make very cautious use of the downwind brake, and smooth use of the windward engine. Never blast out roughly with the throttle, as this just aggravates the control of the ship and strains the landing gear. Use of throttles increases the length of roll considerably.

Where there is a strong drift, land on the upwind side of the runway. The drift will carry you toward the center of the runway.

Common Errors

1. Failure to correct properly for drift when turning into the approach.

2. Failure to correct completely for drift, thereby turning onto the runway at an angle. This makes a good landing difficult or impossible.

3. Failure to recognize drift. This occurs frequently in moderate or slight crosswinds, although seldom where there is a runway to land on.

4. Failure to push the airplane straight on the actual landing, thus putting a side load on the gear. Avoid the tendency to straighten the plane out too high off the runway. If the plane stays in the air long enough it will drift off course and may land with one wheel off the runway.

Correct for Drift

LAND ON THE RUNWAY

Stalls

The B-25 stalls from the wing root to the wingtip. Thus there is no unstable tendency except a slight lateral rolling, easily corrected by coordinated control pressures.

The plane breaks cleanly through the stall, with no tendency to drop a wing, and makes a relatively rapid recovery.

When stalling with power on, the tail surfaces give a warning of the approaching stall by a pronounced buffeting. When stalling with power off there is no warning except the sluggish feel of the plane as it loses lift and control.

Stalls in the B-25 must be practiced because:

1. You must determine for yourself the stalling characteristics of the plane.

2. You must know the speeds at which the plane stalls to set up properly the speeds for slow flying, short field work and normal landings.

The stalling characteristics are not altered by changes in gross weight, amount of power used, raising or lowering the flaps, opening and closing the cowl flaps, or operating the de-icer boots. The stalling speed, however, is changed by these variables.

Operation of the de-icer boots raises the indicated stalling speed 4 mph. With the wing flaps full down, the stalling speed drops approximately 20 mph at normal gross weight. The application of power lowers the stalling speed still further, depending on the amount of power used.

Changes of the CG position in the plane greatly affect the stall characteristics. Do not stall the plane when the center of gravity approaches its fore-and-aft limits.

The stall speeds of the B-25 are approximately:

LEVEL FLIGHT	**101 MPH**
30° BANK	**134 MPH**
60° BANK	**154 MPH**

3. You must know the best recovery for the plane you fly.

There are many more reasons, chief among them the confidence you derive from flying your plane through its low speed limits.

Furthermore, you will trust your plane completely and fly it more accurately in the precision maneuvers that come later in your training.

High-speed stalls and those brought on by rough and uncoordinated movement of the controls are dangerous in the B-25. If you try this type of stall, execute it at reduced power, and avoid it after the characteristics have been determined.

Practice at various flap settings, with wheels up and down, straight and level, and in turns.

When practicing power-on stalls, keep the power at a maximum of 20″ Hg. If you exceed this power limit, the stalling attitude of the plane restricts visibility and tends to make the stall more vicious. This teaches you nothing and only adds unnecessary strain to the airplane.

Stalls and stalling speeds are directly related to maximum performance and to a wide variety of maneuvers you will meet later in training. Understand this relationship thoroughly.

It gives you a basis for setting up proper gliding attitudes, gliding speeds, approaches and landings. It determines the type and method of corrections to be made in changing gliding speeds.

A good method of determining correct gliding speed is to add 20% or 25% to the wheels-down, flaps-down, (45°) power-off stalling speed and use that as a gliding speed to remain within safe flight limits.

Perform all stalls at an altitude to permit recovery 8000 feet above the terrain. Practice with the propeller set at the maximum climbing rpm and power settings varying as necessary.

Perform power-on stalls in this manner: from level flight, reduce the manifold pressure to a maximum of 20″; then bring the nose of the airplane slowly and smoothly to approximately a tail-low landing attitude, maintaining a constant back-pressure until the stall is reached. Do not pull up too rapidly, as this gives a false indicated stalling speed, caused by the momentum built up in flight. Hold the plane in a stalling attitude and allow it to fly into the stall.

Do not use excessive power, as this makes the reaction of the airplane violent.

As already mentioned, the B-25 stalls from the wing root to the tip; the stall is straight ahead and is not violent. You have aileron and rudder control all the way to the stall. When you reach the stall, recover by nosing down. Counteract any rolling or yawing tendency by use of the rudders. Apply only enough aileron to keep the controls coordinated. Increase power slowly when control is regained.

Do not attempt to make a straight power recovery. The B-25 is too heavy to recover safely in this manner. You will get a series of secondary stalls and possibly an unintentional spin.

Don't hurry your recovery. Make it smooth and sure, with coordinated control pressures to prevent a secondary stall. Reach a safe airspeed before attempting to level out.

Use a power-off, nose-down recovery to recover from violent stalls in which the airplane starts to roll or spin out of control. You will lose a great deal of altitude in this type of recovery. Make the pullout gradually to keep a safe wingloading.

Practice glide stalls in the B-25 to familiarize yourself with the feel of the airplane under landing conditions.

Perform them by establishing a power-off glide at normal gliding speeds and then flaring off exactly as you would to make a landing. Hold the plane at a constant altitude in a landing attitude until it stalls. The stalling characteristics are the same as in a power-on stall except that the elevators and stabilizer will not buffet as they do in a power-on stall.

Again, the recovery is a combination of nose-down and increased power. This stall simulates landing conditions exactly when practised with the wheels and flaps full down. The recovery should be made above 8000 feet to give ample room for emergencies.

Recover from Stall Smoothly

SLOW FLYING

ADVANCE RPM TO 2400
GRADUALLY REDUCE POWER
BRING NOSE UP

AS AIRPLANE APPROACHES
LANDING ATTITUDE ADD JUST ENOUGH
POWER TO PREVENT A STALL

Slow flying increases your confidence in the B-25 as few other maneuvers will. It demonstrates more effectively than anything else the effect of applying power.

You can fly the plane at almost a stall attitude and at low airspeed, and by the manipulation of power, continue to keep the plane in safe flight.

It teaches lighter control and the necessity for smooth control movements at low speeds. It teaches stall prevention and recovery by using throttle and a minimum change of attitude. It is one of the most helpful exercises to teach you to fly by feel alone, and in the last phases of every landing, you must fly by feel alone as you do not have time to watch your instruments.

Slow flying is good training for all types of short-field landings and takeoffs.

The technique is as follows: Gain sufficient altitude to allow for safe recovery from an unexpected stall. At cruising setting, advance the rpm to 2400 rpm, gradually reduce the power and at the same time bring the nose up and allow the airspeed to drop. As the airplane comes to a landing attitude and approaches the stalling point, add just enough power to prevent a stall. Approximately ⅔ power is the maximum to be used in the B-25 in this type of maneuver. Do not get into an exaggerated attitude, as the airplane is heavy and slow to respond.

Hold the airplane in this attitude, increasing power when needed to prevent a stall and decreasing power when the airspeed becomes too great. Smooth coordination of stick and throttle is needed to hold the airplane in this landing attitude just above the stalling speed.

During a maneuver of this type, the engines have a tendency to overheat; watch the cylinder-head temperature carefully, and do not allow it to rise dangerously.

Practice this maneuver, checking the air-

PRACTICE SLOW FLYING TURNS

speed indicator only occasionally. Learn to fly through it by feel alone. Practice it with the flaps up and down. Practice it in turns, noting that to hold airspeed and altitude you must increase power. Normally, in an actual short-field landing, the gear is extended and the flaps down; after determining the characteristics with the flaps and wheels up, practice the maneuver with the wheels and full flaps down.

In this maneuver, smoothness and coordination come first. When used, it will be a precision maneuver; make it one. Practice it at a safe altitude and perfect your technique. Do not attempt to use it in turbulent air unless it is an emergency landing.

Common Errors

1. A reluctance to keep a low airspeed.
2. A tendency to drop the nose or apply more power than is necessary. Practice will overcome this and give you confidence.
3. A tendency to prevent stalling by dropping the nose alone, rather than breaking the stall by the use of power and relaxed pressure. Here again, practice is the answer.

SHORT-FIELD TAKEOFF

The short-field takeoff is an important operational maneuver. You can easily understand its importance if you stop to consider that the first Tokyo raid could never have been made without its use.

Many tactical fields have been kept open after a severe bombing simply because our pilots were proficient in this maneuver.

Heavy planes with high wing loadings must often be flown from small fields. The combination of large bomb loads, full fuel cells, loaded ammunition boxes, and poor runways, makes high demands on your skill. Since these loads are gone at the completion of a mission, the landing must take second place to the takeoff wherever the combat operation of the airplane is concerned. Successful short-field takeoffs call for maximum use of every favorable characteristic of the plane. They are directly related to your future as an operational pilot.

The short-field takeoff is a maximum performance maneuver. Know your stalls and slow flying before practicing it.

How

After completing the cockpit check, line up at the extreme end of the runway and set the flaps to the maximum lift-drag position—30°. Set the parking brakes, advance the power to within 5" Hg. of the maximum allowed, and wait for the rpm indications to become constant.

Check to see that the nosewheel is pointed straight ahead and release the brakes. Use the remaining 5" Hg. to control the direction until rudder control is effective, then neutralize the throttles.

Under conditions of high ground friction, heavy grass, sand, or mud, you must make this run with the nosewheel well off the ground. On smooth runways make the takeoff run in a tail-level or minimum drag attitude.

You will take off more quickly on soft runways if the nosewheel is lifted as quickly as possible, and on hard runways if you allow the speed to build up; then apply lift to the wings.

The airplane should leave the ground just after the flaps-down, wheels-down, power-on stall speed is reached. When definitely airborne, retract the wheels, allow the airspeed to build up slightly, and climb until clear of any obstacle. Lower the nose to pick up CSE speed. When you have sufficient altitude, raise the flaps to 15°. When you attain a safe flying speed and altitude, reduce the power to maximum climb and raise the remainder of the flaps.

Prolonged climbs at low airspeeds raise the engine operating temperature dangerously—do not practice them.

Short-Field Takeoff

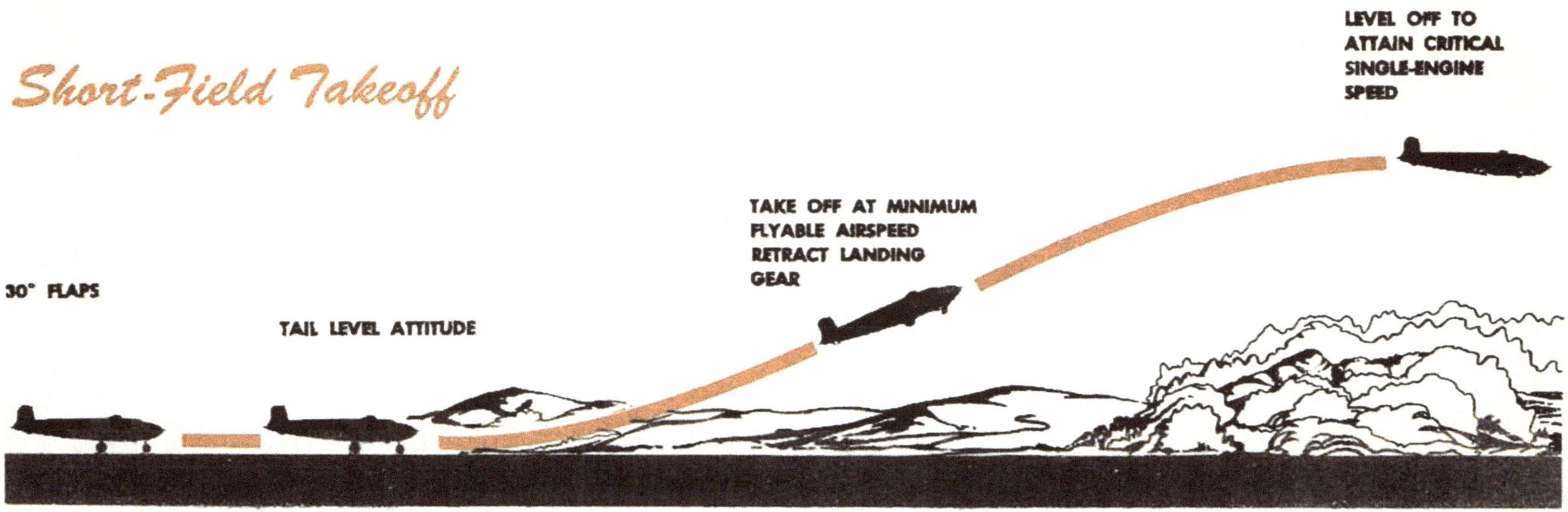

30° FLAPS

TAIL LEVEL ATTITUDE

TAKE OFF AT MINIMUM FLYABLE AIRSPEED
RETRACT LANDING GEAR

LEVEL OFF TO ATTAIN CRITICAL SINGLE-ENGINE SPEED

Muddy or Rough Ground Takeoff

30° FLAPS

TAKEOFF RUN WITH NOSEWHEEL WELL OFF THE GROUND

RAISE LANDING GEAR AS SOON AS AIRPLANE IS AIRBORNE

SHORT-FIELD LANDINGS

You have all heard a lot of discussion on the importance of accurate short-field landings. Combat requires that you be able to operate under conditions that are close to the absolute limit of the airplane's performance.

But even at home, if you took off this afternoon and the hydraulic system failed in flight, you would have a perfect example of the necessity for short-field landings in everyday flying. You would have to make an accurate short-field landing to be sure that there was ample room to stop with the emergency air brake.

Short-field landings are necessary where:

1. The field is unobstructed but small.
2. The runways are blocked by obstacles, power lines, trees, etc.

Training in short-field landings improves your technique and builds up confidence for normal landings.

Short-field landings are closely related to power-on full-flap stalls and power-off full-flap stalls, with the gear down.

Practice slow flying before trying this type of landing. The technique is as follows:

For the field without obstructions:

1. Place the base leg farther from the field than normal.
2. Establish a normal full-flap glide.
3. **Undershoot the field.**
4. Hold the usual speed to the roundout and gradually pull up the nose, increase the power and go directly into slow flying.

Since no obstruction is present, do this close to the ground, enabling you to land almost immediately when the power is cut.

As you approach the desired point of landing, reduce power. Since the plane is in a landing attitude and approaching the power-off stalling speed as you reduce power, you must land almost immediately.

A maximum use of brakes is permissible in this type of landing.

Remember—You are deliberately flying toward a chosen point of landing at approximately power-off stalling speed. When power is cut, you must be ready to land.

For the field with obstructions:

The type of approach you just made is obviously impractical for this landing.

1. Establish a normal full-flap power glide.
2. Plan this glide to clear the obstruction with power. Don't depend on your judgment from too high an altitude.
3. Control the attitude of the plane to gain a level or slightly nose-high attitude as you clear the obstruction.

4. Reduce the airspeed to slightly above the power-off stalling speed.

As the obstacle is cleared, use power in accordance with the height of the obstacle. Place the plane in a tail-low attitude and use the throttles to control the rate of descent. Do not reduce power too quickly or the plane will drop in for a hard and dangerous landing.

Caution—Do not use a dragging approach. Study the diagrams carefully and use them in your planning.

Maintain at all times on the approach a speed not less than the power-off stalling speed of your plane. The exaggerated attitude of the B-25 at lower speeds makes recovery difficult.

In this type of maneuver, don't cut your power suddenly. The plane stops flying and starts falling when the power is completely cut. If the power is reduced gradually, the airplane slowly settles down to a soft, short landing.

Maximum use of brakes is permitted on this maneuver.

This procedure is used by airline and military pilots where field conditions make it imperative. Pilots use it often in tactical flying. Its sole purpose is to approach the field at the lowest safe airspeed and land accurately as soon as the power is cut.

If you lack sufficient feel of the airplane to do this, practice slow flying, stalls, and this type of approach at a safe altitude before it is used.

Common Errors

1. Excessive speed on the approach.
2. Crossing the obstruction too high and landing longer than necessary.
3. Slow flying from traffic altitude to the ground.
4. Cutting power upon crossing the obstacle regardless of altitude, and dropping in. This is extremely dangerous with the B-25.
5. Poor coordination of throttle and airspeed.

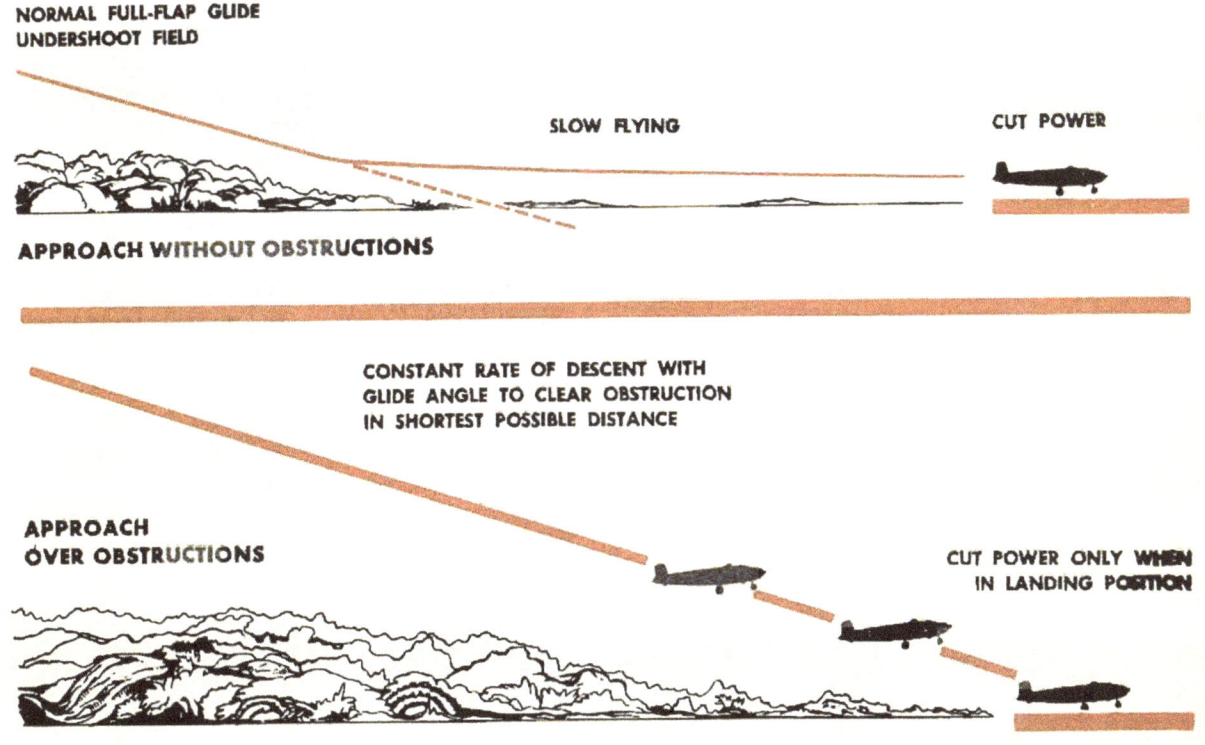

SINGLE ENGINE OPERATION

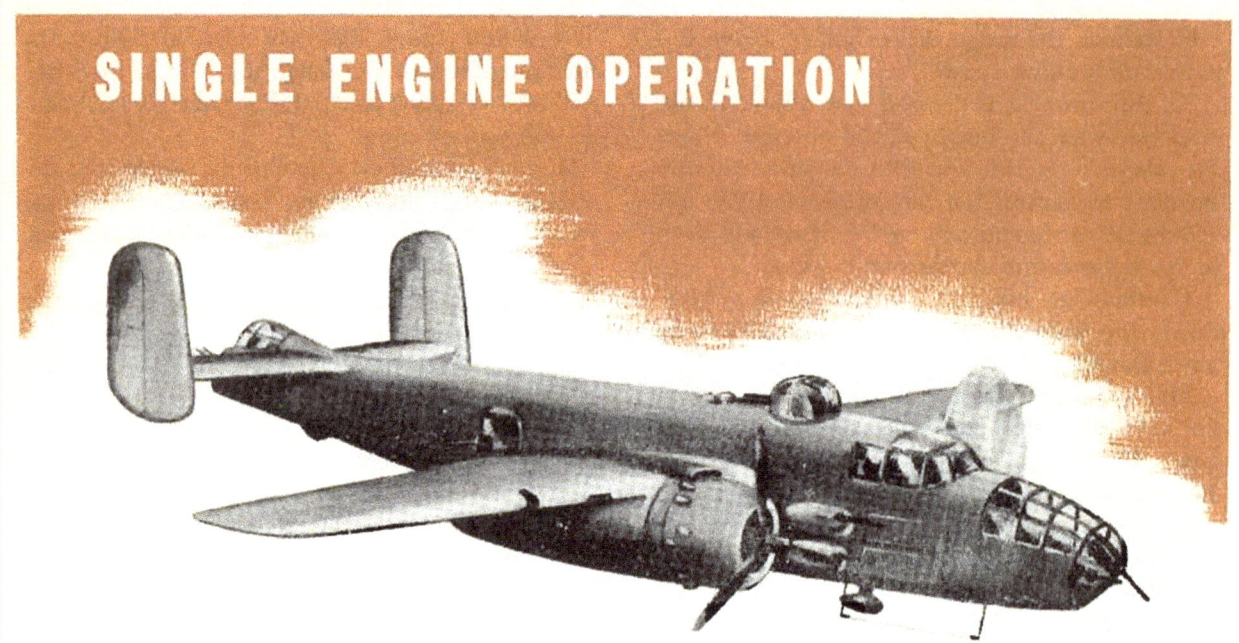

Single engine operation of the B-25 follows a logical pattern of procedure. The plane flies efficiently on one engine at a reduced speed.

Beyond a weight of 32,000 lb. you will experience some difficulty in maintaining altitude. This should never be a serious handicap, since you can always correct it by ridding the plane of excess weight.

Competent ground and air instruction must precede any single engine practice or operation. On the ground your training should include a detailed account of the technique of single engine flying and cockpit drill in the sequence of operation.

You can't get too much cockpit time.

Accidents never just happen. They are the culmination of a chain of events. Don't be cocksure; this breeds a lack of respect for your plane, and this is the first step toward trouble.

In the air you must know what to expect from aerodynamic forces: the difference in handling at different speeds, the effect of open and closed bomb bay doors, the dropping of excess weight, and the futility of using flaps except in landing.

Each airplane has a critical single engine speed. In the B-25 it is 140 mph for normal load weights.

Critical single engine speed is the slowest speed at which the rudder has a safe margin of control over the unbalanced thrust of the one live engine, at maximum power.

Maximum power settings for single engine flight depend on the particular conditions. You can apply power in direct relation to the airspeed. At high speeds it is possible to use take-off power settings for a short time.

For all normal single engine operation, keep your power settings at maximum climb or below. The airplane becomes difficult to control beyond this power setting unless you have excess airspeed. If you have excess speed, you don't need excessive power.

CRITICAL SINGLE ENGINE AIRSPEED MUST BE MAINTAINED AT THE SACRIFICE OF ALL OTHER CONSIDERATIONS

Procedure

1. **Airspeed**—Maintain or get 140 mph by diving if necessary.
2. **Directional control**—Obtain and hold directional control by using rudder. Slight aileron aids coordination but excessive use raises the stalling speed.

Use the trim tabs to help you hold the plane if manual control is too difficult.

Make these checks:
   a. Check your ignition switches.
   b. Check your fuel cut-off valves.
   c. Move mixture control to "FULL RICH."
   d. Turn the booster pumps "ON."

You can make these checks in far less time than it takes to read these lines; they may save the engine, and they prevent featheritis.

3. **Increase power to the limit allowed by airspeed and rudder control**—Advance both prop controls and both throttles. It is sometimes difficult to tell which engine is out. As a precaution, apply power to both engines.

A good method when you are not sure: If the plane wants to turn to the right, the right engine is dead; to the left, the left engine is dead. If you are on instruments, your bank-and-turn needle points to the dead engine.

4. **Reduce drag. Throttle back. Decrease rpm. or feather the prop. Mixture "IDLE CUT-OFF"** gear and flaps up, generators on—Feather the propeller by pushing the feathering button down. The prop will feather, and when it does the button will return to normal position.

Close cowl flaps on dead engine.

5. **Reduce fire hazard**—After the prop stops turning, cut off the fuel and ignition on that engine. Set the Lux system to the dead engine, and be prepared if a fire breaks out.

6. **Trim**—Trim the plane for hands-off flight.

This may seem a complicated procedure; however, when you have practiced it a few times, when you know exactly what you are going to do, the entire procedure requires less than 10 seconds.

Trouble Search

First—Switch the vacuum selector to the good engine to get accurate readings of instruments.

BEFORE YOU FEATHER

✓ IGNITION

✓ FUEL CUT-OFF

✓ MIXTURE

✓ BOOSTER PUMPS

With the plane under control, try to find out what caused the trouble, and, if possible, make temporary repairs. Check all fuses, cut-off valves, pop-out switches, lines and wiring as well as you can.

Don't try to re-start the engine if you don't know what is wrong. It is much simpler to make a single engine landing than to fight a fire.

Adjust the cowl flaps and the oil cooler shutters as desired. Reduce weight if the plane is excessively heavy. Drop bombs, bomb bay tank, tools; in fact, anything that will come loose, if necessary. Make final adjustments on the trim and power setting.

Single Engine Practice

Remember that you are trimmed for single engine flight at one airspeed only. If the airspeed or power setting is changed you must re-trim.

On a practice flight try this: Trim the plane for a speed of 160 or 170 mph. Then advance or retard the throttle. Allow the plane to fly itself—it will immediately start hunting a stable flight condition. It will turn, climb, and dive all over the sky, finally falling off into a spiral or spin if you do not take over the controls.

Now return the controls to the power setting for which you are trimmed. Hold the plane manually until the airspeed returns to its proper setting. The airplane will again fly hands off.

Now for the single engine turns. The old theory that you must never turn into the dead engine is false. You can turn in either direction. If you can make a good coordinated turn into the good engine you can do the same thing into the dead engine.

Practice some turns in both directions. You will find no difference as long as the airspeed is constant. Lose a slight amount of altitude in the turn to keep the airspeed constant. Do not blast roughly on the throttles to maintain airspeed. This is a dangerous fault, leading to loss of control when carried too far.

Steep turns on a single engine are not necessary. The weight of the plane increases rapidly as the angle of bank increases, and as no benefit is derived from steep turns, it is foolhardy to try them when full power is not available.

Engine Failure on Takeoff

This is a tricky proposition for any pilot to handle. When the engine fails before you gain CSE speed, retract the wheels and land straight ahead. There is far less danger in a belly landing than in attempting to go around with too low an airspeed.

If you are in the air, however, and have CSE speed, you can go around without too much difficulty.

You must know your procedure and your airplane. Work quickly, accurately, and efficiently. **Don't get panicky.**

Don't get featheritis—be sure the engine is out, not just spitting a little.

Use the same procedure, but notice that the first three parts of it are already accomplished.

1. **Airspeed**—You either have CSE speed or you land straight ahead.

2. **Directional Control**—This is an instinctive reaction. Use rudder pressure at the first feel of yaw.

3. **Increase power**—Takeoff power has already been applied. It may be necessary to reduce power to maintain control.

A TURN INTO THE DEAD ENGINE IS OK

4. **Reduce Drag**

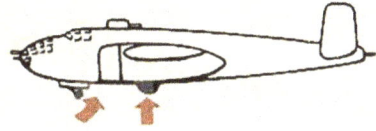

a. Raise the wheels

b. Feather the prop

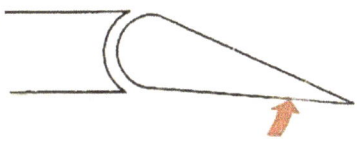

c. Raise flaps to 15°

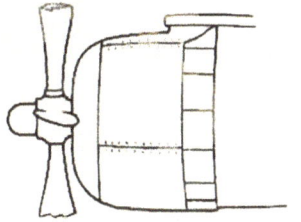

d. Close cowl flaps on dead engine

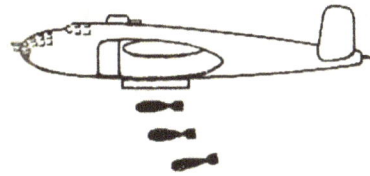

e. Drop weight if necessary

5. **Reduce Fire Hazard**
6. **Trim**
7. **Trouble Search**

EFFECT OF POWER AND AIRSPEED ON SINGLE ENGINE OPERATION

To fly safely on single engine you must know the effect of power on rudder control at various airspeeds. This is vital to your safety when practicing go-around procedures and other maneuvers that require quick changes in power settings.

At 140 mph (CSE speed) directional control can be maintained with takeoff power on the good engine. At airspeeds below 140 mph the plane will turn into the dead engine if power is not reduced. When power is reduced in accordance with the airspeed, directional control can be maintained until normal stalling speeds are reached.

Practice this maneuver with the propeller unfeathered at a safe altitude before attempting single engine landings. Perform this maneuver straight ahead and in turns to the right and left. Practice from level flight and in a simulation of a landing glide, with various degrees of flap settings to determine limits at which a go-around may be made.

You may practice this maneuver with wheels and flaps up to determine its characteristics, but, since this maneuver is used to practice for single engine landings and go-arounds, perform it with wheels and flaps down after its effect is determined.

With power set for normal climb reduce the airspeed below 140 mph until the plane starts to turn toward the dead engine, even though you are holding full opposite rudder.

Recover by reducing power and lowering the nose.

For practice, hold definite airspeeds (for example, 115 mph or 120 mph), and add as much power as you can control.

This maneuver is excellent practice for single engine landings, and go-around procedures. When the airspeed is below CSE speed you know how much power you can safely add to prevent undershooting and to start a go-around procedure.

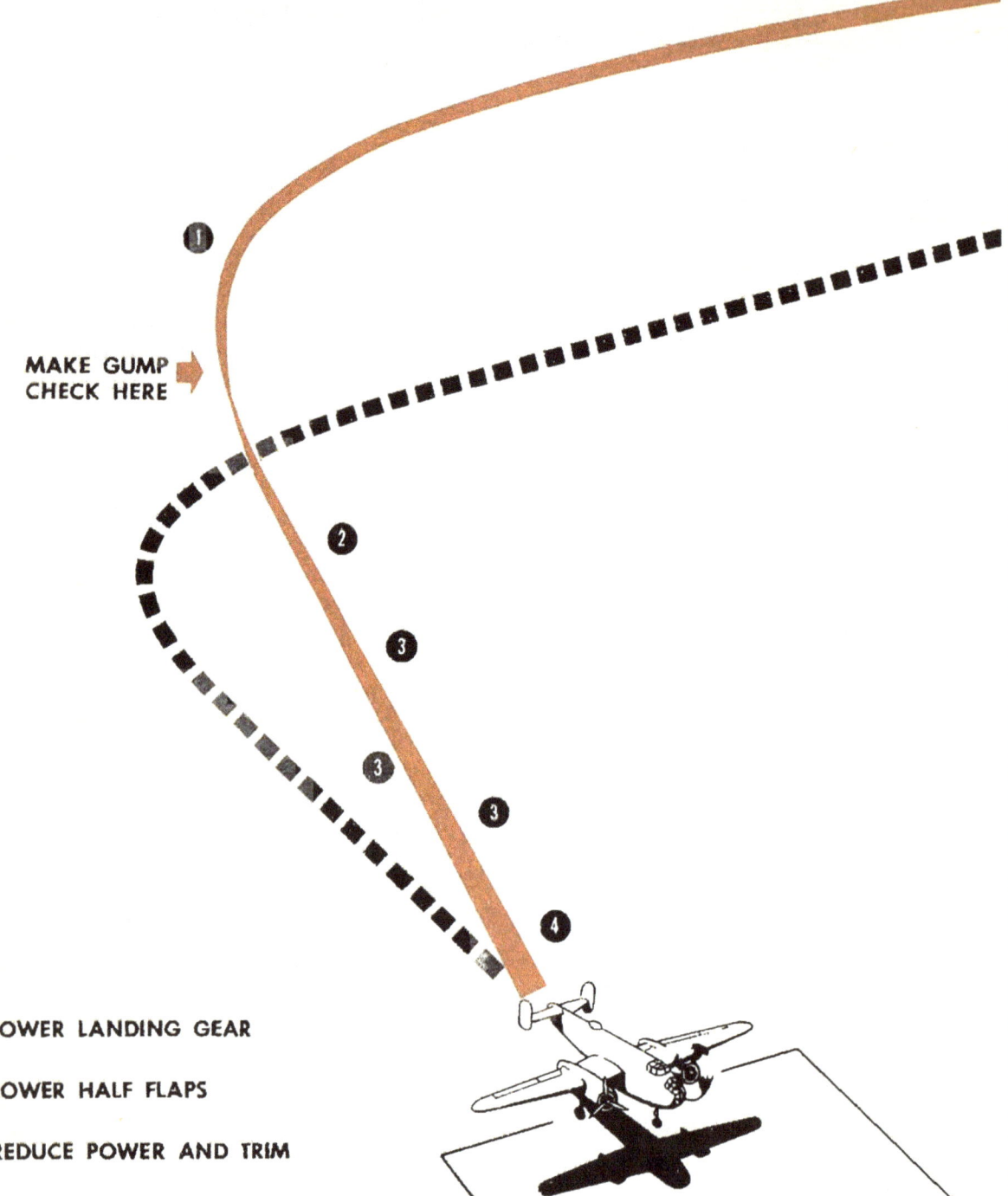

Single engine landings should remove any lingering doubts you may have about the B-25 and its ability as a single engine performer.

You have flown on one engine, turned on one engine. Now you will make single engine landings. This maneuver is simple, safe, and vital for your continued safety.

Fly this maneuver with the propeller unfeathered to allow for recovery from a bad approach. By following this simple procedure you get an exact simulation of single engine flight:

1. While practicing single engine flight set the prop at "DEC. RPM" and feather an engine.

2. Trim the plane for hands-off flight.

3. Unfeather the engine, leaving the prop control set at "DEC. RPM," and apply enough power to the engine you feathered to again have the plane trimmed for hands-off flight.

You have, in effect, found out exactly how much the feathered propeller reduces drag on the airplane. By adding only enough power to return the plane to a trimmed condition without changing the trim tabs, you have simply applied power to offset the drag caused by a windmilling propeller.

This is an exact simulation of single engine operation, including the landing effect of the feathered prop. With a feathered prop, when the power is cut on the good engine, drag is induced, making the plane slew into the good engine during the last stage of landing.

Set the prop at 2400 rpm on the approach so that you have maximum climbing power available for a go-around if it is needed.

The landing procedure is as follows:

1. Fly a normal traffic pattern, except that you do not lower landing gear until you are on the approach.

2. On the approach, lower and check the gear, check brake and hydraulic pressure, set props at 2400 rpm.

3. Lower half flaps—use the rest of the flaps and the power to increase the accuracy of the approach.

4. Never let the airspeed fall below 140 mph on the approach until you are positive the landing can be made.

5. Reduce power and reduce trim. Never allow the power reduction to get ahead of the trim. The ideal approach is one where the power is reduced, then the trim, then power, then trim—and so on throughout the approach.

6. Maintain 140 mph until the landing is in the bag, then lower the remaining flaps and reduce power to make an accurate landing.

The plane will have a tendency to yaw into the good engine as the power is cut off completely. This yaw is present when the propeller is feathered and so should not be changed by cutting power on the engine you have set up to act as a feathered prop. This yaw is easily controlled with the rudder; since you expect it, you will have no trouble.

This technique is sound as it does not make too great a demand on the pilot's judgment. As you approach the ground your ability to properly gage distance and depth increases, allowing you to make good use of the remaining power and flaps for an accurate landing. This in turn greatly reduces the possibility of overshooting or undershooting.

Never try to recover from a bad approach with one engine. Once the power has been cut and the speed is below 140 mph, go ahead and land.

Common Errors

1. Overshooting — a combination of errors. Setting the base leg improperly, Airspeed too high on the approach, and taking too much time to accomplish procedures on the approach.

2. Forgetting to lower the landing gear. This is usually the result of the normal habit of lowering gear on the downwind leg, cutting off the warning horn or lights, and not making the landing check properly.

3. Failure to re-trim the airplane properly.

4. Attempting to make an accuracy landing from the top of the approach.

5. Undershooting and using too much power.

Single Engine Go-Around

Successful single engine go-around depends on an early decision that a go-around is necessary. You can start a go-around procedure at a low altitude and from a low airspeed on the approach, but it is difficult and dangerous.

Make Your Decision Early

The procedure is:
1. Maintain CSE speed at all times on the approach.
2. Apply normal climbing power, this will be sufficient if the procedure is started early on the approach.
3. Reduce drag.
    a. Wheels up.
    b. Prop "DEC. RPM" (on bad engine).
    c. Flaps up to 15° until safe altitude and airspeed are obtained.
4. Trim the plane for hands-off flight.

If you have to go around under emergency conditions, apply all the power you can hold without losing directional control.

Note: Keep flaps ½ down when practicing this, since in emergency conditions the maneuver will start before you have lowered full flaps.

If sufficient altitude is available, nose down to increase airspeed when power is applied to start a go-around.

TIPS ON SINGLE ENGINE OPERATION

Practice single engine operation with the propellers feathered and unfeathered.

Keep the prop feathered for a maximum of 5 minutes in cold weather and 15 minutes in warm weather. If you exceed these time limits the engine cools too much. The oil drains into the bottom cylinders and makes starting difficult and dangerous.

Warm engines gradually when recovering from single engine practice.

Keep all experiments within safe bounds.

Don't allow your airspeed to vary in turns.

Don't blast the throttles to maintain airspeed in turns.

Hold the nose up when rolling out of turns or you will lose too much altitude.

Remember—When at high altitudes the B-25 may lose some altitude, but when you reach denser air at lower altitudes it will hold altitude easily.

When attempting to make a medium turn, establish the proper degree of bank. Otherwise the turn will be uncoordinated.

Hold the airspeed for which you have trimmed. This will save you a lot of wear and tear mentally and physically. **The B-25 flies easily on one engine if it is properly trimmed.**

Re-starting the dead engine

Turn the ignition switches "ON."

Turn the gasoline "ON."

Prop control (bad engine) full "DEC. RPM."
Mixture "FULL RICH."

Depress the feathering switch until the engine rpm is 800.

Release the feathering switch and resume control with the engine controls.

Move prop pitch and throttles forward slowly —not to exceed 1400 rpm and 15" Hg. until the cylinder-head temperature starts to increase.

Warm the engine as you would on the ground and apply cruising power after cylinder-head temperature is normal.

Oil shutters and cowl flaps as desired.

Re-trim.

Warning: If no feathering action occurs within 90 seconds, release feathering button to avoid burning out feathering motor.

AUXILIARY HYDRAULIC PUMP AND EMERGENCY HYDRAULIC SELECTOR VALVE

The auxiliary hydraulic pump is a double-action hand pump for use as a source of pressure if the main hydraulic system fails.

It is between the pilot's and copilot's seats and either man uses it.

A selector valve, directly behind the hand pump on the floor, distributes the pressure from the hand pump.

The selector valve has three positions, "NORMAL," "BRAKE," and "LATCH." In "NORMAL" position the pressure from the hand pump is distributed through the normal hydraulic lines. In "BRAKE" position the pressure goes directly to the brake accumulator and then to the brakes. In "LATCH" position the pressure goes directly to the landing gear down-latch pins.

Use this auxiliary source of hydraulic pressure to make all normal hydraulic actions when the engine driven pumps fail.

You can use it to aid or replace the engine-driven pumps.

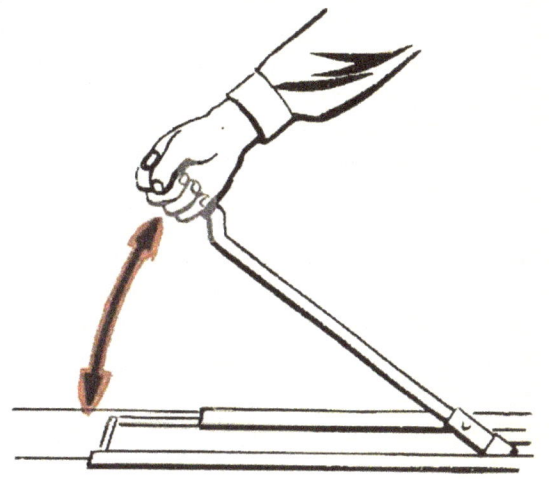

Note

If down-position latchpins of the main landing gear do not engage, turn emergency hydraulic selector valve to "LATCH." Operate the hand pump until position indicator shows main landing gear latchpins in place.

Use this procedure regardless of whether you have employed the main or emergency hydraulic systems for lowering the landing gear.

The yellow flags which show up on the position indicator will always warn you if the latchpins are not engaged.

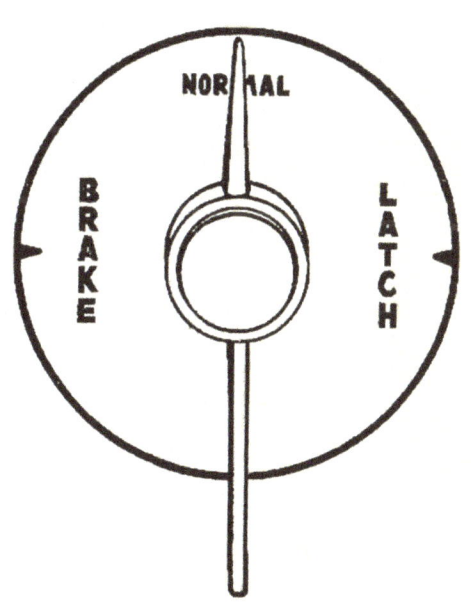

NEVER PUMP THE LATCH PINS INTO PLACE UNLESS THE MAIN WHEELS ARE FULL DOWN

EMERGENCY HYDRAULIC WHEEL LOWERING SYSTEM

The B-25 has an emergency hydraulic wheel lowering system to provide power if the main hydraulic wheel lowering system fails. The system provides for simultaneous lowering of main landing gear and nose gear.

The system consists of an emergency hand pump and a hydraulic fluid reservoir, both in the navigator's compartment. The complete system incorporates automatic valves to regulate normal and emergency flow of fluid to the operating struts, a nosegear up-lock release cable connecting the hand pump handle and the up-lock latch, and fluid transmission lines.

The emergency reservoir fills automatically when the main reservoir is filled, and the fluid is available for the emergency lowering of the landing gear even if the main hydraulic system fluid is completely lost.

Operation

If the hydraulic system fails completely, take the following steps:

1. Return to the home base if possible. Report your trouble briefly to the tower.
2. Climb to an altitude of at least 5000 feet above the surrounding terrain.
3. Reduce your airspeed below 150 mph.
4. Place landing gear control handle in pilot's compartment "DOWN."
5. Operate emergency hand pump one full stroke to release nose gear up-lock. Check landing gear indicator to see whether nose gear is partially extended. If not, give the pump handle another full stroke.
6. Operate the hand pump until gear is down and locked. Employ your normal checks to insure that gear is actually down and locked.

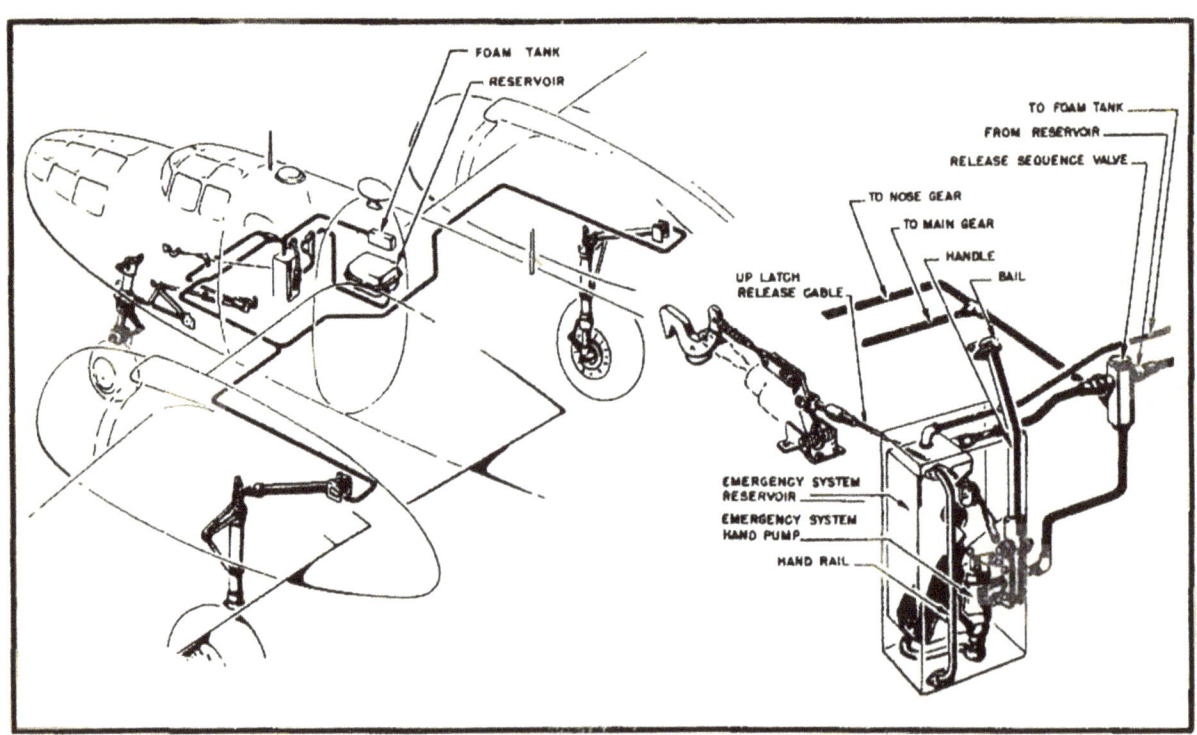

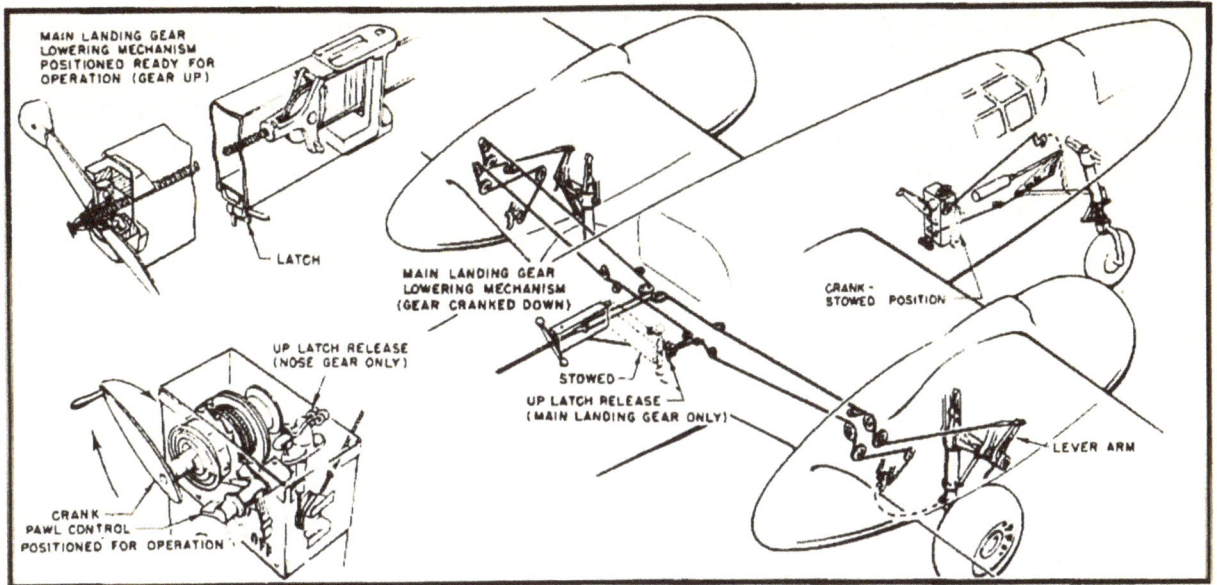

7. Return pump handle to forward position and safety it.

Some earlier models of the B-25 have mechanical emergency wheel lowering controls. In these models, you lower the main landing gear and the nose gear separately. The controls consist of screw jacks and a series of cables which operate directly on the wheels.

In the event of **complete** failure of your landing gear hydraulic system, operate the emergency controls as follows:

1. Establish effective interphone communication between the crew member operating the mechanism and the pilot.

2. Return to the home base if possible. Report your trouble to the tower.

3. Climb to an altitude of at least 5000 feet above the surrounding terrain.

4. Reduce the airspeed below 150 mph (120-130 mph recommended.)

5. Place landing gear control handle in pilot's compartment "DOWN."

6. Swing screw jack in radio compartment to the operating position.

7. Pull up-latch release and check to see that the main gear has released.

8. Operate the screw jack (clockwise) to lower the gear.

9. Use normal landing gear check to see that the gear is down and locked.

10. Release the tension slightly on the screw jack after the gear is down and locked.

Warning: Don't return this system to a stowed position until the plane is safely on the ground, with the landing gear locked to prevent its folding up.

You must stow this system before the wheels can again be operated hydraulically.

Nosewheel

The lowering device for the nosewheel is in the navigator's compartment, on the step into the pilot's compartment.

To operate:

1. Pull nose gear release.

2. Check to see that the gear has released.

3. Turn the nosewheel pawl "ON."

4. Place crank on shaft, turn clockwise to lower.

5. Check locked position normally after the gear is full down.

Warning: The nosewheel lowering cable operates every time the nosewheel is raised or lowered. It is engaged by the pawl to lower the wheels. If the pawl is accidently turned to "ON" the hydraulic system will tear the nosewheel cable out of the plane.

This pawl must be left "ON" after it is used until the plane is on the ground and braced against mishap.

WING FLAP EMERGENCY LOWERING SYSTEM

In the event of **complete** failure of the main hydraulic system, an emergency mechanical flap lowering mechanism is available. It is important to remember to use the emergency mechanism only when the hydraulic system failure is **complete**, as the two systems oppose each other. Use of the emergency system while hydraulic pressure is still available will seriously damage the mechanical system.

The emergency mechanism is in the radio compartment. Be sure the interphone communication between the crew member operating the mechanism and the pilot is 100% effective.

Before entering the traffic pattern it is advisable to lower partial flaps. This enables you to get desired amount of flaps earlier on the final approach.

Operation

1. Reduce airspeed below 150 mph.
2. Move pilot's flap control "DOWN."
3. Remove hand crank from stowage position on forward wall of radio compartment and engage it with the shaft.
4. Rotate crank clockwise until you obtain the desired amount of flaps—14 turns will give you half flaps; 27 turns, full flaps.
5. To lock flaps in position, remove the crank.

Note: If go-around is necessary, turn crank counterclockwise to full stop position. (This operation does not raise the flaps, but releases the pressure on them and the force of the slipstream raises them.)

Warning

Before operating the flaps hydraulically again, be sure that your mechanical system is fully disengaged. To disengage, rotate crank counterclockwise until checked. Remove crank and return to its stowage position.

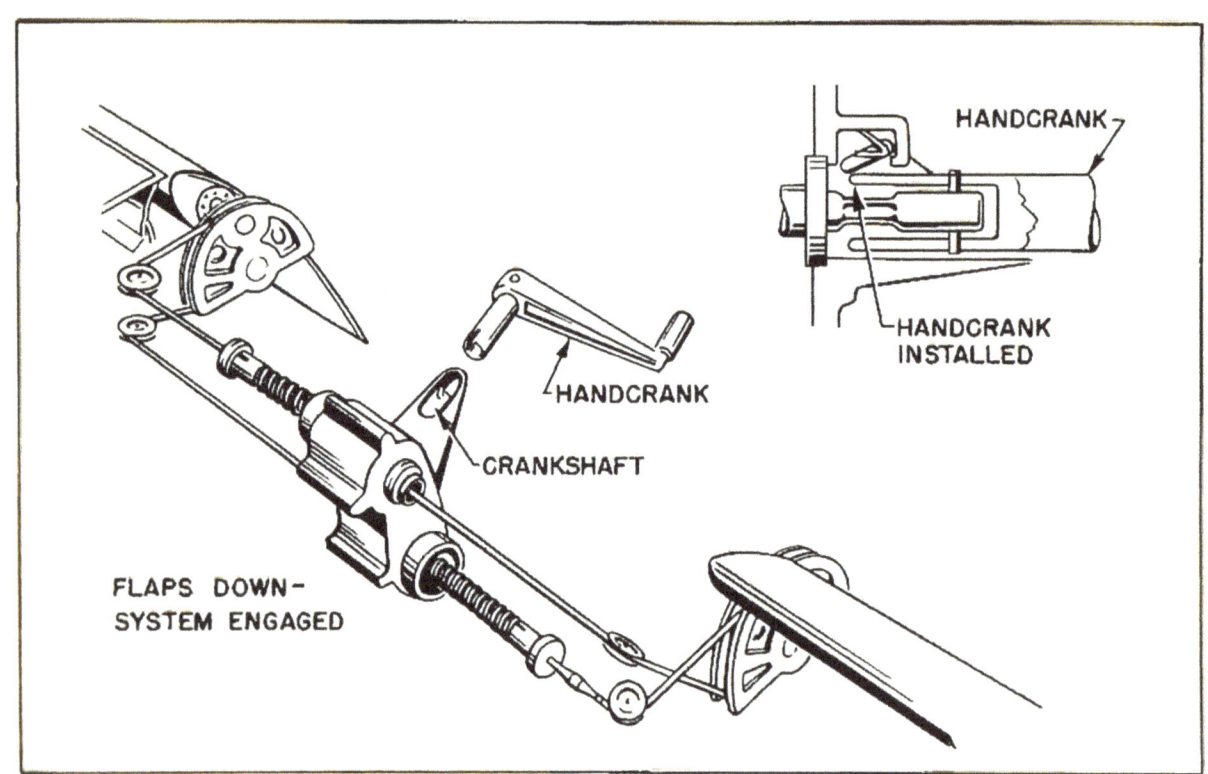

EMERGENCY OPERATION OF BOMB BAY DOORS

Mechanical

The bomb bay doors will automatically open approximately ⅔ of the way in the event of a hydraulic failure.

Use the mechanical system only when hydraulic pressure fails.

1. Move bombardier's control handle to "OPEN." The doors are open and the racks are locked in this position.
2. Install crank on the shaft in the rear of the navigator's compartment, just under the navigator's table. The crank is stowed on the lower right longeron opposite the crank shaft.
3. Turn the crank clockwise to open the doors. Reverse to close them.
4. Thread strap (secured to crank handle) through the down strap on the floor.

Note: The doors are normally held open and closed by hydraulic pressure. The doors will stay open unsecured but must be safetied in the closed position.

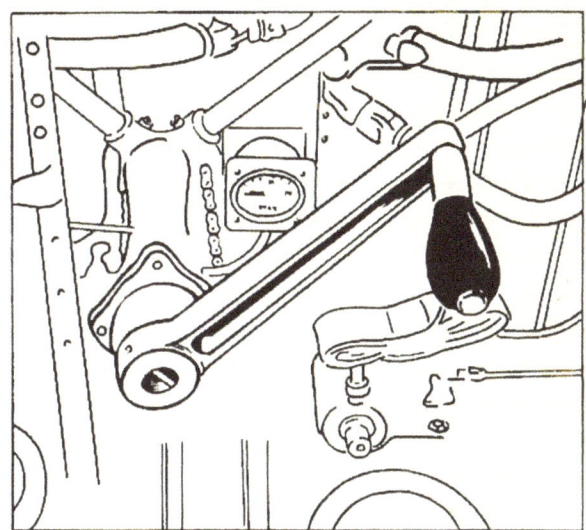

EMERGENCY BOMB BAY DOOR CRANK

EMERGENCY SALVO RELEASE

When your hydraulic system is in operation you can salvo all of your bomb load, both internal and external, by moving the bomb control handle to the "SALVO" position.

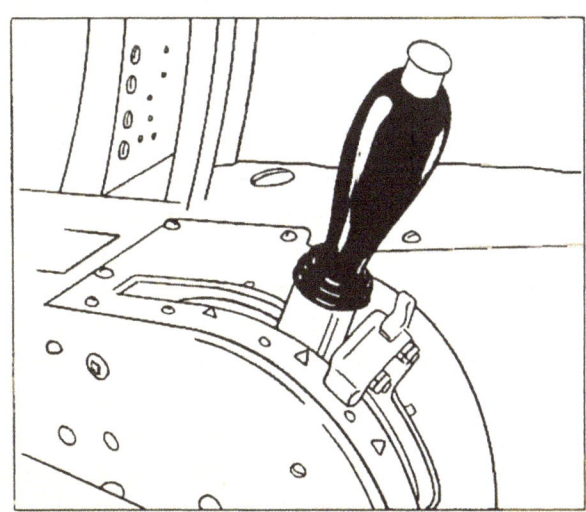

BOMB CONTROL HANDLE

All bombs are dropped safe when salvoed, unless you have an arming control in use on your plane. In that case you can salvo them either armed or safe.

Your bomb bay droppable tank is suspended on bomb shackles in the bomb bay; the pilot and bombardier both have control of these racks and may salvo both bombs and bomb bay tank.

To Operate

1. Push the bombardier's control handle to "SALVO."
2. Pull the pilot's emergency salvo release; this will automatically open the bomb bay doors and salvo your load.

Now to return the system to normal operation.

If the bombardier's control has been used, simply move the control handle to "CLOSED."

If the pilot's emergency release has been used:

1. Move the bombardier's control handle to

"SALVO"; this recocks pilot's emergency release.

2. Move control to "CLOSED."

If your plane has an auxiliary control for torpedo work, you may push down and pull out this control, which is on the right side of the pilot's control pedestal. This enables you to close the doors from the pilot's compartment.

If you use this control, however, you must re-open the doors with it before you can regain control with the bombardier's control handle.

To salvo the torpedo you must:

1. Open the bomb bay doors with the auxiliary control.

2. Pull the emergency salvo release (this also jettisons the wing bombs.)

Warning

On the torpedo only it is necessary to open bomb bay doors to use the emergency salvo release.

Note: On some B-25J and B-25H airplanes the bombing controls are electrical. In the event of electrical failure you cannot salvo the bombs or bomb bay tank.

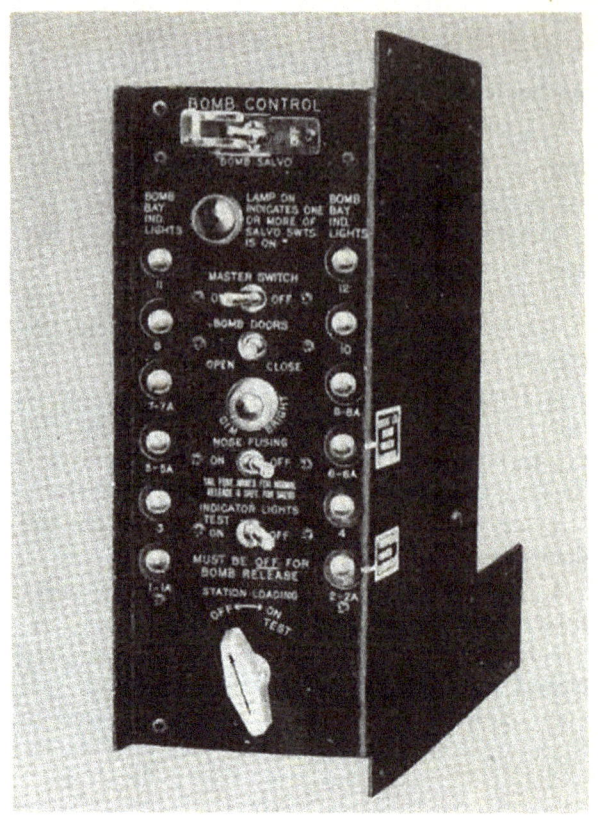

PILOT'S BOMB CONTROL PANEL

EMERGENCY OPERATION—HYDRAULIC BRAKE

EMERGENCY HYDRAULIC SELECTOR VALVE

Before landing, if there is less than 1000 lb. pressure indicated on the brake system pressure gage:

1. Turn hydraulic selector valve to "BRAKE."

2. Operate the hand pump until indicator shows 1000 lb. sq. in. minimum and no more than 1450 lb. sq. in.

3. Operate continuously while landing and taxiing as the initial pressure in the accumulator is insufficient for normal landing.

4. If, on landing, you cannot maintain sufficient pressure, use the emergency air brake system.

5. If you cannot build up 600 lb. pressure in the accumulator, pick a field with at least a one-mile runway, land and use the air brake system.

Always make a short-field landing when your brake pressure is low.

EMERGENCY OPERATION—AIR BRAKES

Use this Air Brake System only in extreme emergencies.

Use it when normal hydraulic system has failed and you cannot develop sufficient pressure with your auxiliary hydraulic hand pump.

When you are sure you must use the air brake system, choose the field with the largest runways within range of your airplane. The runway should be at least one mile long for a safe landing. Make a short-field landing.

Dissipate all the speed you can safely lose before using your air brake, but don't wait until you are out of runway!

You cannot use these brakes selectively. Be ready to counteract any uneven braking action with the throttles.

Operation

1. Pull up sharply on the air brake handle to break the safety wire.

2. Lower the handle immediately. Lower it by hand, as the handle is spring-loaded and will be pulled back past neutral if it is allowed to snap down.

The air pressure is applied to the brakes at the extreme top of the brake handle's travel, and released at the extreme bottom of the travel. In neutral, the air pressure is locked in the brakes and air bottle.

3. Apply braking action in a series of quick, sharp applications. If you apply the brakes continuously for two to three seconds most of the pressure will be transferred to the brake drums and the brakes may lock.

4. To release the brakes, move the brake handle all the way down. It will release pressure in the brakes only at the end of its travel.

5. After you accomplish one complete braking action and the plane stops, there should be a small residue of air still in the emergency air brake bottle. You can use brakes a second time only at a greatly reduced power.

6. You must depend only on the original braking actions and should, on coming to a stop, call the tower and have the plane towed in. Any attempt to taxi with the limited braking action available is extremely dangerous.

Warning

Placing handle in neutral position must be done by hand; the spring load on the handle will snap it into release position and exhaust the air pressure.

Chock wheels before brakes are released.

Bleed hydraulic brake system after using the air brake system.

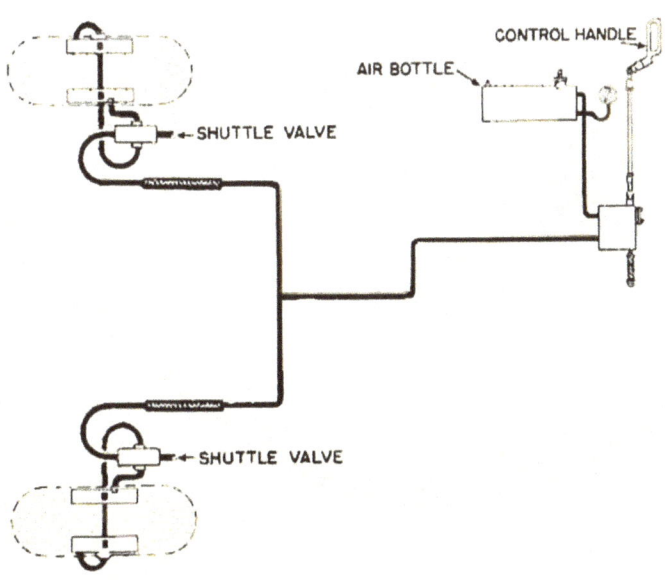

Miscellaneous Emergency Equipment

ALARM BELLS

The alarm bells are located at all crew stations. A switch on the lower left section of the pilot's switch panel controls them.

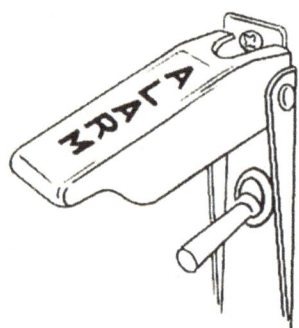

LIFE RAFT

A life raft equipped with a CO_2 cylinder for instantaneous inflation is stowed in the upper forward left corner of the radio compartment. For proper use, see ditching.

LIFE PRESERVERS

The back cushions on the pilot's and copilot's seats are filled with kapok and will serve as life preservers.

EMERGENCY FUEL PUMP

In late-series airplanes there is an emergency fuel transfer hand pump on the floor of the navigator's compartment. If the electric fuel system fails, you can transfer fuel from the bomb bay tanks to the wing tanks with this pump.

PYROTECHNIC SIGNAL PISTOL

On later planes, an M-8 type pyrotechnic pistol is stowed in a canvas holster in the navigator's compartment as loose equipment.

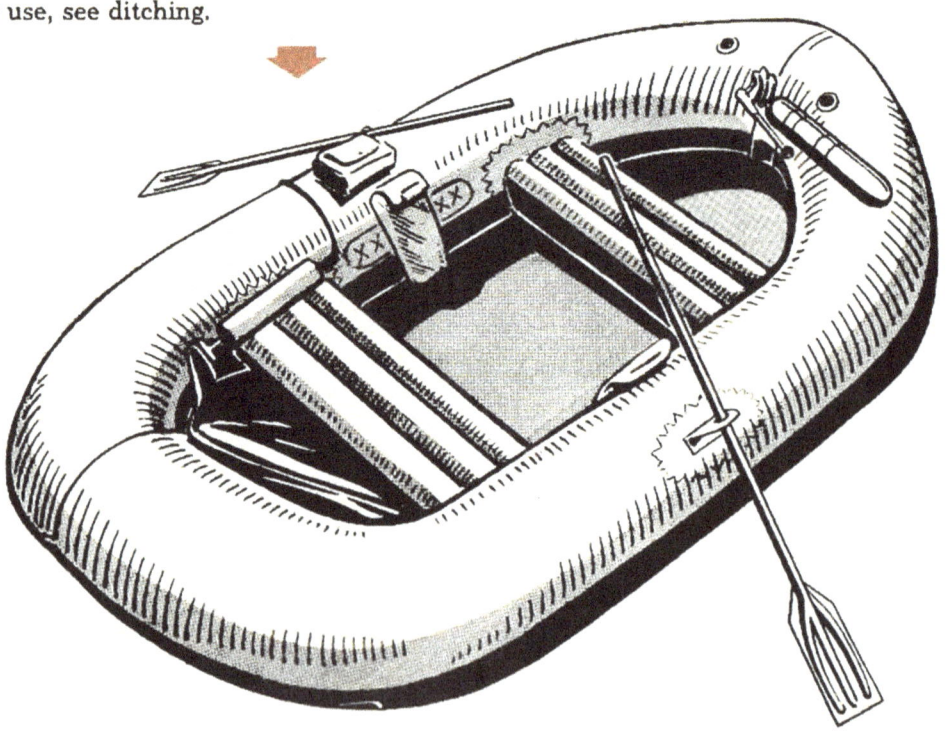

RADIO DEMOLITION SWITCH

On later airplanes, a switch controlling the charge for demolishing the identification radio in an emergency is on the right instrument sub-panel. Depress both buttons simultaneously to set off the charge.

HAND AX

There is a hand ax on the right side of the fuselage in the radio operator's compartment.

FIRST-AID KITS

Two first-aid kits are provided, one on the left side of the navigator's compartment, the other on the right side of the radio compartment. The number of kits is often increased when the ship engages in tactical operation.

Warning

Don't load this pistol except when it has been placed in the mount provided in the upper left corner of the navigator's compartment.

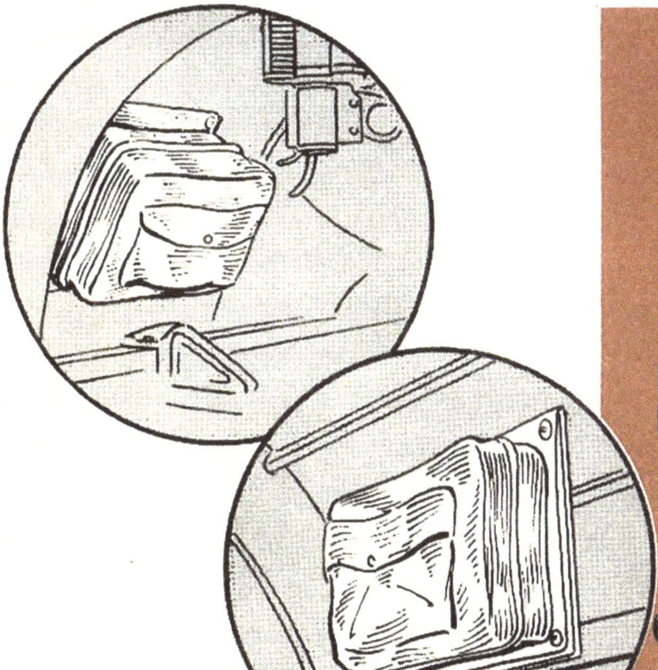

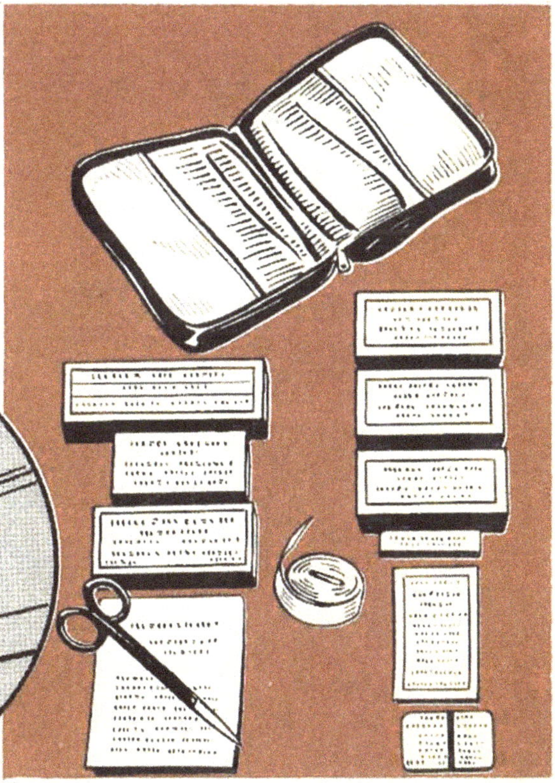

FIRE EXTINGUISHERS

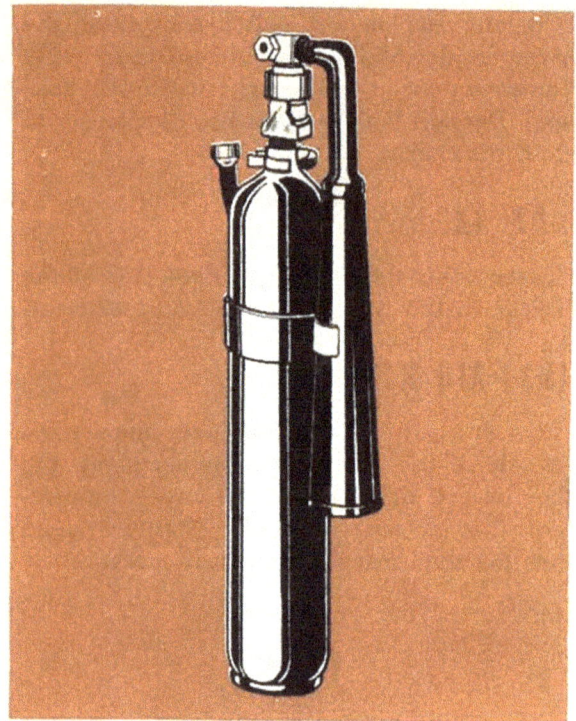

FUSELAGE FIRE EXTINGUISHER

Carbon dioxide fire extinguishers are at the right side of the navigator's compartment and at the right side of the radio operator's compartment.

There is an engine fire extinguisher system for both engines. It is controllable from the copilot's station. A safety fuse for indicating a premature discharge is on the right side of the fuselage above the nosewheel.

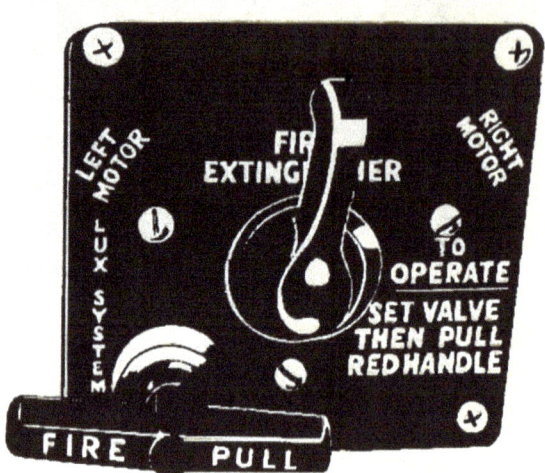

FIRE EXTINGUISHER SYSTEM

Fire in Flight

The deadly enemy of all flyers is fire in the air. All aircraft fires have three main causes:
1. Fire caused by enemy action.
2. Engine fires.
3. Spontaneous combustion.

Enemy Action

The best advice on this is preventive advice. Get them before they get you! If enemy action starts a fire in one of your engines, use the following procedures for fighting it.

Engine Fires

Formerly a great many fires started in the carburetor. To combat a carburetor fire:
1. Cut off gas to the engine.
2. Mixture control in "IDLE CUT-OFF."
3. Throttle full forward.

This quickly empties the carburetor and exhausts the fuel that is burning. In most cases no other action need be taken.

At present, because of the many improvements in carburetion, few engine fires start in this manner. The most common cause today is the mechanical failure of some part.

An immediate use of your CO_2 bottle will only halt the fire momentarily. Don't use it, until:
1. Gasoline cut-off valves "OFF."
2. Prop at "INC. RPM" to blow out the fire.
3. Open the throttle.
4. Feather the prop when the fuel runs out.
5. Cut switches after prop stops turning.
6. Now, if you need it, use the CO_2 bottle.
   a. Set selector switch to desired engine.
   b. Pull the handle. This discharges the CO_2 on the flames.
   (Open the cowl flaps before doing this.)

Don't under any circumstances try to re-start the engine under these conditions. Your CO_2 is exhausted and a recurrence of the fire will leave you with no defense at all.

The danger of fire, other than the natural hazard of the flame, is that the heat may melt or injure the control cables, wing spars, etc.

Do your best to combat engine fires, but don't stay with the ship so long that an explosion traps you.

Spontaneous Combustion

A good, clean airplane prevents spontaneous combustion. Clean off all oil and gas whenever it gets on, or in, a plane. Oily rags, etc., must not be allowed to accumulate. To combat such fires close off the compartment in which they are started and use your hand extinguishers.

Electrical failures and shorts may cause fires. So—if the seat of your electrical pants should start to smoke, take out the plug, take off the pants, and put out the fire.

Remove fuses from inverters, dynamotors, and instruments whenever the fire is localized.

On late-series planes automatic circuit breakers replace the fuses. Excessive heat breaks the electrical contacts and disconnects the source of trouble.

If flames are visible do not re-set the cut-outs.

To combat fire caused by enemy action use the techniques described above, depending, of course, on where they start.

BAILOUT

Take good care of your parachute. Keep it clean and free of grease and moisture.

Preflight Your Chute Before Every Flight.

See that there are no loose threads, rips or tears in the case. See that the seal is intact, the release pins straight, and that the chute has been recently inspected and checked.

Instruct your crew in the use of their parachutes and on the necessity for instant obedience to the bailout order. A few seconds' delay at the escape hatch can easily prove fatal not only to the man who hesitates but to the rest of the crew.

You are the last man out. Have your crew well drilled and instructed.

Check with the ground crew on the condition and operation of the escape hatches. Spot checks show that these hatches are often overlooked on the periodic inspections.

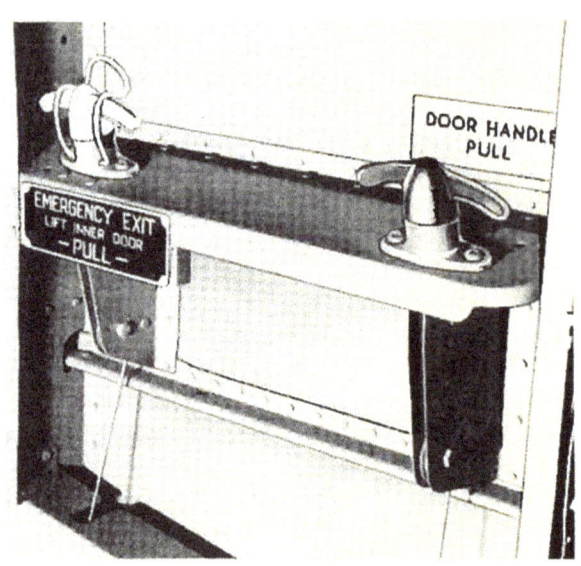

EMERGENCY HATCH RELEASE

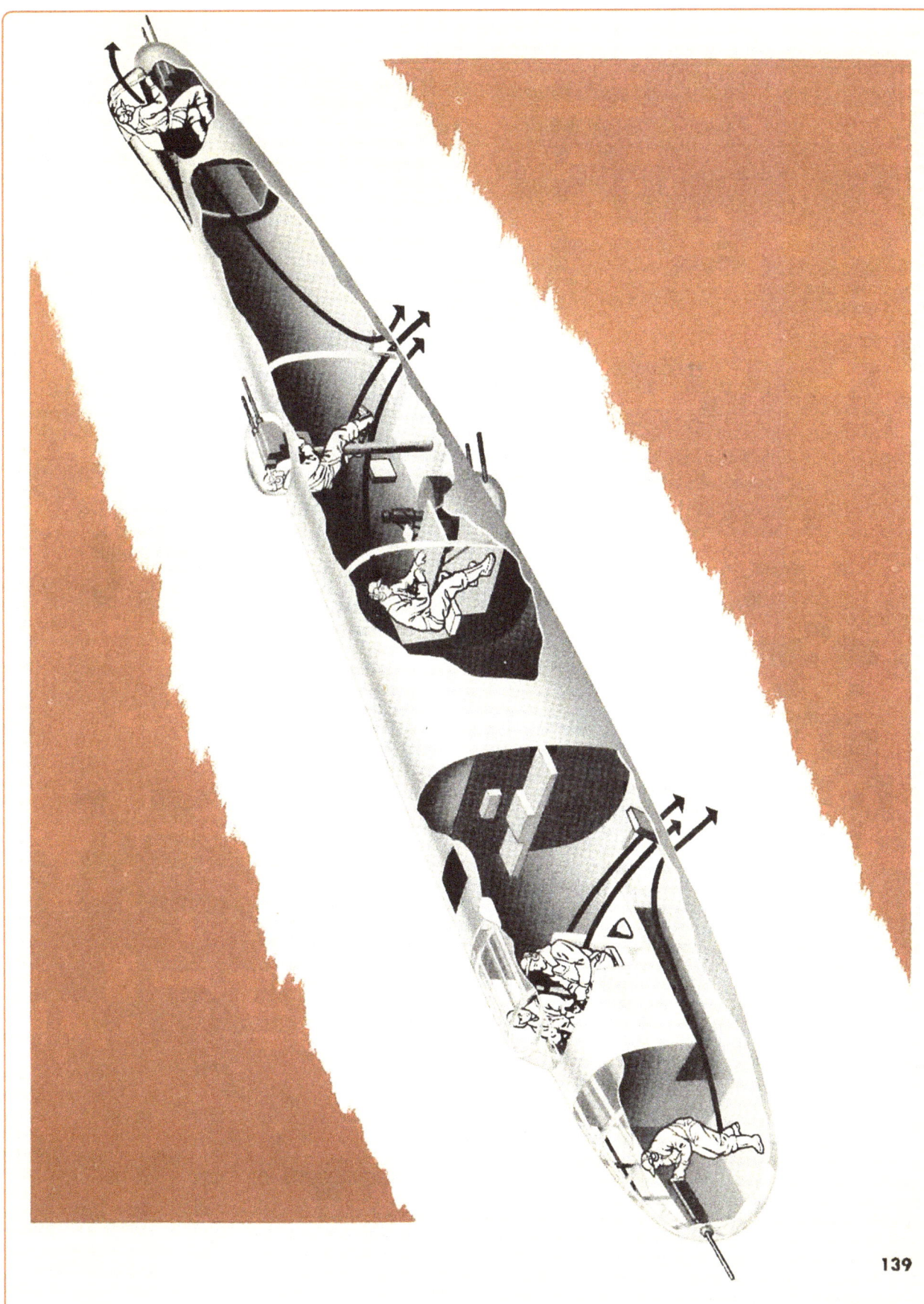

Procedure

When you decide that the ship must be abandoned, give the alarm by interphone and alarm bell, at which time the engineer and rear gunner release the emergency doors.

The first warning informs the crew that they must prepare to bail out.

The second warning is an order to the crew to jump. As each crew member gets ready to leave the plane, he advises you by interphone that he is leaving.

How To Jump

1. Face rear of ship and place hands on structure above rear of hatch.
2. Lower legs through opening. The slipstream will carry your legs up against the underpart of the fuselage. Twist your shoulder to the left to prevent injury to the head on the way out. Push away from the plane with your hands.
3. When you are sure that you are clear of the plane, look directly at the ripcord release and take hold of the handle.
4. Straighten your legs, keeping your feet together, and pull the release. In a low-altitude jump, pull the release as soon as possible.

For further information on bailout technique, consult your **Pilot's Information File.**

The order in which the crew leaves the plane is as follows:

Forward Hatch: 1. Engineer
2. Bombardier-navigator
3. Copilot
4. Pilot

Rear Hatch: 1. Gunner
2. Radio operator.

If you have had a hydraulic failure, be sure that the bomb bay doors are not partially open when you jump. These doors fall open ⅔ of the way when the hydraulic system loses its pressure.

Procedure for Reclosing Bomb Bay Doors

1. Open inner door—this door will not open with the bomb bay door crank installed.
2. Install crank on coupling.
3. Close doors and fasten crank to floor.
4. Complete bailout procedure.

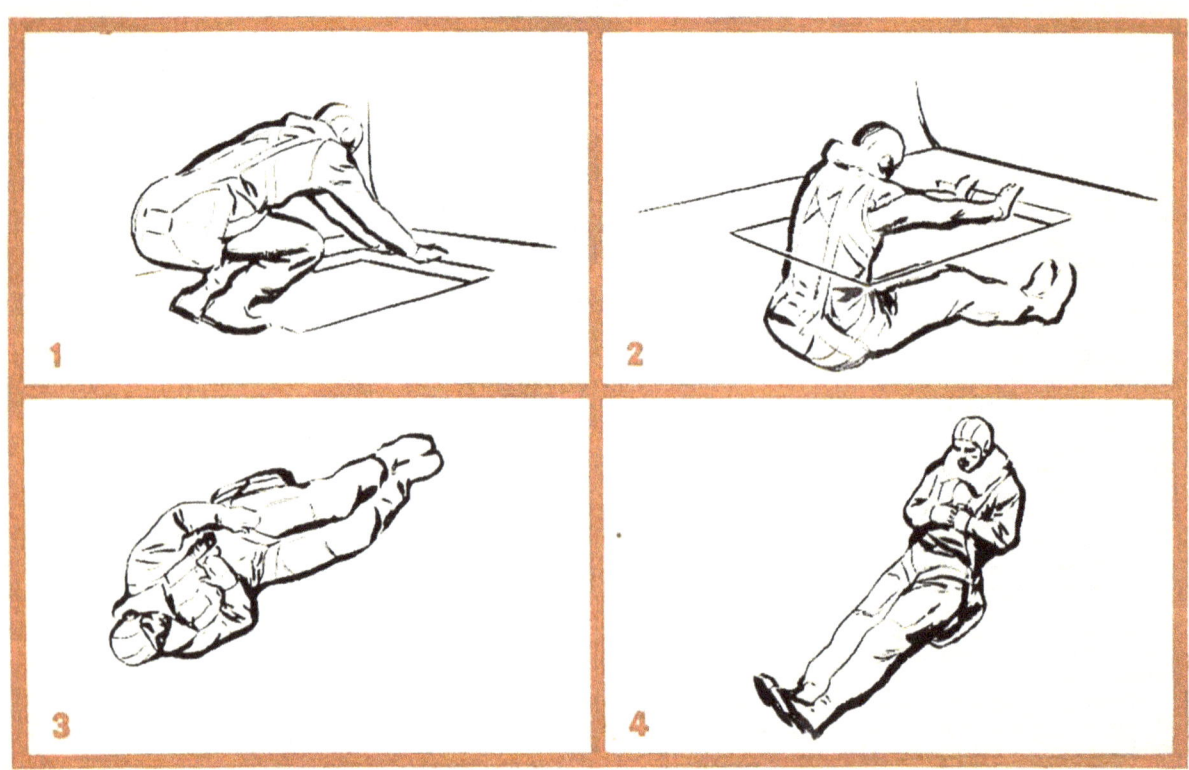

FORCED LANDINGS

Forced landing in the B-25 is at best a difficult job. Fortunately, the B-25's exceptional single engine ability will bring you home unless you have a failure of both engines. You will seldom need to set down in rough country.

Many pilots have made successful landings in wild, rough country. You can get some valuable tips from their experiences.

Never land wheels-up except on a known airfield. Soft ground, plowed fields, ridges, and gullies cause the plane to nose over and tear up, and increase the fire hazard tremendously.

If you make a belly landing the plane will in most cases toboggan over the ground and escape serious damage.

Although the shock and deceleration are less than in a forced landing at sea, they are great enough to necessitate bracing for the impact. Brace and cushion yourself as well as you can. You will save yourself from some hard knocks, if not more serious injuries.

Pick your spot carefully. If you have any control over where you are to land, pick a spot near a road, phone line, small town, or other settlement. This will insure immediate medical attention or quick communication if medical aid is not on hand.

Prepare the Plane

Throw out excess weight, thus lowering the landing speed.

Throw out loose objects to prevent them from flying through the plane on impact.

Keep first-aid kits on your person. In case of fire they will not be forgotten and burned.

Open the escape hatches to prevent jamming on impact.

Inflate your Mae West to help you absorb the shock of landing.

Prepare the Crew

Remove loose cords, parachute harness, radio cords, etc.

Fasten safety belts and shoulder harness.

Proceed to crash stations and remain throughout landing.

Landing the Plane

Make a normal full-flap approach to the landing.

Do not feather propellers unless it is necessary to stretch the glide. If the props are feathered, the tips will not bend aside on impact but will dig into the ground, rupturing wing tanks and engine mounts and adding to the fire hazard. They may also break and throw tips through the fuselage, creating an unnecessary hazard from the flying metal.

Keep wheels up. Remember, however, that the reduced drag from the wheels in a raised position will increase the normal gliding distance of the plane. Make allowances for this in your landing. Don't make a turn close to the ground at low airspeed. Plan your approach to land straight ahead. Before touching down, cut all switches to reduce the fire hazard.

Make a nose-high landing, but do not exaggerate the attitude to the point where there is danger of throwing the nose into the ground when the tail strikes.

Call the roll immediately after leaving the plane. Be sure that no one is left inside in a dazed condition. In the excitement it is easy to lose a man for a few seconds. If the plane starts to burn this may be long enough to prevent his rescue.

Crash stations are the same as those used for ditching.

WHEELS DOWN ONLY ON A KNOWN AIRPORT

WHEELS UP ON ANYTHING ELSE

Ditching

With the tactical needs of World War II calling for the operation of land planes over vast stretches of water, airmen faced a new hazard: ditching—the forced landing of land planes at sea.

From the analysis of actual ditching reports, plus the results of tests made with scale models, there has come a body of information so comprehensive that today ditching is a matter of tried and proven procedure.

Like any procedure, it must be practiced to be effective. Safeguard yourself and your crew by consistent practice.

Successful ditching depends on the speed and efficiency with which each crew member carries out his duties, and on the coordination of all efforts.

The two major factors which may necessitate ditching your airplane are lack of fuel and mechanical failure. It is well to bear in mind, however, that many ditchings have been avoided by thorough knowledge of the airplane and its characteristics under all conditions.

When To Ditch

Start preparation for ditching as soon as you feel the slightest doubt that your mission will be completed successfully.

You are responsible for the welfare of your crew. It is your duty to see that they are prepared well in advance of the actual ditching.

Do not delay your decision too long. Your crew must have as much time as possible to prepare. Once your decision is made, notify the crew by interphone and the alarm bell "Prepare to ditch!"

Radio Procedure

Start emergency radio procedure immediately. Your best chance for rescue lies in correct and speedy radio procedure before ditching. Radio operator and pilot must fully understand the specific radio procedure in their particular theater of operations.

If you transmit distress signals that you are ditching, but are lucky enough to make land,

be sure to notify the Air-Sea Rescue Unit as soon as possible to avoid danger and loss of time for other crews who may be out searching for you.

Prepare the Plane

When ditched, the B-25 loses its forward speed after the second impact in slightly more than its own length. This sudden deceleration makes deadly missiles of all loose objects in the airplane. **Jettison loose equipment.** Also jettison all objects likely to be torn loose by the impact. Lightening the plane reduces the landing speed and lessens the impact. Get rid of oxygen walk-around bottles, kitbags, extra sidearms, cargo. Strip turrets of ammunition,

dismantle and jettison guns and radio sets mounted over the bomb bay. Save at least one parachute for each raft. The silk and shroud lines will prove handy in the raft for sail, cover, and extra line.

Salvo bombs and the fuselage tank if it is more than half full. If fuselage tank is less than half full, keep it in the plane for added buoyancy.

Once the plane is in the water, only the emergency kits and signaling devices are valuable to you. Collect Very cartridges, pistol, smoke flares, all signaling devices and keep them on your person. Don't hesitate to throw out everything else that is loose or can be pried loose. Often the decreased weight will enable you to remain in the air much longer and bring you closer to land.

Drop all equipment through the lower and side hatches. Be careful to avoid damage to tail surfaces.

Before the landing, close all bottom hatches. Leave the right side hatch open to prevent jamming on impact. **If there is not enough time to salvo bombs and fuselage tank (30 seconds), keep the bomb bay doors closed.** Open the pilot's escape hatch only when below 1000 feet. Open hatches create drag.

Prepare the Crew

Remove all entangling cords and lines, parachute harness, radio cords, oxygen masks when below 12,000 feet, and throat microphones. Remove flying boots. Wear all other clothing, regardless of temperature. Loosen the clothing about your neck, particularly ties. Wear life vests at all times on over-water flights, but do not inflate them inside the plane. The escape hatches are small and may damage the vests in the exit.

Accomplish your prearranged duties and go to your ditching station at once. Remain there until the landing is completed. Moving around unnecessarily will change the trim of the plane and make the pilot's job more difficult.

Fasten all safety belts and harness before the landing. Use your headsets and mike at your ditching station but do not fasten them to your body.

Above all, remain in your ditching station

until the plane has stopped moving. More men are injured during the deceleration than at any other time. Terrific forces are generated then; the human body cannot absorb these forces if it is not protected.

Position of Personnel

Pilot—in his seat, seat full forward and locked, cushion protecting chest.

Copilot—in his seat, seat full back and locked to provide easy access to the escape hatch. If his seat is forward it may block the exit of the entire crew. On late-series planes with low-backed copilot's seat, it can be full forward. Copilot braces with his hands on the rubber crash ring on the instrument panel. **Keep elbows flexed.**

Engineer—behind the pilot's seat, facing the rear of the plane, braced and cushioned.

Navigator—on the floor of the navigator's compartment, facing aft, braced and cushioned.

Radio operator—on his seat, back against the bomb bay wall, safety belt fastened.

Gunner—beside the radio operator on the floor. If the airplane has a footwell for the radio operator, up-end a radio coil in this space and sit on that to avoid a cramped position.

If the head protrudes above the support at the back, hold it firmly in position with the hands across the base of the skull, pulling down firmly against the neck muscles. It has been found that the body in this position will absorb shocks far greater than those encountered in ditching.

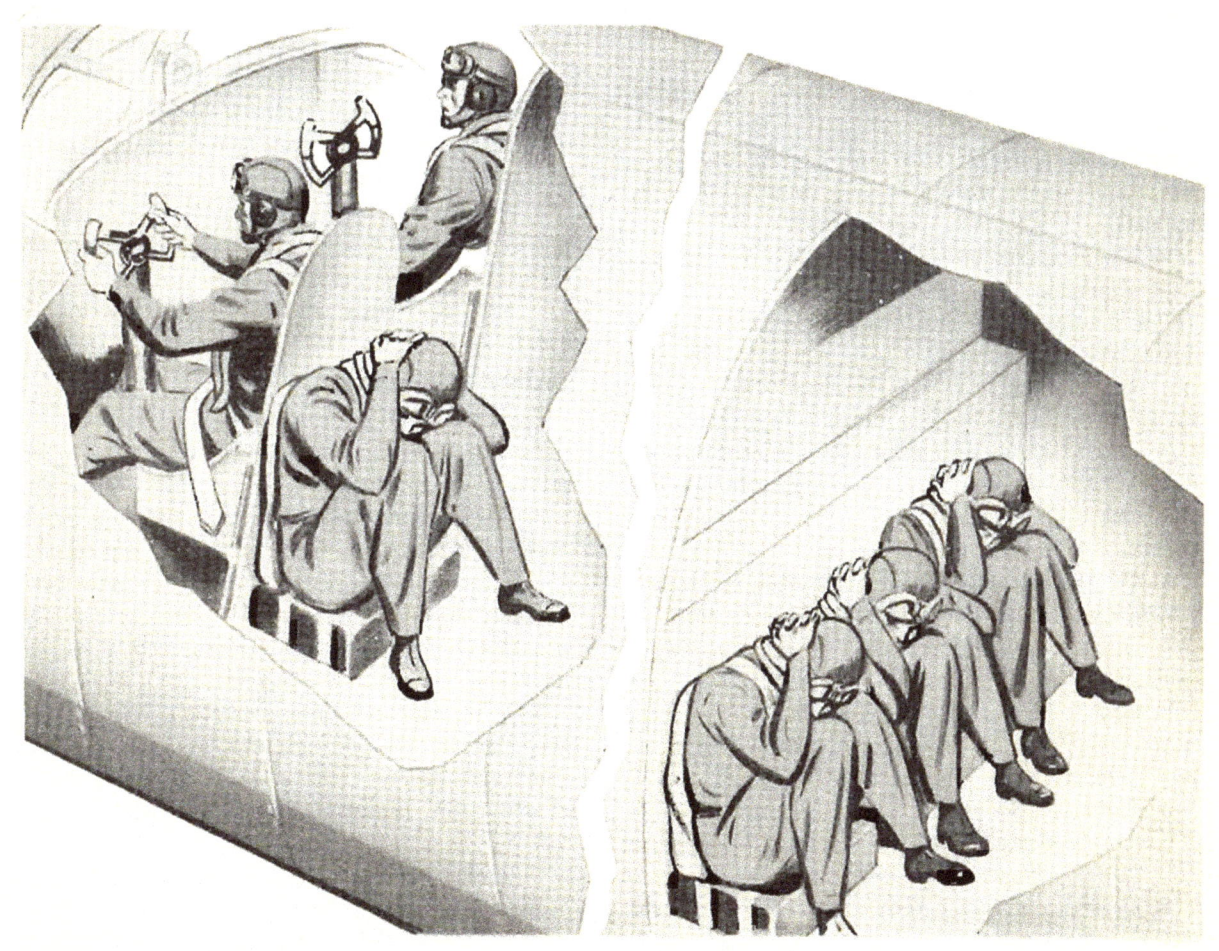

CREW DUTIES

Pilot's Duties

Make the decision to ditch.

1. Warn the crew by alarm bell—this bell is attached to all positive leads on the plane. If either battery-disconnect is on and any current remains in the battery, it will operate.
2. Use the interphone—get an acknowledgment from each crew member.
3. Turn IFF to "EMERGENCY."
4. Check the fuselage tanks and bombs, and salvo if necessary. Close the bomb bay doors—they must not be open for the landing.
5. Landing gear up—check it!
6. Get wind direction and velocity from navigator.
7. Signal copilot to lower flaps as required.
8. Notify crew to brace for the impact (interphone or bell).
9. Cut mixture, cut switches just prior to landing. Leave battery-disconnect switches "ON."
10. Notify navigator to cut gas supply, unless gas cut-off switches are in the pilot's cockpit.
11. Give alarm bell signal to abandon plane after landing.

The rest of the crew must coordinate their duties with those of the pilot. Crew members can practice their duties, and go through a drill, each performing a definite action on a number called by the pilot. For simplification these duties are listed in the order in which they should be done.

Copilot's Duties

1. On the emergency signal switch to interphone and acknowledge the emergency bell.
2. Help the pilot salvo bombs and fuselage tank.
3. Check to see that the gear is up.
4. Assist the pilot in getting wind's direction and velocity from the navigator.
5. Release the pilot's emergency hatch.
6. Lower flaps as required on pilot's signal.
7. Notify the crew to brace for impact.
8. Cut the mixture, cut switches on pilot's signal.
9. Brace for impact.
10. Abandon ship after it has stopped. Check to see that the life raft has released properly. If not, **release it manually.** Proceed to the rear of the ship and assist the men in the rear to abandon ship. Either the pilot or the copilot must take a parachute to the raft.

The Radio Operator's Duties

1. Switch to interphone and acknowledge the emergency bell.
2. Immediately begin sending the distress signal.
3. Receive position from the navigator and transmit it.
4. Receive the probable time and position of ditching from the navigator and transmit it.
5. Obtain first-aid kit. Keep it in your possession.
6. Continue the radio transmission of distress signal, position, course, and probable point of ditching until some further action is necessary.
7. On a signal from pilot to brace for impact, lock the transmitting key, swing around to the side and brace for impact.
8. Abandon ship.

During this period release life raft after the ship has stopped moving, carry out the first-aid kit, and exit through the right lower rear hatch.

Engineer's Duties

1. Acknowledge the emergency bell.
2. Check the fuselage tank and inform the pilot of its condition.
3. Jettison all loose and unnecessary equipment, packages, parachutes, radio equipment, spare tools, parts—**everything that will come loose or that can be torn loose.** Jettison through the bomb bay as the bombs and tank are dropped.
4. If bombs and tank are not dropped, jettison equipment through the entrance port in the lower part of the ship. This must be reclosed after the equipment has been thrown out.
5. Assist the navigator in preparing his equipment for ditching.
6. On the pilot's signal, assume ditching station and brace for impact.

7. Abandon the plane and stand by to assist pilot and navigator.

Gunner's Duties

1. Switch to interphone and acknowledge the emergency bell.

2. Remove the rear escape hatch. Jettison all loose equipment, ammunition cans, guns, chutes, spare coils, etc.

3. Close the hatch. This must be closed for landing, otherwise it will act as a scoop and allow entry of a great mass of water into the rear of the ship. This may damage the structure and cause the rear section to break off, greatly endangering your chances of getting out.

4. See that all rear personnel have their life vests on and that the vests **are not inflated.**

5. Lock rear armor bulkhead open, so that tail position and side windows may be used for escape.

6. Obtain the thermos bottle and keep it in your possession.

7. Brace for the impact on the pilot's signal.

8. Abandon ship. Remove the escape hatch. See that the radio operator releases the life raft. Carry the thermos bottle out and proceed to the raft.

There are two critical periods in ditching:

1. The actual landing and handling of the airplane on the water. This is the sole responsibility of the pilot.

2. The immediate abandonment of the airplane in an orderly manner after ditching. This requires the perfect coordination of the entire crew. Even in a training fuselage in a hangar, this cannot be done efficiently without a great deal of practice. After a severe shock, with the fuselage rapidly filling with water, safe and speedy abandonment is impossible unless the drill has been painstakingly planned and practiced. Every crew member must know his job and the drill to the last detail. Many crews have saved themselves by carrying out a well-executed drill. **This required advance practice and a great deal of it.**

LANDING PROCEDURE

Consult the PIF and your personal equipment officer for general information on landing in the water. They will help you determine wind direction, wind speeds, surface conditions, and other valuable information.

Trim the ship for hands-off flight and establish a normal power approach. Lower the flaps between 20° and 30°. Full flaps will lower the airspeed a few mph but will also increase your angle of descent dangerously.

Retard your rate of descent with the throttles. The flattest approach is by far the best. As you near the water, level off, raising the nose to a nose-high position, and lower the remaining flaps. Make a power landing in the same attitude you would use on a runway.

At high operating speeds the prop tips will strike the water with dangerous force. If they do not rip the engine from the plane they will damage the nacelle and the leading edge of the wing, causing the plane to sink faster.

Because of this, play your approach to enable you to flare off and land with a constantly decreasing load of power. If you have misjudged slightly, **don't blast the throttles open unless you can go around.**

Cut the throttles and switches as the tail strikes the water. There will be a definite impact as the tail strikes. Do not confuse this with the impact that will follow when the nose strikes. **This second impact will be violent.**

The nose will bury itself, and the plane will ship water through the pilot's escape hatch. Don't keep this hatch closed, however, as it may jam on impact and trap you in the airplane.

The bombardier's section, if it is installed, will rupture and water will flow through the crawlway.

The plane will nose up to a 45° angle and settle back to about 15° nose down. Water will enter the pilot's cockpit and fill it to a level with the top of the instrument panel. Expect this, and don't get panicky. Water will enter the right rear escape hatch when it is opened, and the exit may have to be made by ducking into the water to get out.

The length of time the B-25 will float depends on the amount of damage the airplane suffers in landing, and on the condition of the sea. Usually it will float for 5 to 7 minutes. You can safely expect at least 1 minute. Since a well-drilled crew can escape and board the life raft in 15 to 20 seconds, see that your crew is well drilled and you need not worry about how long the plane will float.

Don't make an exaggerated tail-low landing, as the impact of the tail will rupture the rear

fuselage and may snap the nose into the water violently before the plane can lose its excess speed.

Escape Procedure

Front Cockpit

1. Copilot—through top escape hatch. Check, or manually release the life raft. Proceed to the rear of the plane to assist men in their escape.

2. Pilot—through top escape hatch. Aid the crew members in the front cockpit to escape. Take parachute to raft.

3. Engineer—through top escape hatch. Stand by to assist pilot and navigator. Carry equipment to the raft.

4. Navigator—through the top escape hatch. Stand by to assist pilot. Carry equipment to raft.

Rear Compartment

1. Radio operator—through lower right escape hatch. Take equipment to the raft.

2. Gunner—through lower right escape hatch. Take equipment to the raft.

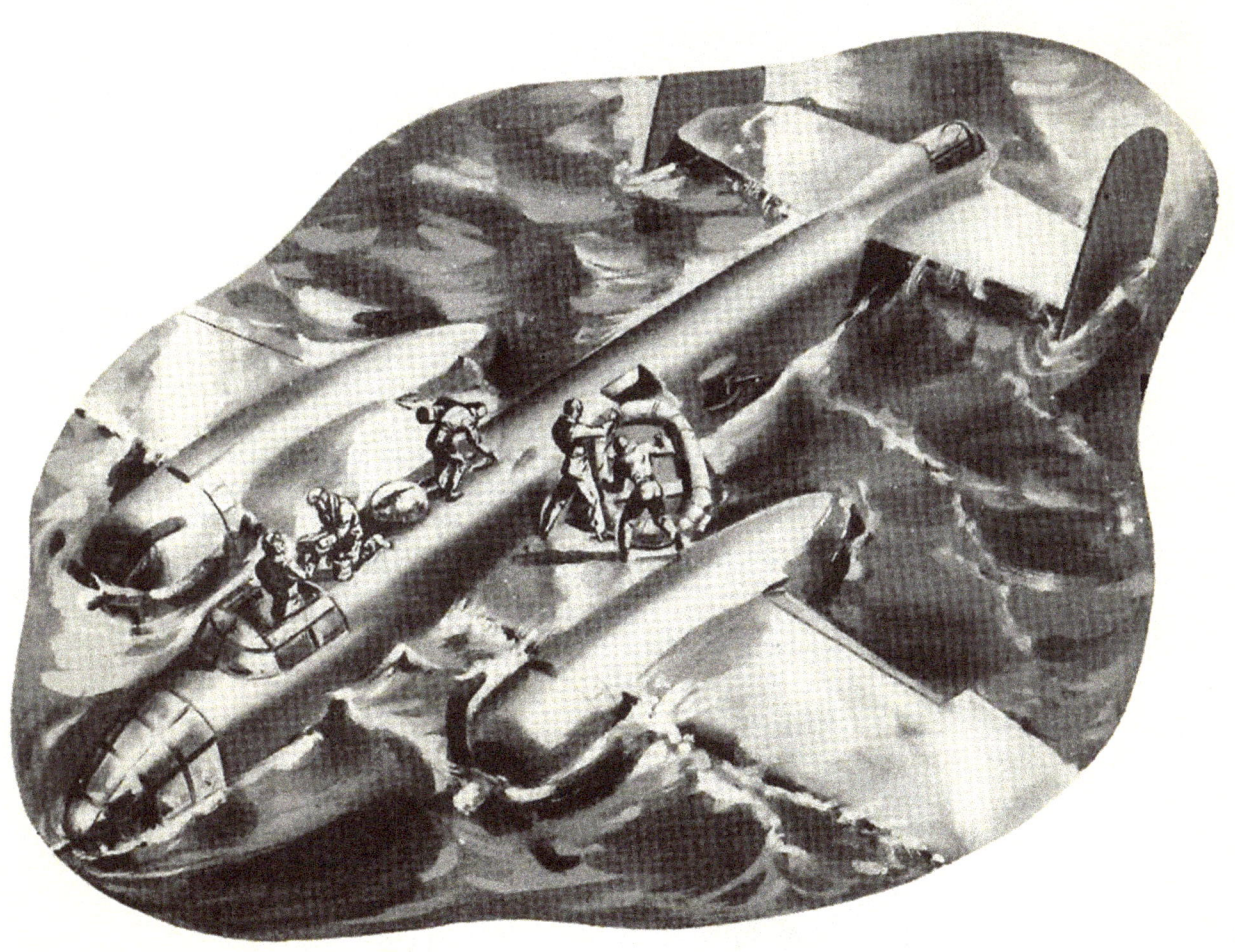

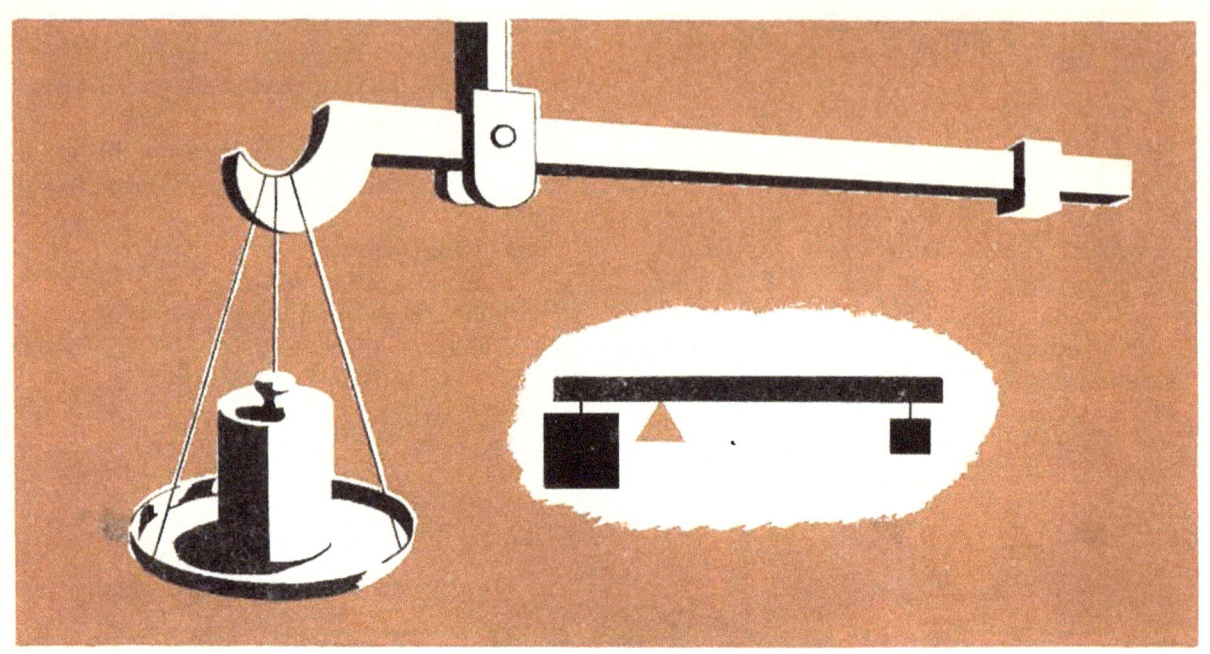

WEIGHT
and Balance

The day when a pilot flew by guesswork is past. One by one the decisions that were made by intuition, hunches, and guesswork have been taken over by an orderly system based on knowledge and understanding. Invariably this has resulted in greater safety and operating efficiency.

In the loading of heavy bombers this is especially true. Ever-changing tactical requirements, calling for more and more complex combinations of cargo, fuel, crew, and armament, have made any but precise, accurate methods too dangerous to consider. This need to get the utmost in efficiency from every flight highlights the need for precise control of weight and balance.

Improper loading, at best, cuts down the efficiency of an airplane. Maneuverability, rate of climb, speed, and ceiling suffer greatly.

At its worst, it may mean failure to complete a flight, and sometimes failure even to start a flight, in most cases with a loss of life and destruction of valuable equipment.

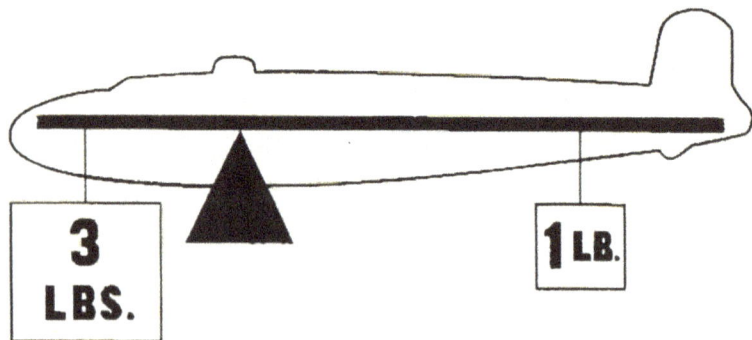

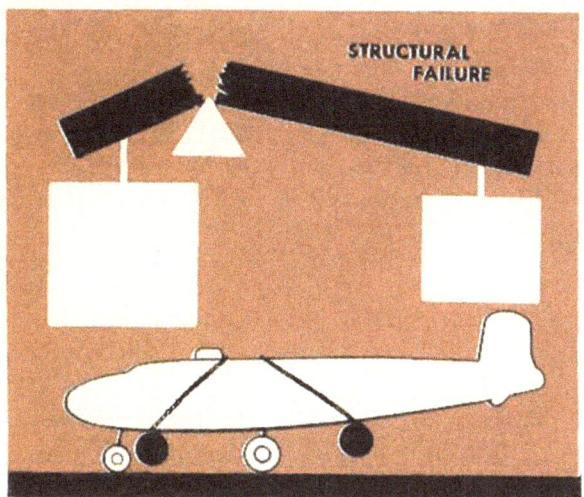

Overload

1. Causes higher stalling speeds.
2. Lowers structural safety limits.
3. Reduces maneuverability.
4. Increases length of the takeoff run.
5. Lowers the angle and rate of climb.
6. Decreases ceiling.
7. Increases fuel consumption for a given speed.
8. Overloads the tires.

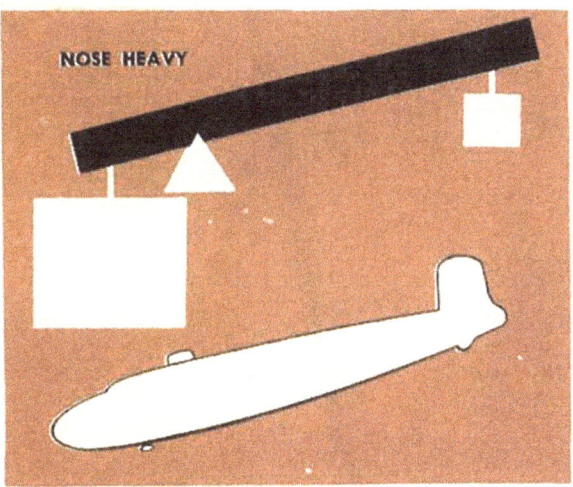

CG Too Far Forward

1. Increases dives beyond control.
2. Causes unstable, nose-down tendencies when flaps are lowered.
3. Increases difficulty in raising nose on landing.
4. Overloads nosewheel and tire.
5. Increases pilot strain in instrument flying.
6. Dangerous if tail structure is damaged.

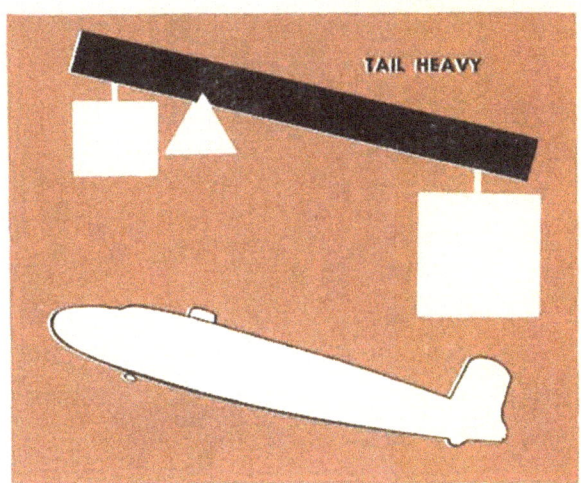

CG Too Far Aft

1. Increases stall tendency.
2. Limits low power operation.
3. Decreases speed.
4. Decreases range.
5. Increases pilot strain in instrument flying.
6. Dangerous if tail structure is damaged.

PRINCIPLES OF WEIGHT AND BALANCE

Proper Balance

An airplane is properly balanced when it will remain approximately level if suspended from a definite point within its center of gravity range.

Center of Gravity Range

The center of gravity range is the maximum fore-and-aft limits within which the balance of the airplane's weight must lie if the plane is to fly safely. This center of gravity range is near the leading edge of the wing where the maximum lift occurs.

Balancing the B-25

Balancing the B-25 is simply a matter of distributing the weight so that the center of the airplane's loaded weight falls within the center of gravity range.

Weighing the B-25

The B-25 is weighed to determine the basic weight of the airplane and to find the point at which this weight is balanced.

Charts and Forms

There are various charts and forms for controlling the weight and balance of the B-25. These may be found in T.O. 01-1B-40. For information on these charts and forms consult your weight and balance officer or T.O. 01-1B-40.

Form F

The Form F vitally concerns the pilot. This is the record of the distribution of weight in the airplane. It will tell you the CG step by step as each item is placed in the plane.

You must fill out this Form F before every flight. One copy is filed and one copy remains in the **Weight and Balance Handbook** of the plane.

For instructions on the use of the load adjuster see the PIF or T.O. 01-1B-40.

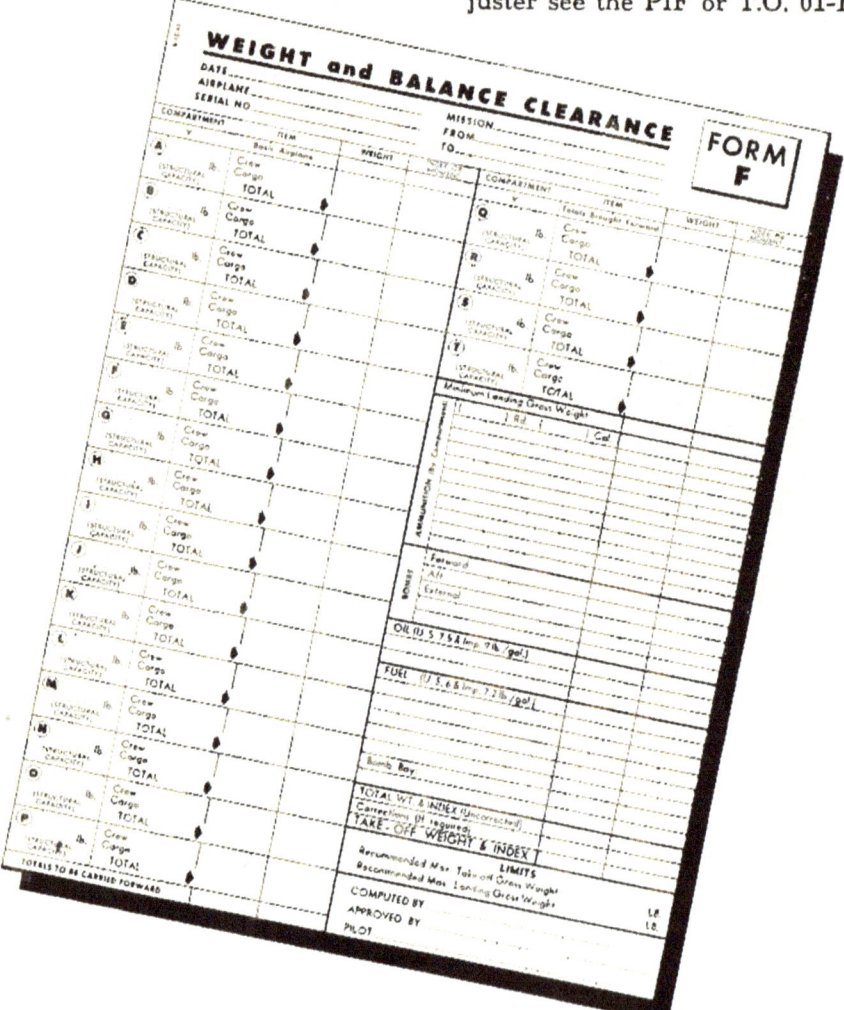

GRADE 91 FUEL

With our entry into World War II, and our operations on fighting fronts the length and breadth of the world, it became apparent that we could not produce high-octane fuels quickly enough to meet the demand.

For this reason, all training and operational flights in the continental United States are made on Grade 91 fuel whenever possible.

The operation of the B-25 on Grade 91 fuel is perfectly safe. With a thorough knowledge of its operating limits you will have no trouble at all.

What Is an Octane Rating?

To properly understand the evaluation of fuels it is necessary to review some basic facts. Let's start with some definitions:

Pre-ignition

Pre-ignition is a condition of premature firing. The fuel charge in the cylinder head is ignited by a hot carbon deposit or other means before time for the electrical firing to occur.

Normal Combustion

Normal combustion is the burning of the fuel charge in the cylinder head as a slow-burning wave, creating power not as an explosion, but as an expansion of the gases.

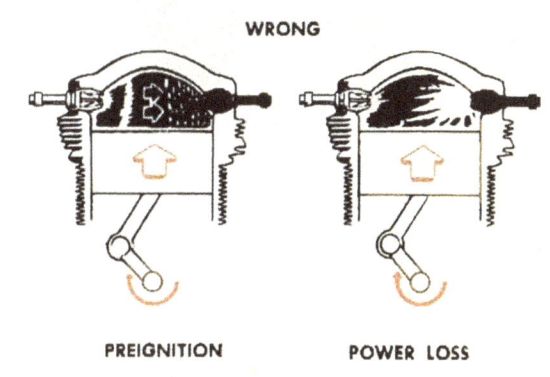

WRONG

PREIGNITION   POWER LOSS

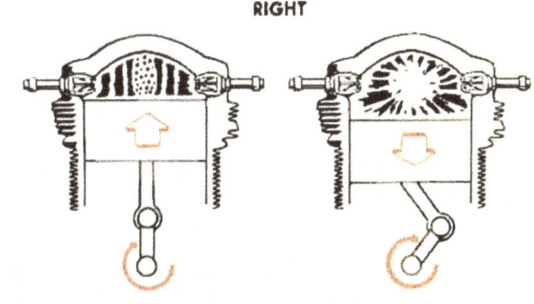

RIGHT

CORRECT COMBUSTION   MAXIMUM POWER

Detonation

Detonation, as the name implies, is an explosion in the cylinder head. The normal burning wave as it travels across the cylinder head subjects the unburned portion of the fuel charge to tremendous temperatures and pressures. If these forces are great enough the remaining fuel charge explodes before it can burn, and the shock waves from this explosion are great enough to blow the cylinder head off the engine.

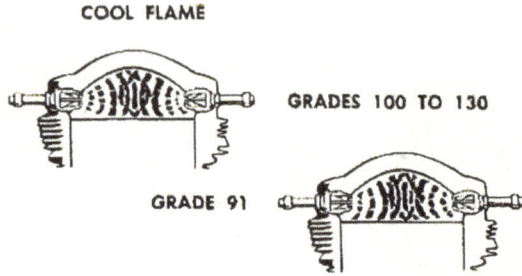

RELATIVE COMBUSTION TEMPERATURES FOR DIFFERENT GRADES OF FUEL

How Does This Affect the B-25?

You control the initial pressure that is allowed to enter the cylinders of the engines. This pressure after entering the cylinders is compressed and fired at a predetermined ratio.

You exercise a control over the temperature at which the engines run. If you allow great pressures to enter the engine, or allow the engine to operate at excessive temperatures, you can be sure of disastrous consequences.

The pressure entering the engine is determined by a relation of manifold pressure and rpm. Temperature is controlled by allowing the engine to get proper cooling.

Learn the power limits you can use with different grade fuels at different altitudes.

The accompanying power control chart shows maximum limits, minimum limits, and the desirable range to increase the life and efficiency of the engines.

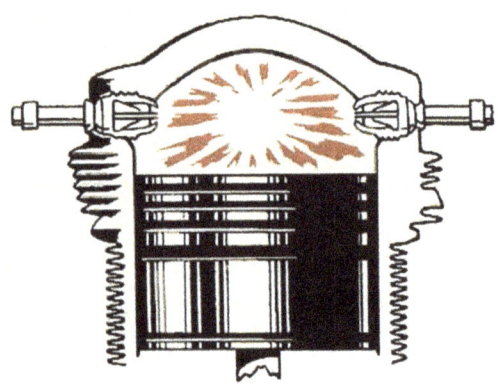

DETONATION

Octane Rating

Octane rating of a fuel is a mathematical grade assigned to a fuel in direct proportion to its ability to withstand pre-ignition and detonation.

Two reference fuels were chosen, iso-octane and normal heptane. Run in a test engine, these fuels respond identically under identical conditions.

To rate a new fuel it is compared to these reference fuels. If it matches the anti-knock ability of iso-octane it is rated as Grade 100 fuel. If its performance is less, normal heptane is added to the iso-octane. Thus, if a fuel matches in performance a mixture of 87% iso-octane and 13% normal heptane it is rated as Grade 87 fuel.

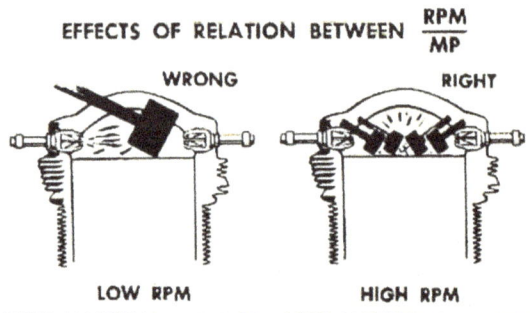

EFFECTS OF RELATION BETWEEN $\frac{RPM}{MP}$

WRONG — LOW RPM HIGH MANIFOLD PRESSURE

RIGHT — HIGH RPM LOW MANIFOLD PRESSURE

POWER CONTROL CHART FOR GRADE 91 FUEL

Power control settings listed in T. O. 02-1-38 are:

	RPM	Manifold Press.	Mixture
Takeoff	2600	39.5" Hg.	Full Rich
Maximum Cruise	2100	29" Hg.	Full Rich
Minimum Cruise	1560	26" Hg.	Cruising Lean

Remember These settings are maximum manifold pressure and minimum rpm. To increase the life of your engine, the following settings are recommended.

Takeoff	2600 rpm	39 inches Hg.	Full Rich	Low Blower
Preclimb	2400 rpm	34 inches Hg.	Full Rich	Low Blower

Climb

Sea Level to 7000 ft	2250 rpm	29" Hg.	Full Rich	Low Blower
7000 ft to 10,000 ft	2250 rpm	28" Hg.	Full Rich	Low Blower
10,000 ft to 16,000 ft	2250 rpm	26" Hg.	Full Rich	Low Blower
16,000 ft to 20,000 ft	2250 rpm	27" Hg.	Full Rich	High Blower

Cruise

1000 ft to 5000 ft	1950 rpm	26" Hg.	Full Rich	Low Blower
5000 ft to 10,000 ft	2050 rpm	25" Hg.	Full Rich	Low Blower
Sea Level to 4000 ft	1560 rpm	26" Hg.	Cruising Lean	Low Blower
4000 ft to 8000 ft	1600 rpm	25" Hg.	Cruising Lean	Low Blower
8000 ft to 11,000 ft	1650 rpm	24" Hg.	Cruising Lean	Low Blower
15,000 ft	1750 rpm	22" Hg.	Cruising Lean	Low Blower
20,000 ft	1850 rpm	24" Hg.	Cruising Lean	High Blower

MAXIMUM RANGE CHART For B-25 C, D, & G AIRCRAFT

Grade 100 Only

Airplane's Gross Weight	Indicated Air Speed	RPM		Manifold Pressure		Mixture Control	Fuel Consumption Gal. per Hour	
		1000 Feet	8000 Feet	1000 Feet	8000 Feet		1000 Feet	8000 Feet
34,000 lb.	175	1680	1925	29.2	27.1	Cruising Lean	107	118
33,000 lb.	175	1640	1885	29.2	26.8	"	103	115
32,000 lb.	170	1590	1850	29.2	26.5	"	99	110
31,000 lb.	170	1515	1800	29.2	26.0	"	93	104
30,000 lb.	165	1490	1740	29.2	25.4	"	88	97
29,000 lb.	165	1460	1710	29.2	25.1	"	85	94
28,000 lb.	165	1425	1680	29.0	24.9	"	82	91
27,000 lb.	165	1410	1660	28.8	24.6	"	79	87
26,000 lb.	165	1410	1600	28.6	24.0	"	78	80
25,000 lb.	165	1405	1525	28.4	23.3	"	77	73

Note: Climb at 2400 rpm, 38" Hg at 155 IAS. Fuel Consumption for Takeoff and Climb:
To 1000 Feet 24 Gals.   To 8000 Feet 84 Gals.

MAXIMUM RANGE CHART For B-25 H & J AIRCRAFT

Grade 100 Only

Airplane's Gross Weight	Indicated Air Speed	RPM		Manifold Pressure		Mixture Control	Fuel Consumption Gal. per Hour	
		1000 Feet	8000 Feet	1000 Feet	8000 Feet		1000 Feet	8000 Feet
34,000 lb.	175	1725	1940	29.2	27.2	Cruising Lean	112	123
33,000 lb.	175	1690	1905	29.2	27.0	"	109	119
32,000 lb.	170	1620	1860	29.2	26.5	"	104	114
31,000 lb.	170	1580	1820	29.2	26.2	"	100	109
30,000 lb.	165	1525	1760	29.2	25.6	"	94	102
29,000 lb.	165	1500	1730	29.2	25.4	"	91	98
28,000 lb.	165	1470	1710	29.2	25.1	"	88	95
27,000 lb.	165	1450	1680	29.1	24.9	"	85	93
26,000 lb.	165	1430	1660	28.9	24.7	"	83	90
25,000 lb.	165	1420	1640	28.6	24.5	"	81	88

Note: Climb at 2400 rpm, 38" Hg at 115 IAS. Fuel Consumption for Takeoff and Climb:
To 1000 Feet 24 Gals.   To 8000 Feet 84 Gals.

COLD WEATHER OPERATIONS

Cold weather operations bring visions of long arctic nights, glaciers, Eskimos, and stories you have heard of the Far North.

But it is well to bear in mind that during the winter months many sections of the United States have climatic conditions requiring just as much specialized maintenance as the Arctic.

Granted that the conditions are not as severe, it is still important that you know how to care for your plane.

Starting Engines

Make a normal start by following the procedure on the pilot's checklist. If you have trouble starting the engines, take the following supplementary measures:

1. Pull the props through about 15 blades before engaging the starter. The engines will need a lot of priming for a cold weather start. If possible use external power for cold weather starting.

2. If the engine fails to start, check plugs for moisture. Make another attempt to start the engine when the plugs are dry.

3. Always make a normal start before using the oil dilution system. If, after the engines are running, your oil pressure is too high or is fluctuating and drops off when the rpm is increased, dilute the oil. (See dilution procedure under After Landing.)

Note: Use this method only if time and extreme temperature conditions do not permit normal engine warm-up.

4. Do not run the engines at more than 1200 rpm until the oil has reached a temperature of 20°C.

5. If icing conditions exist, place carburetor air control handles in "ICING" until the induction system is free of ice.

Takeoff

1. Never take off if there is any snow, ice, or frost on the wings. Even the thinnest layer of frost may cause loss of lift and treacherous stalling characteristics. In extreme conditions it may be necessary to taxi out to the takeoff position before removing the protective covers from the flight surfaces.

2. In ordinary operation, carburetor air controls should be in "NORMAL" for takeoff. In extremely cold weather, however, it is often advisable to place carburetor air control in "ICING" during takeoff to insure proper fuel vaporization.

(You will seldom find these extreme conditions in the continental United States. In arctic zones, consult experienced pilots before employing this procedure.)

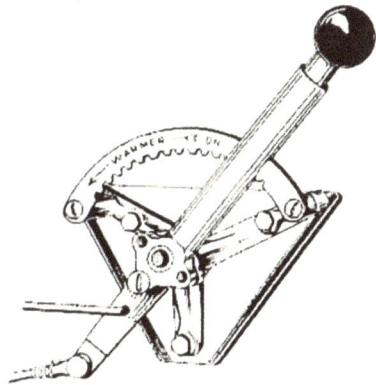

Your cabin heaters must be "OFF" before takeoff.

Flight

1. Your anti-icing and de-icing equipment is primarily intended as a means of getting you **out** of icing levels. Don't fly in icing levels any longer than is absolutely necessary.

2. Check your free air temperature gage before any flight where ice is anticipated.

3. After taking off from snow or slush-covered fields, operate the landing gear and flaps through several cycles to insure against the gear and flaps freezing in the up position.

4. Turn the pitot tube heater "ON" when moisture is present. Pitot tube heat should not be applied until the airplane is on the takeoff run or actually in the air, as there is insufficient cooling in the pitot head while the plane is stationary. **Note:** With pitot tube heat "ON" your magnetic compass may oscillate as much as 15°.

ANTI-ICING

Emergency provision is made to prevent ice formation on the propellers, and on the bombsight window by an alcohol anti-icing system.

The alcohol anti-icing system has two supply tanks, one in each engine nacelle against the outboard wall. They carry isopropyl alcohol. The tank in the right-hand nacelle has a capacity of 10 gallons and supplies fluid through separate line systems for anti-icing of the propeller blades and the bombardier's window. A standpipe reserves 1.5 gallons for the bombsight window after the supply for the propellers is exhausted. The tank in the left-hand nacelle is used for carburetor de-icing. It is similar to the one in the right nacelle except that special inter-rib recesses on the outboard side increase the capacity to 15 gallons. Each system has its own pump, filters, and check valves to keep the fluid readily available near the point of application and to prevent draining of the fluid during dives.

There is no fluid level gage inside the airplane. The fluid level is checked by means of overflow plugs mounted on the tank.

Propeller Anti-Icing

Conventional slinger rings are provided for the propellers. A fluid metering pump in the right-hand nacelle forward of the tank is controlled by a rheostat on the pilot's switch panel. With a slight turn to the right, the control operates the pump at its maximum speed. Further rotation of the control to the right reduces the speed of the pump to any desired volume. The pump is capable of supplying from .36 to 3.17 gallons per hour to each propeller ring.

Whenever icing conditions are encountered, start the pump immediately in order to supply sufficient fluid to coat propeller surfaces before ice formation if possible. However, if ice has already formed—as indicated by rough engine performance—turn the rheostat to fast-flow position until the ice has been removed and the engines run smoothly. **Then turn the rheostat to a position which will supply sufficient fluid to prevent further ice formation.** Use the fluid as sparingly as possible. Remember that the capacity of the supply tanks is only 10 gallons. Keep in mind the length of time you may have to use the pump and the fact that the fluid in the reservoir must also be kept available for anti-icing the bombardier's window. During missions on which the bomb window anti-icing system is not needed, the fluid supply in the reservoir is sufficient for 1 hour and 20 minutes' continual operation with the rheostat turned to the fast-flow position. At the minimum flow setting, the supply will last for 11 hours and 48 minutes.

Bombsight Window

The bombardier's compartment window has perforated anti-icing tubes across the top of the center panel, plus a vertical wiper assembly. Fluid for the spray tube comes from the same tank used for the operation of the propeller anti-icer. The available supply includes the 1.5 gallons reserved by the standpipe within this tank. A rheostat control mounted forward of the instrument panel on the left side of the bombardier's compartment regulates fluid flow.

The check valve in the fluid supply line to the bomb window tubes is in the compartment ceiling and is readily available to the bombardier should minor adjustments be necessary during flight. Turning the visible screw to the right restricts the rate of flow.

The electric motor which drives the windshield wiper through a flexible cable assembly is controlled by two switches in the lower left corner of the box control panel. The first switch may be set to "FAST" or "SLOW" and the motor turned "ON" by means of the second switch. To prevent injury to the motor or the wiper, the switch must not be turned "ON" while the bomb window is dry.

The installation of this equipment precludes the use of a pilot's windshield spray. A field service installation may, however, be made on these aircraft to provide a clear-vision windshield. This is a 6-ply, chemically treated glass window. The outboard sections are in a neutral pressure area and may be removed in extreme icing conditions to provide direct vision ahead.

CARBURETOR DE-ICER SYSTEM

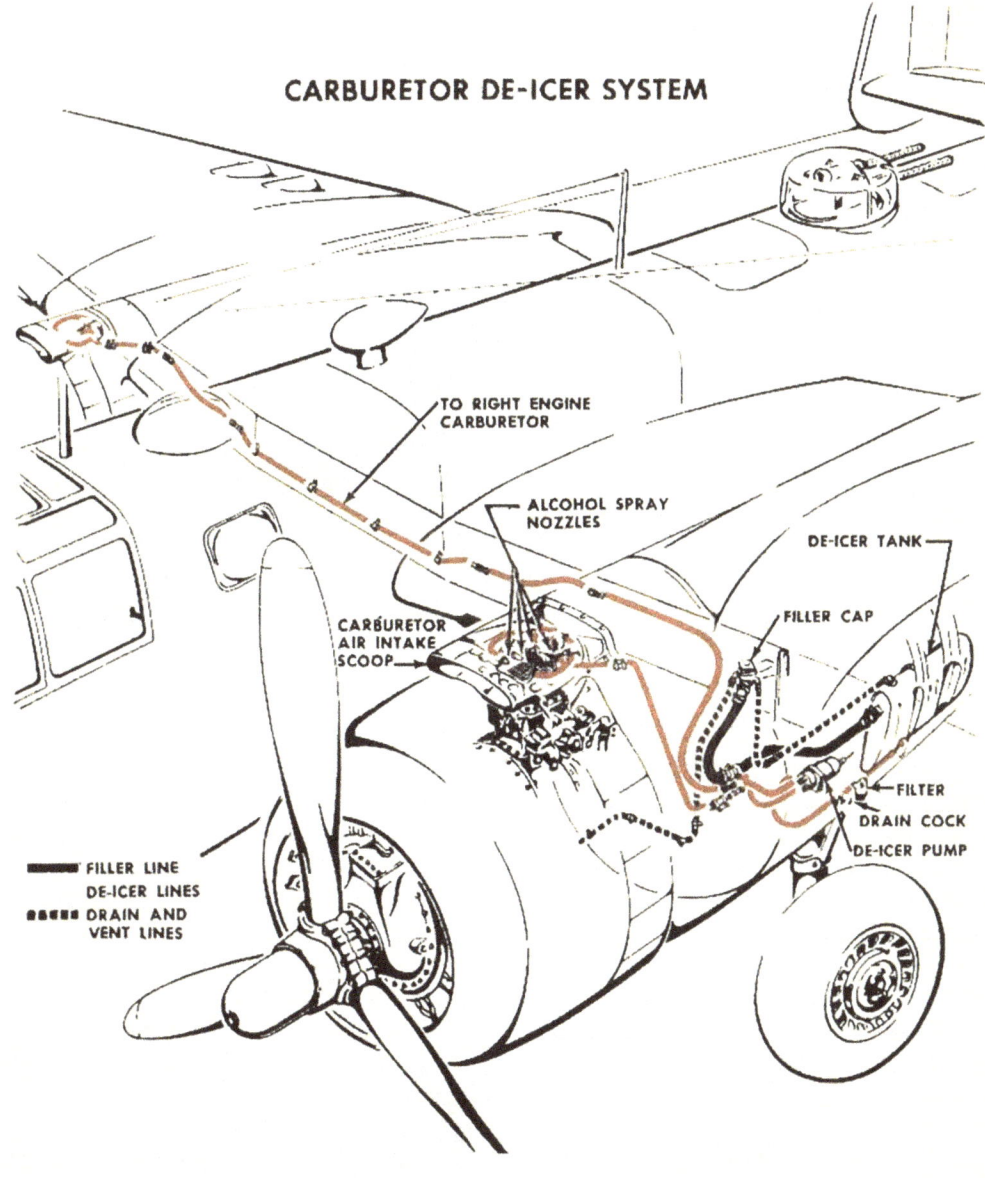

SURFACE DE-ICER SYSTEM

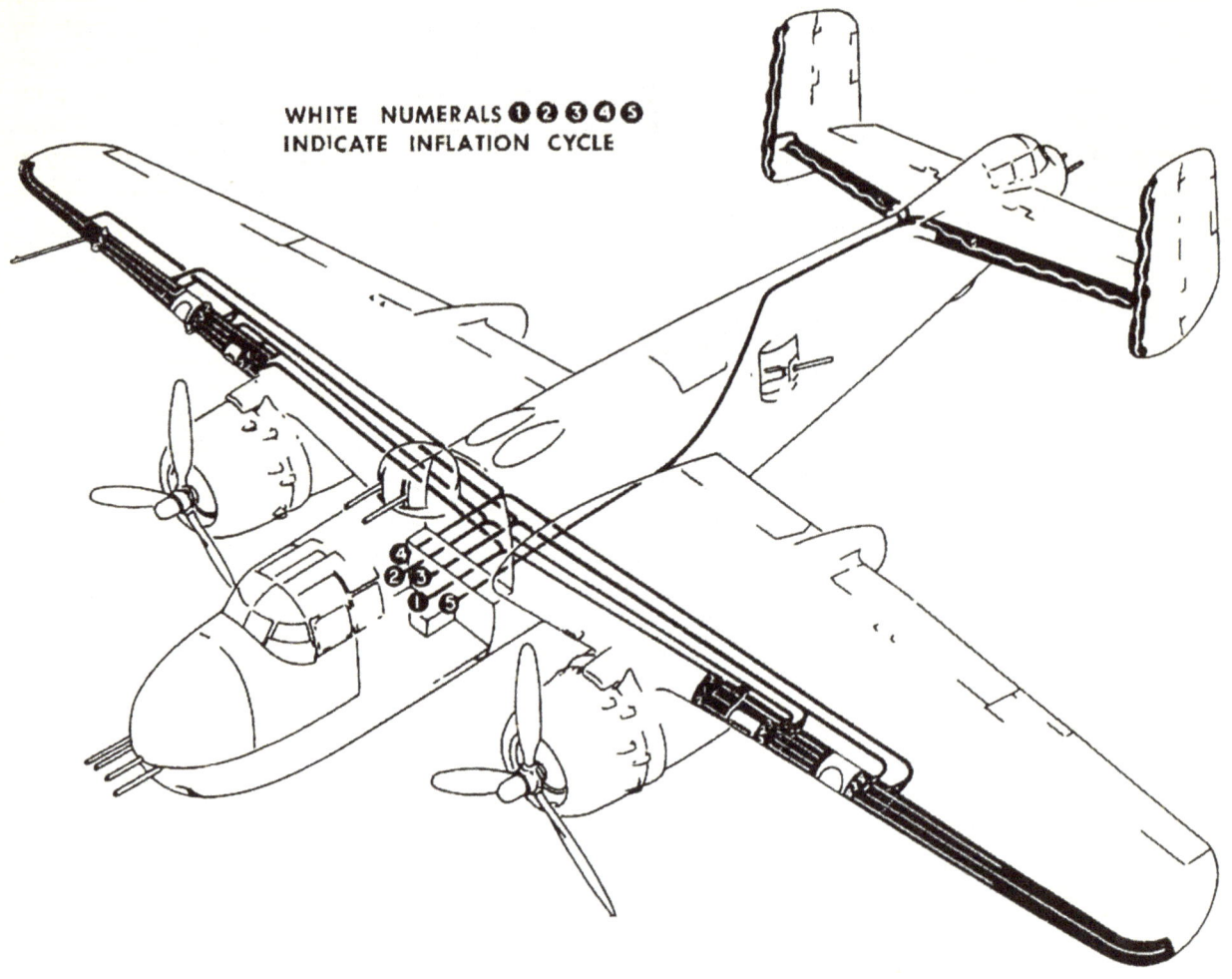

WHITE NUMERALS ① ② ③ ④ ⑤ INDICATE INFLATION CYCLE

Conventional air-inflation de-icer boots are mounted on leading edges of wings and empennage. A rotary distributor valve in the well of the navigator's compartment furnishes air to the boots in a 5-phase cycle every 40 seconds.

When the de-icer system is not in operation, suction provided by the vacuum pumps on both engines prevents aerodynamic negative pressures from raising the de-icer boots.

Operation of the surface de-icing system is automatic when the control is turned "ON."

There is a pressure gage for the de-icer system in the rear of the navigator's compartment. This gage should read approximately 7 lb. sq. in. under normal operating conditions. Should the pressure go above 10 lb. sq. in., the maximum pressure, immediately turn the control "OFF" and check for the difficulty.

Caution: Do not operate the de-icer during landing or takeoff. Never operate the de-icer system at speeds above 230 mph; negative pressure on leading edge of wings will expand the de-icer boots, causing them to rupture.

DEFROSTING SYSTEMS

The pilot's windshield section, bombardier's bombsight window, bombsight, and the navigator's astrodome can be defrosted by warm air from the airplane heating system. The bomb bay window, the astrodome, and the pilot's windshield receive heat whenever the heating system is on.

The bombsight warm air supply is controlled by a lever on the defrosting tube located on the left side of the bombardier's compartment.

There is a door for cleaning the bombsight window. When not in use, the bombsight defrosting tube can be stowed in clips along the left side of the bombardier's compartment.

When not in use, the end of the astrodome defroster tube can be stored on the left side of the navigator's compartment directly inboard of the window on the upper longeron. To use it, attach the end of the tube to the nozzle permanently installed in the astrodome, or place it in the alternate position by hooking it to the rear of the astrodome.

There is a flexible auxiliary defrosting tube on the floor of the pilot's compartment at the base of the control column. You can remove the free end from the storage clip and extend it as needed for defrosting the interior of the top side windows in the pilot's compartment. The push-pull selector control on the lower panel in front of the copilot directs the flow of air either to the windshield or to the auxiliary defrosting tube.

Special blowers assist the flow of air to the pilot's compartment defrosting system and to the bombsight window in the bombardier's compartment. Switch controls for the blowers are on the pilot's switch panel and on the bombardier's control panel.

This heating and defrosting system is slightly modified and adapted for the different series of B-25 planes. There are no provisions for heating or defrosting the nose of the series G and H planes, and other slight changes occur in other models. Information on these changes may be found in the T.O.'s for these planes.

HEATING SYSTEM

The airplane has two independent heating systems; one for heating the navigator's, pilot's, and bombardier's compartments, the other for heating the radio operator's compartment and the interior of the fuselage aft of it. Each system has a Stewart-Warner heater burning a mixture of fuel and air. The forward heating system will operate only when the left engine is running, and the aft system only when the right engine is running.

The heater for the forward system is in the left wing center section and a system of hot air ducts leads forward along the left wall of the fuselage. The pilot may obtain more air at high altitude and slow airspeed by operating the air flow control at the left side of his seat. The air travels from the intake scoop on the leading edge, through the heaters, to valve equipped outlets in each forward compartment.

Controllable cold air scoops are provided for the pilot, copilot, and bombardier.

Do not open any of the three escape hatches during flight to obtain ventilation. The drag these open hatches create lowers the efficiency of the plane and in some flight attitudes will cause unstable flight characteristics.

A direct control for the aft heater system, mounted on the heater itself, is just aft of the lower turret on the left wall of the radio operator's compartment.

There is also a master control switch on the pilot's switch panel for emergency use and to aid the pilot in keeping the heater off during takeoff and landing. The flexible tube leading from the blower and heater unit heats the interior of either the upper or lower turret.

The heating and ventilating system is designed so that you can always obtain hot or cold air when either heater is on or off, respectively, by opening air outlets in the compartment. The temperature of the air is regulated by the air temperature control in the navigator's compartment, which sets the heater in operation and governs its heat output. Both the air temperature control and the pilot's air flow control regulate the heating and defrosting air simultaneously.

The first movement of the heater control in the radio operator's compartment actuates a micro-switch turning the heater igniter on and starting the blower. Additional movement of the control opens the heater throttle for additional heat output.

The heater in the left wing center section will automatically shut off its heating chamber if it becomes too hot, and will re-start when the temperature lowers.

If the temperature in the wing compartment that contains the heater becomes too high, the heater will automatically shut off but will not re-start until it has been serviced.

Warning

WHEN TAKING OFF OR LANDING, IN ORDER TO HAVE FULL POWER AVAILABLE, HEATING SYSTEM MUST BE OFF.

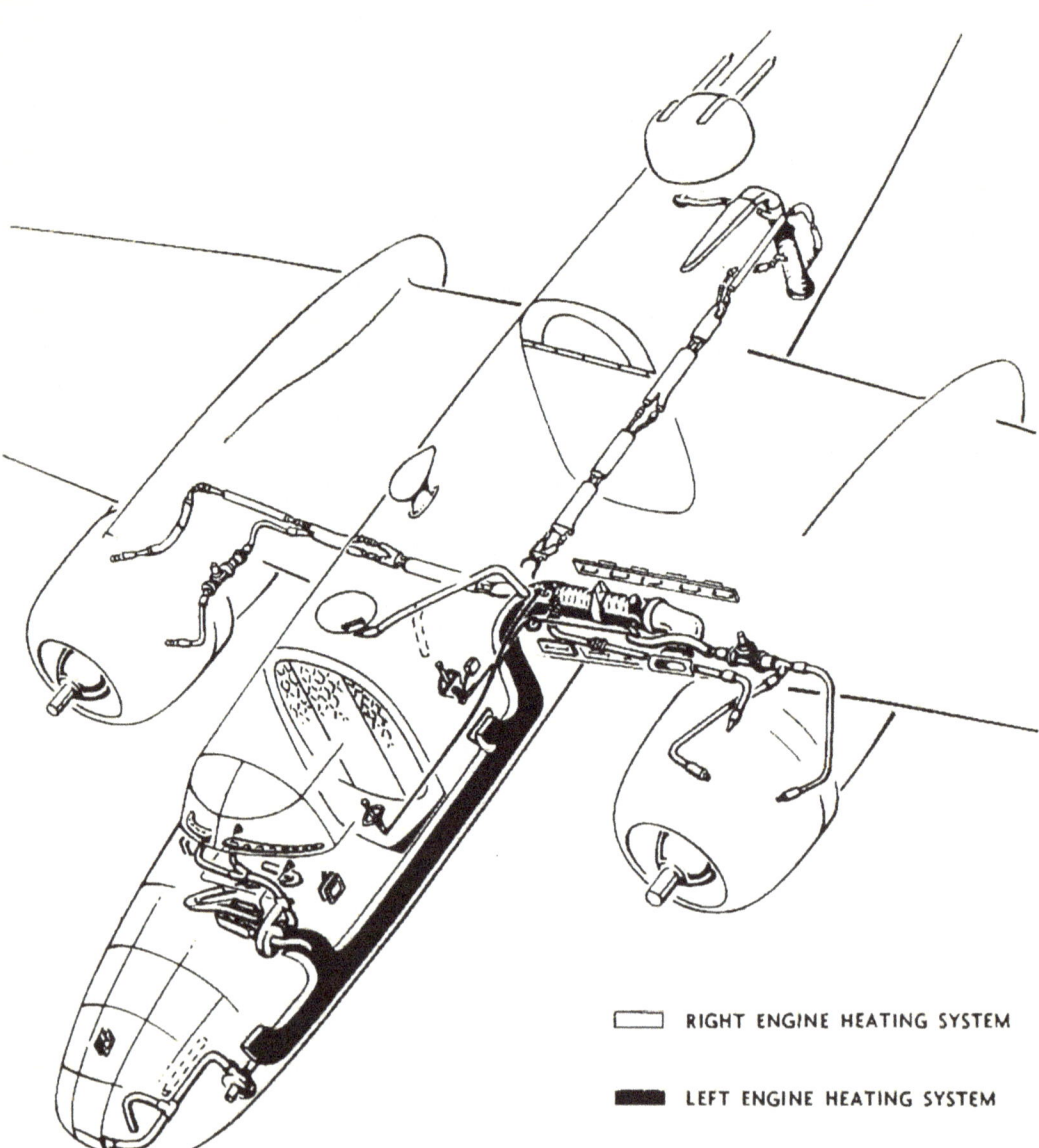

☐ RIGHT ENGINE HEATING SYSTEM

■ LEFT ENGINE HEATING SYSTEM

LANDING

Temperature inversions are common in winter and the ground air may be 15° to 30°C colder than at altitude. Therefore, take care to avoid excessive cooling when letting down. Lower the landing gear and use flaps to reduce airspeed while descending. Retain considerable power, and if possible, maintain oil temperature above 20°C and cylinder-head temperatures above 150°C. Lower readings than these may result in the engines cutting out or the failure of the engines to respond when the throttles are advanced.

Before approaching for a landing, make sure ice is not jamming the carburetor throttle valve. Test by moving throttle back and forth several times. You may have to use carburetor heat on the approach.

AFTER LANDING

Oil Dilution. To obtain sufficient dilution of the oil to facilitate starting, allow the engine to cool either by idling or stopping after flight, before dilution begins. This will prevent rapid evaporation of the gasoline and insure that the viscosity of the oil has been reduced sufficiently. In most cases you will find that the engines have cooled sufficiently for dilution by the time the airplane reaches the flight line.

Dilute the engines at 1000 rpm for the time indicated below, consistent with the lowest expected air temperature.

Temperature	Time—Minutes	Maximum Allowable Temperatures Cyl. Head	Oil
+4 to —12°C (+21 to 0°F)	6	150°C	50°C
—12 to —29°C (0 to —20°F)	10	145°C	45°C
—29 to —46°C (—20 to —40°F)	14	140°C	40°C

Warning

UNRELIABLE DILUTION OCCURS AT THESE TEMPERATURES IF THE OIL TANK IS MORE THAN ¾ FULL.

At the completion of the above dilution period, run both engines up to 1700 rpm, continuing dilution, and with propellers in full "INC. RPM" feather and unfeather each propeller through one complete cycle. Operate each propeller governor through one complete cycle. Release dilution switch and decrease engine speed. Stop engines and install engine covers.

Tactical Uses of the B-25

The combat record of the Mitchell has been printed in the newspapers of all the world for every man to see. Little can be added to that story except the developments of the future.

You and your buddies will write that story in the skies of the world.

You have been taught to fly the Mitchell accurately and safely under all conditions. Now you must learn to use the B-25 as a weapon, for that is the ultimate purpose of military flying.

All the skill and determination you can bring to this job will be none too much. How well you learn to punish the enemy and to protect yourself will in the final analysis determine whether you are a successful pilot.

The B-25 has been used for every purpose that need has demanded. Bombing, strafing, torpedoing, and even the evacuation of wounded, are listed in her duty roster. Whatever the need, the B-25 was either ready or quickly converted to do the job.

Her primary duties have been many:
Bombing, both low and medium altitude.
Strafing, with cannon and machine gun.
Smoke missions.
Gunnery, both for defensive and offensive fire.

The following pages illustrate the duties and responsibilities which are yours when using the B-25 as a weapon. They are typical of the actual orders and instructions issued to B-25 crews in training for combat duty.

PREPARING FOR YOUR MISSION

Before a mission is undertaken, the entire crew will be briefed. Upon completion of the mission the entire crew will again report to the S-2 officer for interrogation.

As commander of your airplane, it is your duty to brief your crew before the flight, pointing out to each crew member the specific duties he is expected to perform.

DUTIES OF THE AIRPLANE COMMANDER

1. Coordinates and supervises duties performed by crew members.
2. Pilot and copilot will practice hooded instruments (on day navigational missions), pilotage navigation, or radio navigation on all missions. Either the pilot or copilot will navigate at all times. Contact radio range stations on all navigation missions when possible.
3. Directs bailout, crash landing, and ditching drills on the ground and in flight.
4. Determines that crew members are receiving the necessary training to make them proficient in their assigned duty.
5. Has a complete knowledge of the assigned mission, and the duties of each crew member.
6. Makes proper use of **all** pilot's checklists.
7. Flies at all times in accordance with rules and regulations as outlined in AAF Regulation #60-16, and per scheduled Operations Orders.
8. Sends RON's on X-Country Flights. Understands necessary security measures regarding confidential equipment in the airplane.
9. When remaining overnight away from the home station, determines that crew members are properly housed and fed and are readily available in event takeoff is advanced.
10. Insures that each crew member is properly briefed on the mission to be performed.

COPILOT

1. Is ready to assume the duties of pilot at any time during the flight and acts as **deputy airplane commander.**
2. Aids pilot in his duties and remembers that the time will come when he assumes the responsibilities of airplane commander.
3. Keeps constant check on engine instruments and controls, notifying pilot of any discrepancy.
4. Makes preliminary check of airplane and crew prior to flight.
5. Aids pilot in accomplishing proper checklist.

BOMBARDIER-NAVIGATOR

1. Responsible for knowing exact position of the aircraft at all times.
2. Becomes proficient in his primary duty as bombardier and navigator.
3. Records weather report during mission.
4. Acts as principal observer, recording all pertinent data for S-2.
5. Keeps complete and accurate log of flight.
6. Furnishes radio operator with position reports.
7. Able to assume duties of fire control officer.
8. Checks sights, racks, intervalometer, control panel, driftmeter, and other allied equipment prior to takeoff as per bombardier-navigator's checklist.
9. Familiar with rack malfunctions that may occur during a mission and understands corrective action to be taken.
10. Understands importance of keeping navigation instruments correctly calibrated.

RADIO GUNNER

1. Thoroughly understands all communications equipment in the assigned airplane. Understands failures that are likely to occur and supplies the corrective action.
2. When outside local flying area the radio operator gunner sends position reports to his home base.
3. Contacts AACS stations when unable to contact group ground station.
4. Records all broadcasts weather data and maintains complete log.
5. Assists navigator by taking radio fixes.
6. Furnishes pilot with courses from the D/F station.
7. Checks location of head sets, and operation and condition of all communications equip-

ment as per radio operator's checklist prior to takeoff.

ENGINEER GUNNER

1. Before each flight, checks airplane for proper loading, stowage of life rafts and emergency equipment, and visually inspects the airplane as per engineer's checklist.

2. Has thorough knowledge of the engines and airplane in general. The occasion will arise when the airplane is away from its assigned ground crew and the engineer must be able to perform necessary maintenance and make required inspections.

3. Ready to assume duties of copilot at any time.

4. During flight will complete the engineer's log and practice fire control on all missions. Engineer gunners will also practice turret operation in flight.

ARMORER GUNNER

1. Before flight he is responsible that ammunition is properly loaded and that all gun positions are in working order.

2. On way to target he checks with other crew members to see that guns are properly working (to be simulated during training).

3. Acts as assistant observer, reporting via interphone to pilot any unusual activities and all airplanes they see during flight while on cross-country.

4. Preflights airplane as per armorer gunner's checklist.

The clock system will be used in reporting position of other aircraft seen in flight.

The pilot of an airplane on an individual flight or the leader of a formation flight will make it standard procedure to contact all radio ranges en route to give a position report, and in case of doubtful weather to receive a weather report especially at the field of intended landing.

On cross-country flights, either the armorer-gunner, radio-gunner, or the engineer-gunner will be in the turret at all times.

On low altitude missions, pilot will not fly below altitude specified as minimum for the particular mission being flown.

On all low altitude missions, course will be corrected to avoid flying over towns, cities, and thickly inhabited rural areas.

Some Typical Missions

FORMATION BOMBING

1. This is a day, 6-ship formation bombing mission. A Norden sight will be used in the lead ship on each element and D-8 sights will be used in wing ships. Bombardiers in lead ships will sight for both range and deflection. Bombardiers in wing ships will drop bombs on **lead ship**.

2. Flight leader will take off at a predetermined time; other ships will take off at 30 second intervals and join formation.

3. After formation has been satisfactorily joined, one circle will be made of the field. During this circle, formation will climb at 170 mph.

4. Flight leader should have an approximate power setting of 32″ MP at 2200 rpm. Climb will continue on course until an altitude of 10,000 feet is obtained. High blower will **not** be used and all ships will keep mixture controls in "FULL RICH" position.

5. Upon reaching the desired altitude, the leader will assume that anti-aircraft fire has been encountered, and evasive action will be used.

6. Upon approaching the target, a gentle left turn, diving at 1000 feet per minute onto the target, will be executed. This final turn requires judgment and precision timing on the part of the lead ship. After diving to the correct bombing altitude (8000 feet), and onto the target, the lead ship should be in a position to allow approximately a 20 second bomb run, straight and level. Immediately upon the closing of the bomb bay doors, the leader will again make a left turn, diving at 1000 feet per minute with a bank not to exceed 15 degrees. This dive will be held until 7000 feet altitude is reached. The following data should be strictly observed:

A. The lead ship should climb at 170 MPH, with approximate power settings of 32″ MP and 2200 RPM. The wing ships should use 2400 RPM.

B. After altitude is reached, power settings of lead ship should not exceed 1900 RPM and 27″ at any time. The wing ships should use at least 2000 RPM.

C. Copilots must be sure that RPM is increased if the MP dictates it.

D. The bombing run should be made at an indicated airspeed of 230 MPH, and upon leaving the target, should not exceed 250 MPH.

E. Wing ships will open bomb bay doors immediately upon seeing doors of lead ship open, and bombs will be dropped on the lead ship. **The Bombardier-Navigator must be quick in releasing bombs after he sees the first bomb leave the lead ship.**

F. Caution must be used by the lead ship at all times. Turns and maneuvers must be gone into gently and slowly.

G. After bombing is completed, flight will return to home base and break up into three-ship elements for landing.

GUNNERY MISSION

1. In this and all ensuing gunnery missions when both ground and water targets are used, extreme care must be exercised to see that the field of fire is clear of other planes.

Instructions for Firing

Ground Targets

A. Five rounds of 75MM ammunition from a range of 2000 yards, firing one round on each approach, plane to turn away from target immediately after firing while using additional evasive action.

B. Five rounds of 75MM ammunition from a range of 2000 yards, firing one round on each approach, using evasive action before and after reaching the 2000-yard point. Approach from 1000 yards and until passing over the target will be covered with short intermittent bursts of 50-Caliber fire.

Water Targets

A. Eleven rounds of 75MM ammunition from a range of 3000 yards, firing one round on each approach, plane to turn away from target immediately after firing while using additional evasive action.

2. The following course will be flown to and from Gunnery Range at a minimum altitude of 200 feet above the terrain. Flight will be made in 2- or 3-ship formations. Formation will go into column for gunnery.

X Base	To	33°38′N; 80°32′W (Bridge over X River)	39 Miles
33°38′N; 80°32′W	To	34°04′N; 79°56′W (Fork in H River)	46 Miles
34°04′N; 79°56′W	To	34°08′N; 79°13′W (H River, 6 Miles after crossing railroad line)	42 Miles
34°08′N; 79°13′W	To	I.P. 33°39½′N; 79°09½′W	33 Miles
Initial Point	To	Gunnery Control	12 Miles
			172 Miles

3. Ammunition
21 rounds of 75 MM ammunition
1000 rounds of 50-Cal. ammunition

CHEMICAL SPRAY MISSION

1. This is a chemical mission, using MR and FS.

2. The plane will be equipped for the mission with a bomb bay chemical spray tank containing MR and two chemical wing tanks—one on each wing—containing FS.

3. The MR target for the mission will be the X Target. The FS target will be the Z target.

4. The MR target is located approximately in the middle of the target area and is marked by an **orange cross in its center.**

5. Chemical tanks will be loaded into the plane. Plane will then be flown to the Z target, making an attack with FS, **using one wing tank,** from an altitude of 100 ft. normally, with the intention of covering the center of the target with a screen of smoke.

6. The plane will then fly to X target, making an attack with MR from an altitude of 150 ft. after inspecting the field to see that the target is in place.

7. The plane will then return to Z target and release the second smoke screen from the remaining FS wing tank.

8. All crew members will be equipped with gas masks while in the performance of this mission. Copilot will wear gas mask beginning 30 seconds before release of chemical until ship has been landed and brought to a stop.

9. This mission will not be flown when the wind velocity is greater than 20 mph.

10. Magnetic course to X target, 197 degrees; distance 50 miles.

11. Special attention should be given to direction of wind. Chemicals should be dropped from a flight path perpendicular to the wind.

12. Mission will be flown at 500 feet above terrain. Towns along route will be avoided.

13. The crew will be interrogated upon return to Home Base as to results of the mission.

DAY NAVIGATION, PHOTO-RECONNAISSANCE, AND INSTRUMENT LET-DOWN MISSION

1. This mission will consist of a controlled ground speed day navigation and photo-reconnaissance mission, at the end of which the pilot will orient himself by the X Radio Range and simulate a let-down to Home Base. If first attempt is unsuccessful, a second orientation and let-down will be accomplished.

2. **Conduct of Mission:**

A. This mission will be briefed by the Squadron S-2. All crew members will take careful notes as directed by S-2, and will be interrogated upon return as to observation. Oblique and pinpoint photographs will be taken. Target maps are available for the localities directed below and photographs will be taken of each given target.

3. **Specific Duties of Crew Members:**

A. Pilot—will aid and direct crew in obtaining observations; give careful attention to best photographic procedures; direct photographs be taken as briefed; and communicate on interphone at all times.

B. Copilot—will take notes on installation noted by himself and pilot, and accomplish all normal copilot duties.

C. Navigator-Bombardier

(1) Will navigate by DR Navigation on a V-P chart except within 10 minutes of target area where pinpoint pilotage will be used on a sectional chart.

(2) Act as observer and perform duties as briefed by S-2.

(3) Maintain and submit navigation log, weather observations, and other data to Squadron Navigation Officer.

D. Radio Operator—will transmit position reports submitted by Bombardier-Navigator, and practice tracking from all gun positions.

E. Engineer-Gunner—will perform all normal duties and also act as observer.

F. Armorer-Gunner—will preflight and install photo equipment; take photos as directed by pilot; make observations of ground activity; and man battle station at all times, taking careful observations and reporting to the pilot all aircraft and ground installations sighted.

Index

	PAGE		PAGE

Air Induction System.................... 30
Airplane Commander 8-9
Air Work, Advanced....................101
Anti-Icing 158-159
Armament 50-53
    B-25G 51
    B-25H 52
    B-25J 52-53
    Bombing 50
    Gunnery 51
Automatic Pilot 45-46
    Operation 98-100
Auxiliary Hydraulic Pump 127
Bailout 138-140
Bombardier-Navigator 10-12
Carburetor Air Filter.................... 97
Carburetor Air Heat..................... 97
Checklist 59-61
Checklist, Abbreviated.................. 62
Checks and Inspections..............63-67
Climb 79
Cold Weather Operations 157-163
Communication Equipment 47-49
    Command Set 47
    Interphone 49
    Liaison Set 48
    Marker Beacon Receiver........... 49
    Radio Compass Receiver........... 49
Comparison Equipment Chart............. 58
Controls, Location of................19-27
    Bombardier's Compartment—Left Side. 19
    Control Pedestal Panel 22
    Hydraulic Hand Pump 24
    Instrument Panel 21
    Navigator's Compartment, Forward.... 24
    Navigator's Compartment, Rear....... 25
    Pilot's Compartment, Forward........ 20

Pilot's Compartment, Left............ 23
Pilot's Compartment, Right.......... 23
Radio Operator's Compartment,
    Forward 26
Radio Operator's Compartment, Left... 27
Switch Panel 22
Copilot 10
Crosswind Landing 111-112
Crosswind Takeoff 110
Crosswind Taxiing 72
Defrosting Systems 161
De-Icer System 160
Dimensions 18
Ditching 143-149
    Crew Duties 146-147
    Landing Procedure 148-149
Dives 102
Electrical System 35-36
Emergency Equipment, Miscellaneous..134-136
Emergency Hydraulic Selector Valve......127
Emergency Hydraulic Wheel
    Lowering System 128-129
Emergency Operation—Air Brakes.........133
Emergency Operation—Bomb Bay Doors...131
Emergency Operation—Hydraulic Brake...132
Emergency Salvo Release.............131-132
Emergency Wing Flap Lowering System...130
Engine Power Ratings 28
Engineer 13-14
Feathering 39
Fire in Flight 137
Forced Landings 141-142
Formation 104-108
    Javelin 105
    Echelon 106
    Stagger 108
Fuel System 31-32

	PAGE
Crossfeed	94
Emergency Fuel Transfer	94
Operation	91-95
General Description	16-18
Go-Around	88-89
Single Engine	126
Grade 91 Fuel	153-155
Power Control Chart	155
Gunners	14
Hamilton Hydromatic Propeller	38-40
Heating System	161-162
History of the Mitchell Bomber	5-7
Hydraulic System	40-41
Ignition System	35
Inspections and Checks	63-67
Instrument Flying	103
Instruments	44
Landing	81-87
Crosswind	111-112
Forced	141-142
Formation	107
No-Flap	87
Power-Off	86
Power-On	83
Short-Field	118-119
Single Engine	124-125
Strange Field	109
Landing Gear	42-43
Let-Down	79
Lighting Equipment	36-37
Maximum Range Charts	156
Models and Changes	57
Night Flying	103
No-Flap Landing	87
Oil System	33-34

	PAGE
Oxygen	54-55
Parking	90
Photographic Equipment	56-57
Power Changes	78
Power-Off Landing	86
Power-On Landing	83
Power Plant	28-30
Priming	97
Radio Operator	13
Rules to Be Enforced on Every Flight	15
Run-Up	74
Short-Field Landing	118-119
Short-Field Takeoff	116-117
Single Engine Go-Around	126
Single Engine Landing	124-125
Single Engine Operation	120-126
Slow Flying	115-116
Spins	102
Stalls	113-114
Starting Engines	68-69
Strange Field Landings	109
Supercharger	96
Tactical Uses	164-166
Takeoff	75-77
Crosswind	110
Formation	107
Short-Field	116-117
Taxiing	69-73
Crosswind	72
In Mud or Sand	72
Tips	73
Trimming	80
Typical Missions	167-169
Unfeathering	40
Weight and Balance	150-152

www.ingramcontent.com/pod-product-compliance
Lightning Source LLC
Chambersburg PA
CBHW080507110426
42742CB00017B/3029